The Apress Certification Study Companion Series offers guidance and hands-on practice to support technical and business professionals who are studying for an exam in the pursuit of an industry certification. Professionals worldwide seek to achieve certifications in order to advance in a career role, reinforce knowledge in a specific discipline, or to apply for or change jobs. This series focuses on the most widely taken certification exams in a given field. It is designed to be user friendly, tracking to topics as they appear in a given exam and work alongside other certification material as professionals prepare for their exam.

More information about this series at https://link.springer.com/bookseries/17100.

# Certification Study Companion Series

# CompTIA Linux+ Certification Companion

## Hands-on Preparation to Master Linux Administration

Ahmed F. Sheikh

Apress®

*CompTIA Linux+ Certification Companion: Hands-on Preparation to Master Linux Administration*

Ahmed F. Sheikh
Miami, FL, USA

ISBN-13 (pbk): 979-8-8688-0127-3        ISBN-13 (electronic): 979-8-8688-0128-0
https://doi.org/10.1007/979-8-8688-0128-0

Managing Director, Apress Media LLC: Welmoed Spahr
Acquisitions Editor: Susan McDermott
Development Editor: Laura Berendson
Project Manager: Jessica Vakili

Cover designed by eStudioCalamar

Distributed to the book trade worldwide by Apress Media, LLC, 1 New York Plaza, New York, NY 10004, U.S.A. Phone 1-800-SPRINGER, fax (201) 348-4505, e-mail orders-ny@springer-sbm.com, or visit www.springeronline.com. Apress Media, LLC is a California LLC and the sole member (owner) is Springer Science + Business Media Finance Inc (SSBM Finance Inc). SSBM Finance Inc is a **Delaware** corporation.

For information on translations, please e-mail booktranslations@springernature.com; for reprint, paperback, or audio rights, please e-mail bookpermissions@springernature.com.

Apress titles may be purchased in bulk for academic, corporate, or promotional use. eBook versions and licenses are also available for most titles. For more information, reference our Print and eBook Bulk Sales web page at http://www.apress.com/bulk-sales.

Any source code or other supplementary material referenced by the author in this book is available to readers on GitHub (https://github.com/Apress). For more detailed information, please visit https://www.apress.com/gp/services/source-code.

If disposing of this product, please recycle the paper

*This book is affectionately dedicated to all IT experts, professionals, and students.*

# Table of Contents

About the Author ...........................................................................................**xxi**

About the Technical Reviewer ...................................................................**xxiii**

Introduction .................................................................................................**xxv**

**Chapter 1: Introduction to Linux and Linux Certification** ...................... 1

What Is Linux? ........................................................................................... 1

MULTICS Project ........................................................................................ 2

UNIX ......................................................................................................... 2

GNU Project ............................................................................................... 3

Linux Created ............................................................................................. 3

Licensing ................................................................................................... 3

Linux Distributions ..................................................................................... 4

Reasons to Use Linux .................................................................................. 4

    Reduces Total Cost ............................................................................... 4

    Software Availability .............................................................................. 5

    Increases Security and Stability ............................................................. 5

    Runs on Multiple Hardware Platforms ..................................................... 5

Linux Certification: Why Get Certified? .......................................................... 6

    CompTIA Linux+ ................................................................................... 6

    Linux Professional Institute (LPI) ............................................................ 7

Summary ................................................................................................... 7

**Chapter 2: Installing Linux** ................................................................... 9

Preparing for Installation ............................................................................. 9

    Step 1: Talk to Key People ..................................................................... 10

    Step 2: Distributions ............................................................................ 10

Resource Requirements for Ubuntu and Fedora ................................................................. 11

Step 3: Naming Conventions ............................................................................................ 12

Step 4: Partitioning .......................................................................................................... 13

Step 5: Default Bootloader ............................................................................................... 15

File System ...................................................................................................................... 16

Windows and Linux File Systems ..................................................................................... 16

Step 6: Additional Installation Needs .............................................................................. 17

Methods of Installation ..................................................................................................... 18

Summary ........................................................................................................................... 18

Resources ..................................................................................................................... 19

Chapter 3: Shells, Scripts, and Data Management ............................................. 21

Linux Review ..................................................................................................................... 21

Shell Environment ............................................................................................................ 21

Shell Configuration .......................................................................................................... 22

Environmental Variables .................................................................................................. 23

PATH Variable .................................................................................................................. 24

Special Characters ........................................................................................................... 25

BASH Functions ............................................................................................................... 26

Function: Call from Library Example ................................................................................ 26

Function Example: Call from Inside Script ........................................................................ 27

Scripts .............................................................................................................................. 28

Types of Scripts ............................................................................................................... 29

Script That Executes Commands ..................................................................................... 30

Scripts That Take Input and Use It to Perform an Action ................................................. 32

The Execute Permission ................................................................................................... 33

Constructs ........................................................................................................................ 33

if Statement ...................................................................................................................... 34

Case Construct ................................................................................................................. 39

Difference Between if and case ........................................................................................ 41

Testing Using if and case ................................................................................................. 41

| | and && Chaining Operators ......................................................................................... 43

Repetition Construct .................................................................................... 45

while Statements ........................................................................................ 47

Status of Script ......................................................................................... 49

Databases & SQL Commands ......................................................................... 51

Database Services ..................................................................................... 51

Client/Server Model ................................................................................... 53

SQL Commands .......................................................................................... 54

Verifying MySQL Is Installed ........................................................................ 55

Summary ........................................................................................................ 56

Chapter 4: Boot Process and Shutdown ................................................. 57

Boot Process ................................................................................................. 57

Fedora Boot Process ................................................................................... 57

BIOS ........................................................................................................ 58

Boot Loader .................................................................................................. 59

Kernel ..................................................................................................... 59

Common Boot Loaders ............................................................................... 60

LILO ........................................................................................................ 60

GRUB ....................................................................................................... 60

GRUB Parameters ...................................................................................... 61

GRUB2 ..................................................................................................... 62

Common Options Used in the /etc/default/grub File ....................................... 64

Runlevels ...................................................................................................... 65

Runlevels on Fedora ................................................................................... 66

Runlevels in Ubuntu ................................................................................... 66

Runlevel Commands ................................................................................... 67

Kernel Options .......................................................................................... 67

Init Scripts .................................................................................................... 68

System V Distros ....................................................................................... 68

BSD Distros .............................................................................................. 69

Managing Init Scripts ................................................................................. 69

Configuring Init Scripts .............................................................................. 70

Additional Scripts ........................................................................................ 72

Upstart ........................................................................................................ 73

Systemd ...................................................................................................... 74

Shutting Down Linux ........................................................................................ 74

Summary .......................................................................................................... 75

**Chapter 5: Desktop and User Interface .................................................... 77**

X Window System ............................................................................................ 77

Video Hardware ......................................................................................... 78

X Server ..................................................................................................... 79

Window Manager ....................................................................................... 79

Desktop Environment ............................................................................... 80

Gnome Desktop Example ........................................................................... 81

X Client ...................................................................................................... 83

X Font Server ............................................................................................ 83

Configuring X Server ....................................................................................... 84

Editing xorg.conf Files in Fedora ............................................................. 85

Editing XF86Conf File in Fedora .............................................................. 86

Restart X Server ....................................................................................... 87

Configuring Window Manager and Desktop Environment ............................. 88

GUI Problem-Solving Utilities ................................................................... 89

Display Manager .............................................................................................. 90

Configuring Display Manager .................................................................... 90

X Terminal or X Station Support ............................................................... 91

Configuration Steps on X Server .............................................................. 92

X Display Manager (XDM) .......................................................................... 93

XDM Configuration Files ........................................................................... 93

Remote X Window ..................................................................................... 94

KDM ............................................................................................................ 96

GDM ............................................................................................................ 96

Accessibility ............................................................................................... 97

Mouse Accessibility ................................................................................. 102

Preferred Applications Menu .................................................................. 104

Desktop Themes ..................................................................................... 107

Summary .................................................................................................. 108

**Chapter 6: Hardware and Process Settings ................................ 111**

Device Drivers ......................................................................................... 111

Two Ways to Implement .......................................................................... 111

The /proc Directory ................................................................................. 112

The /sys Directory ................................................................................... 113

Tools to Manage Device Drivers ............................................................ 113

Managing Kernel Modules ...................................................................... 114

Configuration Files .................................................................................. 114

Manually Managing Kernel Modules ...................................................... 115

Tools to Manually Manage Kernel Modules .......................................... 115

Hotplug and Coldplug Devices ............................................................... 116

Hotplug ..................................................................................................... 116

Coldplug ................................................................................................... 117

Components That Manage Devices ........................................................ 117

Processes ................................................................................................. 118

What Is a Process? .................................................................................. 118

Process ID ................................................................................................ 118

Forking and Zombie ................................................................................ 119

The ps Command ..................................................................................... 120

The pstree Command .............................................................................. 120

Top Command .......................................................................................... 120

Process Management .............................................................................. 120

Foreground Processing ........................................................................... 121

Background .............................................................................................. 121

The nohup Command ............................................................................... 121

Prioritizing Processes ............................................................................. 122

Terminating a Process ................................................................................ 122

    Kill Command ....................................................................................... 123

Summary.................................................................................................. 123

**Chapter 7: Users and Groups ............................................................... 125**

User Accounts .......................................................................................... 125

    Account Locations ................................................................................ 125

    Types of User Accounts ........................................................................ 126

    User Account Files................................................................................ 126

    /etc/passwd File.................................................................................. 127

    /etc/shadow File.................................................................................. 127

    Synchronize passwd and shadow Files.................................................... 129

Groups..................................................................................................... 130

    Group Accounts ................................................................................... 130

    Group Account Types ........................................................................... 131

    Group Account Files............................................................................. 132

Managing User/Group Accounts.................................................................. 134

    Default Configurations.......................................................................... 134

    add Command ..................................................................................... 135

    Skeleton Directory............................................................................... 135

    useradd Command ............................................................................... 136

    Password ............................................................................................ 136

    Modifying User Accounts...................................................................... 137

    CHAGE................................................................................................ 138

    Lock/Unlock User Accounts .................................................................. 139

    Deleting a User Account ....................................................................... 140

    Group Accounts .................................................................................. 141

Best Practices .......................................................................................... 143

Summary.................................................................................................. 144

**Chapter 8: Administrative Tasks** ........................................................................... **147**

Task Management ........................................................................................................ 147

    ATD Daemon ......................................................................................................... 147

    at Command ......................................................................................................... 148

    Shell Script ........................................................................................................... 148

    at Optional Additions .......................................................................................... 149

    Cron Command ..................................................................................................... 151

    Cron Jobs .............................................................................................................. 152

    Configuration Files ............................................................................................... 152

    Content for cron Files .......................................................................................... 154

    Working with cron Jobs ....................................................................................... 154

Localization ................................................................................................................. 155

    Locale .................................................................................................................... 155

    Locale Code .......................................................................................................... 155

    Environmental Variables ..................................................................................... 157

Time Management ...................................................................................................... 158

    Linux Clocks ......................................................................................................... 158

    Local Time and Universal Time ........................................................................... 158

    Time Zone ............................................................................................................. 159

    Changing the Time Zone ...................................................................................... 160

Summary ..................................................................................................................... 160

**Chapter 9: Working with Linux: Part 1** ................................................................... **163**

Kernels, Terminals, and Shells ................................................................................... 163

    Kernel ................................................................................................................... 163

    Shell ...................................................................................................................... 164

    Terminal ............................................................................................................... 164

    Shells Available in Linux ...................................................................................... 164

    Kernel Architecture ............................................................................................. 166

    Terminal Session .................................................................................................. 166

Environment Variables ............................................................................................... 167

    Two Types of Variables.......................................................................................... 167

    Variables Used in Linux ........................................................................................ 168

    Path Variable.......................................................................................................... 168

Working with Shell Commands ................................................................................. 169

    Shell Commands: Case Sensitive ......................................................................... 170

    Shell Commands: Path........................................................................................... 170

    Good to Know ........................................................................................................ 171

    History File ............................................................................................................ 171

    Purpose of Configuration Files ............................................................................. 172

    Basic Shell Commands.......................................................................................... 173

    Metacharacters ..................................................................................................... 174

How to Get Help ....................................................................................................... 175

    Man and Info Pages.............................................................................................. 175

Summary.................................................................................................................... 176

    Resources.............................................................................................................. 176

**Chapter 10: Essential System Services ............................................................ 177**

System Time Management ........................................................................................ 177

    Hardware Clock ..................................................................................................... 177

    System Clock.......................................................................................................... 178

    Network Time Protocol (NTP)................................................................................ 179

System Logging ........................................................................................................ 180

    Logrotate ............................................................................................................... 182

    Mail Transfer Agent (MTA)..................................................................................... 186

    Mail Protocols........................................................................................................ 187

    MTAs...................................................................................................................... 188

    Redirecting Mail .................................................................................................... 189

Print Management ..................................................................................................... 190

    Linux Printing Systems.......................................................................................... 190

    LPD Printing System ............................................................................................. 191

    Common Unix Printing System (CUPS) ................................................................. 191

Print Job Flow..................................................................................... 192

CUPS Configuration ........................................................................... 193

CUPS Print Job Management............................................................... 194

Summary.................................................................................................. 195

Resources ............................................................................................... 197

**Chapter 11: Working with Linux: Part 2.............................................. 199**

Directory Structure.................................................................................. 199

What Is a Directory Structure? ........................................................... 199

Filesystem Hierarchy .......................................................................... 200

File Types ............................................................................................ 202

Common Filename Extensions ............................................................ 203

More Linux Commands ........................................................................... 203

Wildcard Characters ........................................................................... 204

Regular Expressions ............................................................................... 205

Common Regular Expressions............................................................ 205

Extended Regular Expressions ........................................................... 205

Compression ........................................................................................... 206

Compress Utility ................................................................................. 207

GNU Utility ......................................................................................... 208

Bzip2 Utility ........................................................................................ 209

Archiving.................................................................................................. 210

Tar........................................................................................................ 211

Cpio ..................................................................................................... 212

Summary.................................................................................................. 213

Resources ........................................................................................... 214

**Chapter 12: Networking Fundamentals .............................................. 215**

Internet Protocol ..................................................................................... 215

Networking Models ............................................................................. 216

OSI Model ........................................................................................... 217

TCP/IP Model ...................................................................................... 217

TCP and UDP ................................................................................................ 218

Internet Control Message Protocol (ICMP) ............................................ 218

Addressing ..................................................................................................... 219

Physical and Logical Addresses ............................................................. 219

IPv4 ............................................................................................................. 220

Binary Values ........................................................................................... 222

IPv4 Address Classes .............................................................................. 223

Subnet Mask ............................................................................................. 224

ANDing Process .......................................................................................... 224

Default Gateway ...................................................................................... 225

Broadcast Address ................................................................................... 225

Lack of IPv4 Addresses .......................................................................... 226

Comparing IPv4 and IPv6 ....................................................................... 226

IPv6 Addressing ....................................................................................... 228

Converting Hex to Decimal or Binary ................................................... 229

Parts of an IPv6 Addresses .................................................................... 230

Ports ............................................................................................................... 231

Port Numbers ........................................................................................... 231

Configuring an Interface ........................................................................... 233

Network Interface Card (NIC) ................................................................. 233

Static Settings ......................................................................................... 234

DHCP Settings .......................................................................................... 235

ifconfig Command .................................................................................... 236

Configuring Routes ..................................................................................... 236

Routers ...................................................................................................... 236

Configuring DNS .......................................................................................... 237

Name Resolution ...................................................................................... 237

/etc/hosts ................................................................................................. 238

/etc/resolv.conf ....................................................................................... 238

/etc/nsswitch.conf ................................................................................... 239

Configuring with GUI ................................................................................................ 239

    Network Configuration Tool ............................................................................ 239

    Troubleshooting .............................................................................................. 239

Summary.............................................................................................................. 242

## Chapter 13: Software Installation .................................................................. 245

Package Managers ............................................................................................... 245

    Source or Binary............................................................................................. 246

    Red Hat Package Manager (RPM)................................................................... 247

    Yellowdog Updater Modified (YUM) ............................................................... 249

    YUM Configuration Files ................................................................................ 250

    Debian Package Manager............................................................................... 251

    Debian APT .................................................................................................... 251

    KPackageKit Package Manager...................................................................... 252

    Libraries......................................................................................................... 252

    Troubleshooting ............................................................................................. 253

Summary.............................................................................................................. 255

## Chapter 14: Security ...................................................................................... 257

Root User Security .............................................................................................. 257

    su Command .................................................................................................. 257

    sudo Command............................................................................................... 258

    Sudoers File.................................................................................................... 258

    User Security Administration .......................................................................... 259

    Best Practices................................................................................................. 260

User Limits ........................................................................................................... 261

    Changing Limits.............................................................................................. 262

Auditing Files ....................................................................................................... 263

Host Security........................................................................................................ 264

Open Network Connections (Sockets) ................................................................ 265

Open Ports ........................................................................................................ 266

Firewalls .......................................................................................................... 267

User Running a Service .................................................................................... 268

TCP Wrappers ................................................................................................... 268

Encryption ............................................................................................................ 269

Asymmetric Key Encryption .............................................................................. 270

Symmetric Key Encryption ............................................................................... 270

Secure Shell ..................................................................................................... 271

Connection with SSH ........................................................................................ 272

Key Pair ............................................................................................................ 272

SSH-Agent Utility ............................................................................................. 275

SSH Configuration Options ............................................................................... 275

SSH Port Tunneling ........................................................................................... 276

SSH Authentication .......................................................................................... 276

GNU Privacy Guard ........................................................................................... 277

Key Exchange and Encryption Example ............................................................ 278

GPG Options ...................................................................................................... 279

Summary ............................................................................................................... 280

**Chapter 15: Working with Files, Directories, and Permissions ............................ 283**

Managing Directories and Files ........................................................................... 283

Finding Directories and Files .............................................................................. 284

Structure of Files ................................................................................................. 285

Linking Files ..................................................................................................... 286

Ownership and Permissions ................................................................................ 286

Directory and File Permissions ......................................................................... 286

Ownership ........................................................................................................ 287

Setting Up Permissions and Ownership ........................................................... 288

Default Permission ........................................................................................... 288

Special Permissions ......................................................................................... 289

Text Editors .............................................................................................................. 290

    The vi Editor.......................................................................................................... 291

    Gedit Editor........................................................................................................... 292

Summary.................................................................................................................. 292

Index........................................................................................................................ 293

# About the Author

**Ahmed F. Sheikh** is a Fulbright alumnus and has earned a master's degree in electrical engineering from Kansas State University, USA. He is a seasoned IT expert with a specialty in network security planning and skills in cloud computing. Currently, he is a Research Fellow at Energy Systems Research Laboratory.

As an experienced IT professional with a passion for Linux, Ahmed Sheikh has spent several years working in various roles, including system administration and network engineering. Throughout his career, he has witnessed the growing demand for Linux expertise and the need for comprehensive resources in the field. This has motivated him to share his knowledge and experience through writing this book.

Ahmed's goal is to provide readers with a practical and accessible guide that covers essential concepts, best practices, and real-world examples to help them succeed in their Linux journey. He is excited to contribute to the Linux community and empower individuals with the skills they need to excel in this ever-evolving field.

# About the Technical Reviewer

**Ayesha Nisar** is a seasoned Linux expert with over five years of hands-on experience in Linux system administration. Her proficiency spans various distributions, including Ubuntu, CentOS, and Red Hat, where she has successfully designed, implemented, and maintained Linux-based infrastructures across diverse industries.

Holding certifications such as Linux+, RHCSA, RHCA, and RHCE, she prides herself on not only troubleshooting but strategically solving complex problems. Her skill set includes proficient shell scripting and automation, allowing her to streamline tasks and optimize system performance. She specializes in implementing robust security measures to safeguard against vulnerabilities.

Throughout her career, she has led successful migrations, implemented effective backup and recovery strategies, and provided expert guidance on Linux best practices. She is the go-to professional for ensuring the reliability and security of Linux environments.

# Introduction

The *CompTIA Linux+ Certification Companion* is the ultimate guide to mastering Linux system administration in preparation for the **CompTIA Linux+ Certification**. Whether you're a beginner or an experienced professional, this comprehensive resource is designed to equip you with the knowledge and skills needed to excel in the world of Linux.

With its comprehensive coverage, this book delves into essential Linux concepts, commands, and techniques, providing you with a complete reference guide. You'll review how to customize and navigate the shell environment, write powerful scripts, configure user interfaces, perform administrative tasks, configure system services, establish network connections, and secure your system. No stone is left unturned in this in-depth exploration of Linux administration.

What sets this book apart is its practical approach. Real-world scenarios and practical applications take center stage, ensuring that you not only understand the theory but also know how to apply it effectively.

Troubleshooting common issues becomes second nature as you gain the skills to diagnose and resolve system problems with ease. You'll discover industry best practices and standards, enabling you to optimize systems, implement robust security measures, and adhere to compliance regulations.

## CHAPTER 1

# Introduction to Linux and Linux Certification

In this introductory chapter, you will learn about the history of Linux. You will gain an understanding of licensing, Linux distributions, reasons to use Linux, and exams related to Linux certification.

By the end of this chapter, you will be able to

1. Explain the history of Linux

2. Identify reasons why individuals and organizations use Linux

3. Discuss Linux certification requirements

## What Is Linux?

To better understand the history of Linux, you will need to be able to identify what it actually is. You likely are familiar with Microsoft's operating systems, but there is another operating system that you should familiarize yourself with – it is called Linux. One way to understand it is to equate it to cars. A car is a car, but there are various brands of cars. There is the Mercedes, and then there is the Ford, and each one is purchased for a different reason. You have to look at what each operating system has to offer and pick the one that best suits your needs.

The Linux roots began in the 1960s with the Multiplexed Information and Computing Service (MULTICS) project created by the Massachusetts Institute of Technology (MIT), General Electric, and AT&T Bell Labs. Over the next 25 years, thanks to many dedicated programmers and engineers, the operating system created by that project evolved into the original version of Linux created by Linus Torvalds in 1991. Today, there are millions of Linux users worldwide, and this number continues to grow.

1

© Ahmed F. Sheikh 2024
A. F. Sheikh, *CompTIA Linux+ Certification Companion*, Certification Study Companion Series, https://doi.org/10.1007/979-8-8688-0128-0_1

# MULTICS Project

The MULTICS (MULTiplexed Information and Computing Service) project was created in 1965 by a group of programmers and engineers from higher education and corporate settings. Their purpose was to create an operating system that could control the amount of time each process could use a mainframe's processor. Even though the project was abandoned a few years later, the operating system (OS) was used into the twentieth century and greatly influenced the future development of operating systems. It is a pioneering time-sharing operating system based on the idea of a single-level memory.

# UNIX

One of the developers of the MULTICS system, Ken Thompson, made changes to the original operating system (OS) to create what we now know as UNIX. Unix is a modular operating system comprising essential elements, such as the kernel, shell, file system, and a fundamental set of utilities or programs. Unfortunately, it only ran on Digital Equipment Corporation's PDP-7 hardware. Not too long after Thompson's new OS was available in 1969, Dennis Ritchie developed a new programming language (called C) that allowed code to run on multiple hardware platforms. UNIX was then rewritten in that language.

Richie and Thompson were both working for AT&T Bell Labs when the new UNIX was created, and AT&T was legally restricted from selling this new OS. To best ensure the use of the new knowledge and technology, the source code was sold to several companies with the requirement that each would continue to maintain a specific standard set by AT&T. Afterward, even though the standard was usually maintained, each company added their own modifications thus creating different flavors of UNIX.

AT&T gave some universities copies of UNIX in an effort to promote the use of UNIX. Between 1977 and 1995, the University of California at Berkeley created its own version called BSD Unix – Berkeley Software Distribution, and it is still widely used today. Sun Microsystems, one of the companies that purchased the source code from AT&T, started selling its version of UNIX on relatively inexpensive hardware, which established it in many companies and universities. UNIX is rarely used as a home computer but is still widely used in business. Hewlett Packard's HP-UX and IBM's AIX are other versions of UNIX that are still very popular.

# GNU Project

UNIX was not free to the public, which meant that all the techies that loved experimenting with an operating system and other software did not have a free platform they could use. In an effort to meet the needs of these techs, also known as hackers, Richard Stallman started the GNU project ("GNU's not Unix!"). Through a collaborative effort, a new and free operating system was created.

Although the GNU OS did not gain much acceptance, it led to the new licensing format called GNU Public License (GPL). By licensing a new product, it would be legal to distribute it along with its source code. Any modifications to this free software would also have to be distributed for free.

# Linux Created

Linus Torvalds took advantage of the GNU Public License (GPL) and created the operating system now known as Linux in 1991. There are lots of disagreements over whether it is pronounced "Linux" or "Lenux," but most people refer to it as "Lenux." Torvalds improved on what was known as MINUX, or the mini-UNIX OS, which was mainly developed for use with the Intel X86 platform. Linux is used in homes and businesses today.

# Licensing

Linux is licensed as open-source software, which is code that is freely distributed to anyone that wants to use it or improve it. Thanks to the collaborative efforts of many Linux users, changes and improvements are constantly being made in the current versions of Linux as the need arises. One of the good things about open-source software is that errors are usually very quickly corrected. This software takes advantage of the GPL format, which means the source code is freely available, and any changes to this source code are also free.

# Linux Distributions

To understand Linux distributions, you must first identify what a distribution is. A distribution, or distro, is a collection of Linux kernels, libraries, and additional software that has been added for a specific purpose.

The following list includes the most well-known distributions. If you look closely, you will find that many of them are versions of another distribution. For instance, Ubuntu is a derivative of Debian. Fedora is a derivative of Red Hat. This example demonstrates how one distribution can morph into another distribution and then morph again into yet another distribution.

**Common Linux Distributions**

| | |
|---|---|
| Red Hat | SuSE |
| Fedora (Red Hat) | Debian |
| Slackware | Ubuntu (Debian) |
| Mint (Ubuntu & Debian) | CentOS (Red Hat) |
| Bodhi (Ubuntu) | Gentoo |
| OpenSuse (Slackware) | Mageia (Mandriva) |
| Manjaro | Elementary |

# Reasons to Use Linux

You may wonder why a business owner would want to use Linux when Windows is so popular with businesses today. The following information helps answer that question.

## Reduces Total Cost

One of the main reasons to use Linux is that it reduces the total cost of ownership (TCO). Licensing is free, as are upgrades and fixes. Software that runs on the Linux platform is either very low in cost or free. Support for Linux can be quickly found on the Internet in how-to documents, FAQs, news groups, blogs, and Linux user groups (LUGs). One good practice to adopt when you do not know how to do something in Linux is to go straight to the Internet and search for information. You often will find the answer. Overall, the TCO is a lot less than when using another operating system.

# Software Availability

Another important reason that businesses like to use Linux is that most of the software that is needed in their business is free and readily available for installation. Most installations are not for the desktop user but for a business server. Linux can be used as a desktop since it has a GUI and all of the normal office-type applications, such as text editors, presentation software, and spreadsheets. Linux software also offers audio and video editing software as well as various security options. One prominent reason that Linux is used is to provide web services.

# Increases Security and Stability

Linux tends to be a very stable and secure operating system for a couple of reasons.

First, any vulnerability found is fixed very quickly. There are numerous people involved with maintaining the security of Linux. This is very different than the timeframe involved for an OS vendor to prepare and test fixes and then push them out to the public. Businesses like Linux because they want secure assets and information.

Another reason is there are not as many Linux systems in use as there are Windows. Hackers go after what can provide the biggest impact with the least effort. Until Linux becomes more widely used, it will not be as big a target as Windows.

# Runs on Multiple Hardware Platforms

Almost every hardware platform can run Linux. In comparison, how many can you put Windows on? Intel and Itanium are present, but it cannot be installed on any of the other platforms. The specifications of the hardware are not nearly as stringent for Linux as are on other OSs. As a result, you can get by with less RAM and slower processors – even less hard drive space. Think about what that could do for businesses, as they usually have older hardware that cannot run another OS. They become too slow or do not have enough resources to satisfy the minimum requirements. These are still good machines on which to install Linux. Just imagine how much money that could save a business.

Some of the hardware platforms on which Linux can run are:

- Intel

- PowerPC

- SPARC

- Ultra-SPARC

- Itanium

- ARM

- MIPS

- Alpha

- ARC

- m68k

Some people have gone so far as to point out its benefit to the environment. Linux is not boxed and sold to users, as is most software. It is downloaded from the Internet. This keeps the boxes and packing materials from ending up in a landfill.

# Linux Certification: Why Get Certified?

Earning certification shows prospective and current employers that you have the skills and knowledge needed to work with Linux. It also shows you want to continue learning so you can do better in your career. Linux certification is backed by a couple of well-known global Information Technology (IT) associations that have the respect of the industry. CompTIA's Linux+ is the most widely known Linux certification. The Linux Professional Institute (LPI) also has several Linux certifications.

## CompTIA Linux+

The most widely known certification is CompTIA's Linux+, covering the following topics:

- System Management

- Security

- Scripting, Containers, and Automation

- Troubleshooting

For more details on this certification, visit www.comptia.org/certifications/linux.

# Linux Professional Institute (LPI)

Another organization called the Linux Professional Institute, or LPI, produced four different certifications. The first certification is the Linux Essentials, which proves you understand the basics of Linux as a user. Next, Professional Certifications are available that cover a junior, advanced, and senior level of Linux. These certifications prove your ability to work with Linux at a specific level.

## Introductory Certification

- Linux Essentials – Basics of Linux

## Professional Certifications

- LPIC-1 – Junior Level Linux Certification

- LPIC-2 – Advanced Level Linux Certification

- LPIC-3 – Senior Level Linux Certification

For more information on these certifications, check out `www.lpi.org/our-certifications/summary-of-lpi-certifications/`.

# Summary

In this chapter, you learned about the history and real-world applications of Linux, as well as certification requirements. Keep the following in mind:

- The MULTICS operating system was created in 1965 to allow multiple processes to time-share.

- UNIX was created in 1969 and could run on multiple hardware platforms.

- Linux was created from MINUX as a free, open-source operating system for home or business use.

- Linux continues to be modified and made available to the public, including the source code, due to GPL licensing.

- There are hundreds of flavors of Linux available today.

# CHAPTER 2

# Installing Linux

In this chapter, you will gain an understanding of the preparation needed and the methods used to install Linux.

By the end of this chapter, you will be able to:

1. Create a plan for installation

2. Identify methods of installation

3. Install Linux

## Preparing for Installation

Before starting an installation of Linux, it is important that you begin with project management. You have to meet with numerous people and ask lots of questions. Here are some important questions that you should prepare to ask:

- What tasks will be performed on this host?

- What distribution of Linux do I need to install?

- Will the hardware I have now run the selected version?

- What type of hard drives am I going to use?

- How am I going to partition those hard drives?

- Which bootloader will be used to load the OS?

- What filesystem am I going to install?

- What information do I need to connect the host to a network?

- What method of installation will be used?

© Ahmed F. Sheikh 2024
A. F. Sheikh, *CompTIA Linux+ Certification Companion*, Certification Study Companion Series,
https://doi.org/10.1007/979-8-8688-0128-0_2

You can see there are lots of things that have to be determined before you should start an installation. This section will cover each of the steps in more detail.

## Step 1: Talk to Key People

The first thing you need to do in planning for your installation is to talk to all of the key players. Talk to management and especially the end users. What management envisions may not be what works for the end users. The end users are the people on the front line; they know exactly what they need. It is important to determine the tasks the host will need to perform or what problem will be satisfied with this installation. Does the host need to be a server or a desktop? Make sure everyone is in agreement as to what the host is expected to do before you move to the next step.

## Step 2: Distributions

Picking the distribution, or distro, that will be used can be a challenge. The first step to determine is whether the host should be a server or a desktop; this should be identified during preliminary discussions with key people. The answer to this question can determine which distribution will be used. For example, Community Enterprise Operating System (CentOS) is a Linux distribution that acts more as a server than as a desktop. Fedora and Ubuntu are operating systems that act more like desktops. Fedora and Ubuntu can act as servers, but usually do not. Here are some important points to consider:

- Will the end users be comfortable with this distribution, or will modifications be required?

- Will the software the end users need run on the selected distribution?

- Will there be adequate support for the selected distribution?

Distributions (distros) used in this book will include the following.

**Common Distributions**

| Distribution | Provider | Function |
|---|---|---|
| CentOS | Red Hat Enterprise Linux (RHEL) | Used as a server |
| Fedora 38 | Red Hat | Used as a desktop/server |
| Ubuntu 23.04 | Debian Linux | Used as a desktop/server |

# Resource Requirements for Ubuntu and Fedora

It is important to know the resource requirements for Ubuntu and Fedora. The minimum requirements are listed as follows.

## Ubuntu: Recommended Minimum System Requirements

- CPU – 2 GHz dual-core processor
- RAM – 4 GB
- Hard disk size – 25 GB
- 101 keyboard and 2-button mouse
- Monitor
- Network card
- VGA capable of 1024x768 screen resolution
- CD/DVD ROM or USB flash drive

## Fedora: Recommended Minimum System Requirements

- CPU – 2GHz dual core processor or faster
- RAM – 2 GB
- Hard disk size – 20 GB
- 101 keyboard and 2-button mouse
- Monitor
- Network card
- VGA capable of 1024x768 screen resolution
- CD/DVD ROM or USB flash drive

In addition to the minimum requirements, there are three important things that you need to take into consideration as well.

1.  Check the distribution's hardware compatibility list (HCL). You can Google the distribution's HCL and find several places to help in that area.

2.  Use the correct version of the distribution that is based on the host's CPU architecture, such as understanding if you are using 32-bit or 64-bit. Itanium, Alpha, and PowerPC are also considered the CPU architecture.

3.  Make sure you have the hardware you need to run the operating system you want to install and the software that is going to be used to perform the required task.

# Step 3: Naming Conventions

Before you can determine how you are going to partition your hard drives, you need to determine what type of hard drives you are going to use. As a quick review, there are Parallel ATA hard drives (PATA) and Serial ATA (SATA), or the Small Computer System Interface (SCSI). The ATA in these two acronyms stands for *Advanced Technology Attachment*.

## Parallel AT Attachment (PATA) or Integrated Drive Electronics (IDE)

With PATA or IDE, you have a primary channel and a secondary channel, and each can have a slave. You can only have four physical hard drives when using PATA/IDE drives. Notice their naming convention. The /dev directory is where the information about the interface will be located.

- Primary Master (/dev/hda)
- Primary Slave (/dev/hdb)
- Secondary Master (/dev/hdc)
- Secondary Master (/dev/hdd)

## Serial AT Attachment (SATA) and Small Computer System Interface (SCSI)

SATA or SCSI information is also located in the /dev directory, but they have a slightly different naming convention. You are not limited to four physical devices with these interfaces.

- First SATA/SCSI drive (/dev/sda)

- Second SATA/SCSI drive (/dev/sdb)

- Third SATA/SCSI drive (/dev/sdc)

- Fourth SATA/SCSI drive (/dev/sdd)

# Step 4: Partitioning

When using MBR (Master Boot Record) format rather than GPT (GUID partition table) to set up your drives, it is important to know that you can only have four primary partitions or three primaries and one extended partition that can hold multiple logical partitions. This limitation comes from the data structure of the MBR partition table. When you are working with a single hard drive, it is known as hda or sda. Each partition you create on that drive gets a number starting with 1. The extended or logical partition starts with 5. It does not matter which primary partition you select to extend.

For example, the first partition on your first PATA (or IDE) drive would be /dev/hda1. The next three will be /dev/hda2, /dev/hda3, and /dev/hda4. You can then select any of these four partitions to "extend." To compare this to Windows, hda1 would normally be C:, hda2, D:, hda3, E:, and hda4, F:. When you extend a partition (create multiple virtual partitions), they start with /dev/hda5 and continue with /dev/hda6, /dev/hda7, etc. Normally, you the 4th partition is the one that is extended.

If your drives are SATA or SCSI, the "h" in hda is replaced with "s" to make them /dev/sda1, /dev/sda2, /dev/sda3, /dev/sda4, etc.

## Linux Partitioning

Now that you have an understanding of how hard drives are partitioned, you can look at some of the Linux partitions that are located on most Linux systems.

The following are recommendations about directories that should be on their own individual partition and their recommended size.

- / – minimum 8 GB, at least 15 GB recommended

- /boot – 250 MB–1 GB

- /opt – 500 MB–5 GB

- /tmp – size this to match/swap

- /usr – 10 GB

- /var – 2 GB

- /home – as you wish

- Swap – size of RAM

Examining points:

- / – the root directory or top of the directory tree.

- /boot – where all boot-related files are located.

- /opt – stores all software and add-on packages that are installed after the default installation.

- /tmp – where information that is only needed for a short time is kept. Do not store data here, because it is automatically cleared out periodically.

- /usr – where all user applications are stored. This usually ends up being a very large directory, so provide a lot of space here.

- /var – where the system writes data while it is operational – cache, logs, spool, locks, etc. Data in this directory is specific to each computer and is never shared with other hosts on a network.

- /home – where all users' home directories are placed. Give it lots of space.

- swap – space used the same in Linux as in Windows. It holds information that had been stored in RAM until it is needed and is placed back in RAM. This is also called virtual memory. This area should be twice as large as the amount of the installed RAM.

The following directories are required to be on the same partition in order for Linux to work properly.

Examining points:

- /etc – contains all the configuration files for your Linux system including databases.

- /bin – is where binary files are located – images, sound, executable programs, and compressed data.

- /sbin – stands for System Binaries and contains programs most commonly run as the root user – sysadmin tools.

- /lib – holds kernel modules and shared library images. Library files usually end in .so and are very similar to the Windows .dll files.

- /dev – contains device drivers for all devices used by your system.

- /proc – is a virtual directory where information about the current state of the kernel can be located.

- /mnt – holds mount points. Any physical device, like a hard drive or a CD/DVD ROM drive, has an empty directory under /mnt where the contents of the device can be seen and used by the OS. Before a CD/DVD can be read, it has to be mounted into its mount point or /mnt directory.

# Step 5: Default Bootloader

Before proceeding with your installation, you have to decide whether to select the default bootloader for your system or pick another one. A bootloader is a program that starts when you boot your system, which loads the OS Kernal into RAM. You may have set up your home PC where you can boot into Windows or another operating system. The bootloader allows you to control what operating system is loaded. The most common ones are:

Linux Loader (LILO) (/etc/lilo.conf)

- First Linux boot loader

Grand Unified Bootloader (GRUB) (/boot/grub/grub.conf)

- Most commonly used boot loader today

# File System

You have more choices in Linux than in Windows for the file system you want to use. A file system is the format of a hard drive that holds files and directories. The four that you could see in Linux are ext2, ext3, ext4, and reiser.

## Ext2

Ext2 is the first file system that had a way of recovering if the host went down unexpectedly. It uses a lost-and-found directory where information is saved that could help put the system back to a steady state. The problem in this version is that even though it can recover data, it will go through everything before it actually boots. It can take a long time before your system will come back up. That amount of downtime is often not acceptable.

## Ext3

Ext3 is an enhancement over the ext2 and is backward compatible, but instead of the lost-and-found directory, it uses what is called journaling. This is a technique commonly used in databases. Every transaction is recorded, and it is marked as complete after it has been written to the hard drive. So if a system goes down, it looks in this journal, or log, to see what transactions were not committed to a hard drive. This saves the time of reviewing the entire system.

## Ext4

Ext4 is also an enhancement on ext3 and includes several new features, such as allowing up to 1 exabyte of data to be stored on the partition.

## Reiser

Reiser is also based on journaling, but it has a totally different file structure and provides some different features.

# Windows and Linux File Systems

It is important to take a look at the file systems currently used by Windows and Linux.

## Windows

The Windows default is NTFS (New Technology File System), and all drives must use that same file system.

## Linux

With Linux, each partition can have a different file system. This is helpful when you have a program that will not run on a newer file system. The default for Ubuntu and Fedora are ext4 and Btrfs.

- Ubuntu 24.04: ext4

- Fedora 38: Btrfs

# Step 6: Additional Installation Needs

There is additional information needed to put the host on a network. You will need to know the following:

- A host name.

- An IP address and subnet mask.

- A gateway IP address which is actually the router's address.

- The DNS server's IP address.

- Whether you have a DHCP server on your network; if you do, the previously listed information can be dynamically assigned when the system boots, but you must know the IP address of that server.

One final consideration: What software will you need to install during installation? You will be provided with a list of software that can be installed, but recommendations say to only install what you know you are going to use. You can always install additional software later.

# Methods of Installation

Now that you have reviewed the steps for preparing for an installation, it is time to learn how to install Linux. The most common way to install Linux is from a CD/DVD ROM disk. There are alternative locations from which you can install. You can have a package that is loaded directly onto your local hard drive, you can install from an FTP server, an NSF server, or even an HTTP web server. It depends on the configuration selected by your company or what you have available from home.

This section of the chapter includes videos that will show you an installation of Ubuntu and of Fedora into a virtual machine using Virtual Box by Oracle. This is a free program that allows you to install virtual machines on Windows, Linux, and Macintosh. Additional virtual machine software is available such as Virtual PC, Hypervisor, and VMware.

**Ubuntu Installation:** www.youtube.com/watch?v=Ny1GCbqWYWc

**Fedora Installation:** www.youtube.com/watch?v=4eJ3pF4-CN4

# Summary

In this chapter, you learned important concepts relating to installing Linux. Keep the following in mind:

- Be prepared to gather facts before starting an installation. You need to know which distributions of Linux you will need, how it will be configured, and whether your existing hardware can be used.

- All methods for installation should be evaluated to see which fits your needs the best.

- It is important to be prepared and follow the installation steps correctly. This will allow for an easy Linux installation experience.

# Resources

- **Ubuntu Minimum Requirements:** https://help.ubuntu.com/
  community/Installation/SystemRequirements

- **Fedora Minimum Requirements:** https://docs.fedoraproject.
  org/en-US/fedora/latest/release-notes/welcome/Hardware_
  Overview/

- **Virtual Box:** www.virtualbox.org/

- **Partitioning a Linux System:** https://help.ubuntu.com/
  community/DiskSpace

# CHAPTER 3

# Shells, Scripts, and Data Management

This chapter will introduce you to the various shells used in Linux and how to work with them. You will also learn how to do some basic scripting and work with a database.

By the end of this chapter, you will be able to

1. Customize and use the shell environment

2. Create and modify shell scripts

3. Use SQL commands to manage data

## Linux Review
## Shell Environment

The shell is the user interface that acts as a middleman to accept input and pass it on to the kernel for processing. Each user decides what tasks they need to perform, and they pick the shell that performs that task the best. The Borne Again Shell (bash) is the one that is most commonly used (Table 3-1).

© Ahmed F. Sheikh 2024
A. F. Sheikh, *CompTIA Linux+ Certification Companion*, Certification Study Companion Series,
https://doi.org/10.1007/979-8-8688-0128-0_3

***Table 3-1.*** *Linux Shells*

| Shells | Description |
| --- | --- |
| Bash | Bourne Again Shell – default |
| sh | Bourne Shell – bash predecessor |
| ksh | Korn Shell |
| csh | C shell (programming language C) |
| tcsh | Enhanced C Shell |

# Shell Configuration

The appearance of your shell and how it functions is automatically set when the configuration is added to the appropriate file or files. Shell configuration files are summarized in Table 3-2.

When you turn on your Linux machine, you normally will get a login prompt, as you do in Windows. That means you are now working in a login shell that is running a GUI desktop. The most common way to start a non-login shell is when you open a terminal session from the GUI.

Next, you will see two files that are run from the /etc directory: profile and bashrc. The /etc/profile file sets system-wide preferences, such as setting up environment variables. The /etc/bashrc file sets things like system-wide aliases and functions and which file runs will depend on the login type. After the appropriate /etc file is run, a file by the same name located in each individual user's directory is run. All commands found in those files will modify the global settings. Some distributions use the ~/.bash_ profile file rather than or in addition to the ~/.profile file.

The last two, login and logout, are simple to understand.

Recall that a period at the start of a file name indicates the file is hidden. Use the **-a** option with the list or **ls** command to show hidden files.

*Table 3-2.* *Types of Shell Configuration*

| Configuration Files | Shell Types | Description |
| --- | --- | --- |
| /etc/profile | login | Stores system-wide configuration preferences and is used mainly to set environment variables |
| ~/.profile | login | Stores configuration preferences for individual users |
| /etc/bashrc | Non-login (login on some distros) | Stores system-wide shell preferences |
| ~/.bashrc | Non-login (login on some distros) | Stores shell preferences for individuals |
| ~/.bash_profile | login | Stores shell preferences for individuals |
| ~/.bash_login | login | Stores commands that execute at login |
| ~/.bash_logout | login | Stores commands that execute at logout |

# Environmental Variables

Recall that environment variables, often referred to as ENVs (Table 3-3), are used to modify the way your shell functions. You can set new variables, display the list of all your variables, and use them in the appearance of your shell and in scripts you create. These variables act as a means to communicate crucial information to software, influencing their interactions with the environment.

*Table 3-3.* *Commonly Used Environmental Variables*

| Variable | Description |
| --- | --- |
| SHELL | Name of the shell you are using |
| PATH | Search path for commands; list of directories, separated by a colon, in which the shell looks for a command |
| PS1 | Your prompt setting |
| HOME | Home directory of current user |

# PATH Variable

This section includes one of the most important environment variables and shows how it can be used. Be very careful with the PATH variable. If you don't include **$PATH:** at the beginning of the command to change or export the PATH variable, you will overwrite what was already there and create lots of headaches for yourself.

---

### Key Facts

### Environmental Variables

- Modifies the way your shell environment functions

- Begins with $ followed by all capital letters

- Displays the variable with the echo command – **echo $HOME**

- Uses the **set** command to display a list of all variables and their value

### Path Environment Variable

- Sets the PATH variable

    **PATH = $PATH:<newpath>**

- Makes the changes  consistent in all shell sessions

    **export PATH**

- Makes the new values permanent after a reboot, update the following files

    - User only - ~/.bashrc, ~/.bash/login, ~/.bash/profile

    - All users - /etc/profile, /etc/bashrc

- Displays the PATH, type **echo $PATH**

---

# Special Characters

Special characters generally act as shorthand commands, instructing Bash to execute a particular function without the need for more extended and detailed command input. The special characters in Table 3-4 are very important for you to remember. You will use these over and over again while you are working in a shell and especially in writing scripts.

***Table 3-4.*** *Special Characters*

| Symbol | Description |
| --- | --- |
| > | Output redirection |
| >> | Output redirection-append |
| < | Input redirection |
| << | Input redirection-append |
| \| | Pipe – take output of 1 command and send it to another as input |
| # | Comment |

Table 3-5 includes more commands you have seen before that you will definitely use when working in a shell and when you are writing scripts.

***Table 3-5.*** *Shell Commands*

| Command | Task |
| --- | --- |
| **env** | Runs a command with a modified environment |
| **set** | Sets the value of an environment variable |
| **unset** | Removes an environment variable |
| **alias** | Shortcut or abbreviation (rather than typing long command) |

# BASH Functions

When you hear about functions, you might ask the question, "How are they different from creating an alias?" Think of an alias as a nickname for a command string. If you have a command with lots of options that you use often, create this "nickname" for the long command string. That way you do not have to remember the exact syntax of the command every time you want to use it, nor do you have to carefully type a long set of characters repeatedly.

A function is much more powerful than an alias. Functions are actually small mini-scripts. Before you run a script that depends on a specific file being in a specific location, it is nice to know that file is there and that it actually exists. You can create a function that verifies the file exists or tells you if it does not. Stopping the script at that point only makes sense.

Creating a function at the beginning of a script allows the same commands to be executed over and over again in the overall script, just by calling the function. This reduces the size and complexity of a script. If you create a file containing a called function, that function can be used in multiple scripts, saving time and ensuring accuracy and consistency.

# Function: Call from Library Example

Figure 3-1 creates a mini-script which can be classified as a function that displays the message "Hello to all!" Figure 3-2 creates a function that exits a script. Figure 3-3 calls these two functions from a library.

```
#! /bin/bash              #creates a bash subshell in which
                          #the script runs the commands
#Peterson-2023-03-27-Issue a Welcome statement-hello.sh
echo ""                   #adds blank line
echo "Hello to all!"      #Displays a message on the screen
```

***Figure 3-1.*** *Function that displays a message*

```
#! /bin/bash   #creates a bash subshell in which
               #the script runs the commands
#Peterson-2023-03-27-Exits and displays message-quit.sh
echo ""        #adds blank line
echo "I am exiting the script." #Displays message on the
screen
```

***Figure 3-2.*** *Function that ends a script*

```
#! /bin/bash   #creates a bash subshell in which
               #the script runs the commands
#Peterson-2023-03-27-Displays Hello message and
               #exits-sample.sh
./hello.sh     #executes the script created in Figure 3-1
./quit.sh      #executes the script created in Figure 3-2
```

***Figure 3-3.*** *Script that calls functions from a library*

## Function Example: Call from Inside Script

Figure 3-4 shows how you can create functions at the top of a script that can be used over and over inside a script. This is a simple function to demonstrate the concept.

```
#! /bin/bash          #creates a bash subshell in which
                      #the script runs the commands
#Peterson-2023-03-27-Call functions from script-sample2.sh
function cmd {        #creates a function
    echo ""           #adds blank line
    echo " Let's execute a command."
    exit              #If error found, displays error& stops script
}
function quit {       #creates a function
    echo ""           #adds blank line
    echo "I am exiting the script."
    echo ""           #adds blank line
    exit              #If error is found, displays error and stops script
}
echo ""               #adds blank line
cmd                   #calls the function cmd
echo ""               #adds blank line
echo "The ls command lists the names of the files and folders."
echo ""               #adds blank line
ls                    #executes the command ls
echo ""               #adds blank line
cmd                   #calls the function cmd
echo ""               #adds blank line
echo "The ls -l command gives you more information."
echo ""               #adds blank line
ls -l                 #executes the command ls-l
echo ""               #adds blank line
quit                  #stops the script
exit                  #If error isfound, displays error and stops script
```

***Figure 3-4.*** *Functions included in a script*

# Scripts

Scripts can be a great tool for sysadmins! Many routine tasks can be completed quickly and more efficiently using scripts.

A script is nothing more than a collection of commands listed in the order you would do them if you executed them one at the time. Some scripts are complex as they perform multiple commands using multithreading.

When preparing to write a script that will perform a specific task, first determine what commands are necessary and the order in which they should be executed. Create a text file and add each command in the proper order. Execute each of the commands, one at a time, to determine each one works properly and that you received the desired results.

After creating the file, make it executable; otherwise, it is just a normal file that contains information. Next, run the script. Often, the first test run of a script fails. The script may have syntax errors, or it may not do the tasks correctly. Revise the script until it runs without errors and completes the task properly.

The complexity of a script ranges from simple – where the script executes a single command – to complex, where there are multiple commands, the script accepts input at run time, or commands are executed in multiple threads.

As you progress through this chapter, you will look at several scripts.

## Key Facts

Be sure to remember the following steps when working with a script:

- Create the script.

- Assign the Execute permission to the script.

- Run the script.

# Types of Scripts

### Script That Displays Information on the Screen

The following simple script (Figure 3-5) displays the version of BASH being used on the system and the name of the host.

```
#! /bin/bash        #creates a bash subshell in which
                    # the script runs the commands
#Peterson - 03/27/23 - Displays information about system-sysinfo.sh
echo "BASH version: $BASH_VERSION" #displays version of bash used
echo "Hostname:  $HOSTNAME"        #displays the name of the host
exit               #If error is found, displays error and stops script
```

*Figure 3-5.* Script that displays the version of bash being used and the name of the host

---

**Key Facts**

- **#** is used to indicate what follows is a comment.

- **echo** displays what follows on the screen.

- **exit** returns either a success or error message.

---

The second line is a comment that shows who created the script, when it was created, and the purpose of the script. This line is not required and is often omitted; however, it is helpful to others who might use the script. Knowing the purpose of a script quickly can be extremely helpful. Otherwise, a user would have to go through the entire script to determine what it is doing. Knowing who wrote it gives you a place to go for help if that person is still available.

Side note – **#!** is also known as "shebang" to Unix/Linux users. The entire line, **#!** / **bin/bash**, is called a "hashpling."

# Script That Executes Commands

Now that you have seen how the echo command works, you can add some escape sequences to it. There are several in the following list that are often used with **echo ""**.

The most common escape sequences used with the **echo** command are

- **\a** – ASCII beep

- **\c** – prevents adding a new line after a command

- **\e** – enables interpretation of \ as an escape character – not as text

- **\f** – causes a form feed after the command

- **\n** – creates a new line after a command

- **\r** – issues a <return> after a command

For additional escape sequences, see the man pages for the **echo** command (Figure 3-6). (**man echo**)

```
#! /bin/bash    #creates a bash subshell in which
                #the script runs the commands
#Peterson - 03/27/23 - Displays all expense reports submitted
                #for the week-expense.sh
echo ""         # places a blank line before the date
echo -e "Date:  \c" #\c prevents moving cursor to start of new line
date            #executes the date command
echo ""         # puts blank line after date
ls -l /reports/expenses
echo ""         # puts blank line after list command
exit            #If error is found, displays error and stops script
```

***Figure 3-6.*** *Script that executes commands*

The script in Figure 3-6 displays the current date from the computer system and then displays a list of expense reports that were placed in the /reports/expenses folder. You could expand on this script to save this information to a file and even copy these files into another location for processing or archiving.

**Things to note:**

Line one tells the system what shell is to be used. The next line is usually comments; line three is where the actual commands normally start. Comments are placed at the end of most of the commands for clarification.

- **echo ""** creates a blank line

- **echo –e "Date: \c"** puts Date: and two spaces on the screen without moving the cursor to the beginning of the next line. The **–e** causes the \c to be read as an option rather than text that should be displayed.

- The next command, which is date, displays the current date two spaces after Date: and leaves the cursor at that position.

- The cursor then moves to the beginning of the next line and displays all files and directories in the /reports/expenses directory.

# Scripts That Take Input and Use It to Perform an Action

Figure 3-7 accepts two numbers as input from the user and returns their sum on the screen. The script starts with the usual first two lines and then gets into the actual code or commands. The script can ask for something, but if there is no place set up to accept the input, nothing will happen. You must declare the new variable. In this case, we are going to add two numbers together; therefore, you have to indicate the input will be an integer (or some numeric format) as you cannot add characters. This is done by using the **–i** option with the **declare** command. Unless you want to indicate you are using something other than text, BASH does not require that you declare a variable.

After creating the variable, the script can then ask for the input. Use **echo–e** to indicate it will be using an escape sequence in this case **\c** so the input will be shown two spaces after the colon in "Enter a number" – not on the next line. Next the script will accept the input and store the number as the value of the variable.

After asking for the second number and having it stored in the appropriate variable, the numbers are added and used as the value of the TOTSUM variable. The **$((** in the **TOTSUM** command indicates what is inside the double parentheses will be an arithmetic function and not text. That total is then displayed in the last **echo** command.

Setting a variable and reading a value into it is also called command substitution.

```
#! /bin/bash
#Peterson-2023-03-27-Adding 2 numbers-totsum.sh
declare –i NUMA      #the –i creates NUMA as an integer
declare –i NUMB      #the –i creates NUMB as an integer
declare –i TOTSUM    #the –i creates TOTSUM as an integer
echo –e "Enter a number:  \c" #input is put on the same line
read NUMA            #reads input into NUMA variable
echo –e "Enter a second number:  \c"
read NUMB            #reads input into NUMA variable
TOTSUM=$(($NUMA + $NUMB))  #(( ))indicates is a arithmetic command
echo "The sum is:  " $TOTSUM #Displays value of $TOTSUM
exit
```

***Figure 3-7.*** *Scripts that take input and use it to perform an action*

# The Execute Permission

After the script is created, make the file executable; otherwise, it is just a file containing data. Use the **chmod** command to do that. If you run the script and see a message saying "command not found," it means you probably didn't make the script into an executable file.

To execute the command, remember what you learned about indicating the location of the file in Linux. Do one of the following: list the absolute path, use the **./** to indicate the file is in the current directory, add the location to the $PATH variable, or move the file to the user's bin directory (~/bin or /home/<username>/bin) which is usually in the $PATH variable already.

Assign the Execute permission needed to run the script file:

- **chmod u+x <filename>**

OR

- **chmod 744 <filename>**

Ways you can execute the script file:

- /home/<user>/<filename>

- ./<filename>

- Add directory to the $PATH variable

- Move <filename> to ~/bin directory which is usually in PATH

# Constructs

More functionality can be added to the previous scripts by using constructs. These alter the way the script is executed based on the success or failure of a set of commands or on the input from a user. There are three constructs:

- Sequence

- Decision

- Repetition

This section will give you examples of how each is used.

## Sequence Construct

A sequence construct defines the order or sequence in which program commands are executed. Some commands must be run before another can execute properly; with others it doesn't matter. Review the steps you take to get ready for work. Select the clothes you will wear, brush your teeth, take a shower, shave or put on makeup, get out of bed, cook breakfast, eat breakfast are some good examples. There are some steps that have to be taken before another can be completed such as getting out of bed. Until you do that, nothing else can happen. Whether you pick out your clothes, brush your teeth, or take a shower first really doesn't matter. For a man, shaving can go in any order but a woman must at least take the shower before putting on makeup. You also have to cook breakfast before you can eat it. See how important the order in which the commands are executed is when preparing your script?

You have already seen an example of the sequence construct in Figures 3-1 through 3-7. Note how there is an order to how the commands are executed. Figure 3-7 would not calculate the sum of two numbers if you try to add the two numbers before reading them from input.

## Decision Construct

In a decision construct, a condition is tested for true or false. If the condition is true, control (the next command executed) flows to one command. If the condition is false, control flows to a different command. The two decision statements that will be covered in this chapter are the **if** statement and the **case** statement.

# if Statement

The **if** statement tests whether a condition is true or false. Depending on the result, the code branches to one or another path for the next statement (command).

Figure 3-8 uses an **if** statement along with the "equal to" test statement. This can be used in the beginning of more complex scripts to determine if the logged in user is authorized to run the script. This script knows the user Sam is authorized to run the script. The computer first determines if the **value of** $USERNAME variable is Sam. **If the comparison is true, *Welcome Sam* is displayed on the screen.**

End an **if** statement with **fi** – **if** backward.

```
#! /bin/bash
#Peterson-2023/03/27-Welcomes Sam as the authorized user
if [ $USERNAME = "Sam" ]   #test condition
then
    echo "Welcome Sam."
fi                          #end of test condition
```

***Figure 3-8.*** *if statement*

Figure 3-9 uses the **else if**. If the user is Sam, the message *Welcome Sam.* is displayed on the screen. If the user is **not** Sam, *You are not authorized to perform this script.* is displayed.

```
#! /bin/bash
#Peterson-2023/03/27-Welcomes Sam as the authorized user;
#everyone else is told they are not authorized
if [ $USERNAME = "Sam" ]    #test condition
then
    echo "Welcome Sam"
else
    echo "You are not authorized to perform this script."
fi                          #end of test condition
```

***Figure 3-9.*** *if/else statement*

Figure 3-10 uses the **if/then/else** statement. Again, if the user is Sam, *Welcome Sam* is displayed. If the user is Susie, the message *Get out of Sam's work!* is displayed. Then the else part of the **if** statement will be displayed, *You are not authorized to perform this script.*

```
#! /bin/bash
#Peterson-2023/03/27-Welcomes Sam as the authorized user; tells
#Susie to get out of Sam's work; anyone else is told they are
#not authorized
if [ $USERNAME = "Sam" ]
then
     echo "Welcome Sam"
elif [ $USERNAME = "Susie" ]       # elif = else if
then
     echo "Get out of Sam's work!"
else
     echo "You are not authorized to perform this script."
fi
```

***Figure 3-10.*** *if/ else/elseif statement*

Figures 3-11a and 3-11b show a complex **if** construct. Figure 3-11a shows the logic in a flowchart and Figure 3-11b shows the code. This example illustrates how you can combine several of the **elif** (else if) commands when there are only a few choices in your menu.

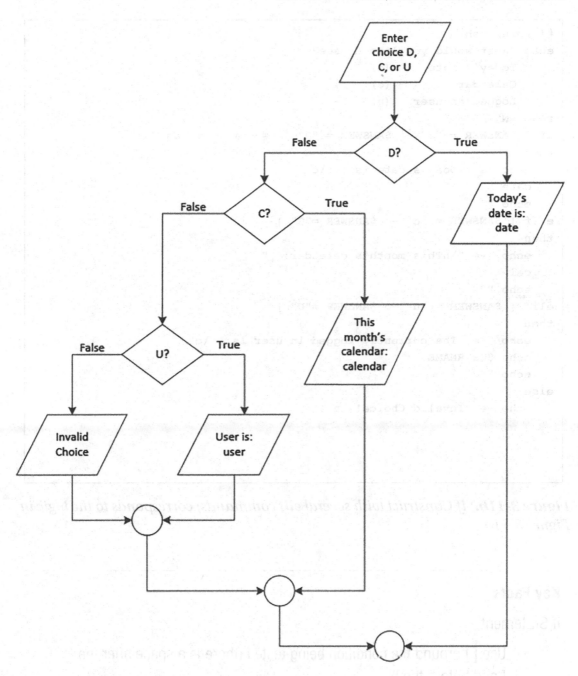

***Figure 3-11a.*** *Complex if logic shown in a flow chart*

```
#! /bin/bash
echo "What would you like to see?
     Today's date        (d)
     Calendar            (c)
     Logged in user      (u)"
read ANSWER
if [ $ANSWER = "d" -o $ANSWER = "D" ]   #-o is same as "or"
then
    echo -e "Today's date is :  \c"
    date
    echo ""
elif [ $ANSWER = "c" -o $ANSWER ="C" ]
then
    echo  -e "\nThis month's calendar:  "
    cal
    echo ""
elif [ $ANSWER = "u" -o $ANSWER ="U" ]
then
    echo  -e "The currently logged in user is:  \c"
    echo $USERNAME
    echo ""
else
    echo -e "Invalid Choice! \a"
```

*Figure 3-11b.* *if Construct with several **elif** commands; corresponds to the logic in Figure 3-11a*

---

### Key Facts

if Statement

- Use [ ] around the condition being tested (there is a space after the [ and before the ]).

- If [ condition ] then action.

- If [ condition ] then action else action.

- If [ condition ] then action elif [ condition ] then action.

- End the if construct with fi.

- Caution: The logic can become complex very quickly.

## Case Construct

A variation of the **if** statement is the **case** statement. It also tests for a condition, and takes action on the results. As with the **if** statement, the **case** statement ends with the reverse of **case** or **esac.**

   As the number of conditions increase, the **case** statement is more functional than the **if** statement. Figures 3-12a and 3-12b use a **case** statement that does the same as the **if** statement shown in Figure 3-11b. With this code, the **case** statement is easier to code and understand than the **if** statement. The flowchart is shown first, followed by the code.

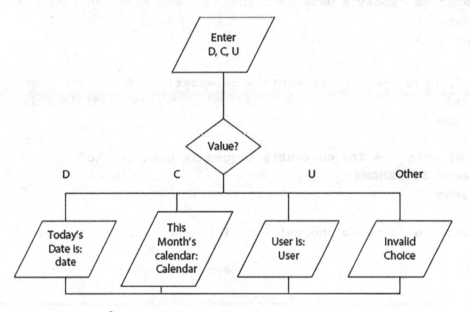

***Figure 3-12a.*** *Menu choice using **case** construct*

This script gives the user a short menu of choices. By selecting the appropriate letter, the command is executed. If you select *u* in Figure 3-12b, the script continues through the code until it finds the appropriate **$ANSWER** and then executes the appropriate command. If none of these three letters is selected, the code displays *Invalid Choice!*.

```bash
#! /bin/bash
# Peterson -03-27-2023-Date/Calendar/Logged in User Menu-menu.sh
echo "What would you like to see?          #creates the menu
        Today's date        (d)
        Calendar            (c)
        Logged in user      (u)"
echo ""
read ANSWER                               #reads the response
case $ANSWER in                           #create the case
d | D )                                   #first option
    echo -e "Today's date is : \c"        #\c stays on same line
    date
    echo ""
    ;;
c | C) echo  -e "\nThis month's calendar:  " #\n - new line
    cal                             #display current month's calendar
    echo ""
    ;;
u | U) echo  -e The currently logged in user is: \c"
    echo $USERNAME
    echo ""
    ;;
*) echo -e "Invalid choice! \a"  #*) test fails - \a makes sound
    ;;
Esac                             #end the menu
```

***Figure 3-12b.*** *Case Statement*

Figure 3-12b will produce the same results as the **if** statement; however, the logic is simpler than in the **if** statement used in Figure 3-11b.

The more choices you have, the more cumbersome the **if** statement will become. When there are more options for a single variable, it is easier to code with a **case** statement.

---

**Tip**   When working with case statements using letters or a combination of letters, add an extra test for both upper and lower case. If you don't, the letter "s" becomes case sensitive.

---

# Difference Between if and case

With **if** statements, you can ask about many different variables. For example, you can ask if the username is Mary AND the day of the week is Thursday AND the value of the variable is greater than 1000, and then do a specific task.

With **case**, the variable must always be the same. This corresponds to a menu choice, or day of the week, or a known list of users. The case statement is helpful when there are multiple different choices.

A **case** statement can always be written as an **if** statement, but an **if** statement may not always be written using a **case** statement.

# Testing Using if and case

**if** and **case** statements commonly use what are called test conditions. The best way to explain their use is by an example.

A script can ask a true/false question. The conditional statement is checked. If the result is true, the script continues. The yes/no shown in Figure 3-13 is the same as true/false.

```
#! /bin/bash
#Peterson-03-27-2023-Ask question, Is this Sam Spade?-sams.sh
echo "Is this Sam Spade?  (yes/no)"
read ANS
if [ $ANS  = "yes" ]
then
    echo -e "\nWelcome Sam."
else
    echo -e "\nSince you are not Sam, you have no access"
fi
```

***Figure 3-13.*** *Demonstrates the test condition A = B*

That example is known as [ A = B ]. Note there must be a space after the first square bracket and before the last square bracket or the expression will not be executed properly. The opposite of that expression is [ A! = B ]. This is read as A is not equal to B.

To perform a numerical comparison (Table 3-6), you must use one of the following rather than the "=" or "!=" symbols that are used with text.

***Table 3-6.*** *Numeric Comparison Operators*

| Term | Comparison Operator | Comparison Operator Symbol | Example |
|---|---|---|---|
| equal | Eq | == | If A = B then echo "You win!" |
| not equal | Ne | != | If A == B then echo "Do not pass GO!" |
| less than | lt | < | If A < B then echo "Do not buy it." |
| greater than | gt | > | If A > B then echo "You have enough to buy it!" |
| less than or equal | le | <= | If A <= B then echo "You pass" |
| greater than or equal | ge | >= | If A >= B then echo "Please include more" |
| true if file exists | [ -f A ] | | If myfile exists then cp myfile mynewfile |
| true if directory exits | [ -d A ] | | If /mydir exists then cp myfile /mydir |

# I I and && Chaining Operators

The || and **&&** chaining operators connect two statement (Figure 3-14). This example shows how to make a directory and copy files into it when using an **if** construct. The scripts that follow show you how to do the same thing using the || and/or **&&** Chaining Operators.

```
#! /bin/bash
#Peterson-03/27/23-Make a directory and copy files to it.
if mkdir scripts      #true if scripts directory was created
then
    cp *.sh scripts      #all script files are copied to scripts dir
    echo "Files were successfully copied to the scripts directory."
else                     #false if scripts directory is not created
    echo "The scripts directory could not be created."
fi                       #end if statement
exit
```

***Figure 3-14.*** *Make a directory and copy files to it using **if** statement*

Follow the scripts in Figures 3-15 through 3-17 carefully. You may have to review them several times before you really understand this logic.

Figure 3-15 uses the **&&** chaining operator. The make directory command is executed. If it works, then the copy command is executed. It no directory is created, the copy command does not execute.

Think of the **&&** chaining operator as "and." Execute the first command AND the second command if the first command is true (or executes properly).

```
#! /bin/bash
#Peterson-03-27-2023-Copy files only if dir is created.
mkdir scripts && cp *.sh scripts
```

***Figure 3-15.*** *Make directory and copy files using && chaining operators*

Figure 3-16 uses the || chaining operator. If the make directory command is successful, the error message is not displayed. If it fails or is false, the error message is displayed. Think of this construct as "or." One OR the other of the commands is successfully executed.

```
#! /bin/bash
#Peterson-03-27-2023-If the dir is not create, show message.
mkdir scripts || echo "The scripts directory could not be created."
```

***Figure 3-16.*** *Make directory using || chaining operators*

Now you will combine the && and the || chaining operations in a single script.

In Figure 3-17, each set of commands is highlighted in a different color so you can "see" the parts better. Both statements are using the || chaining operator, and they are combined with the **&&** chaining operator. Review each statement individually.

- || - Blue highlight – If the directory is successfully created, the error message does not display. If it is not created (fails), the error message is displayed.

- || - Green highlight – If the copy is successful, no error message is displayed. If it fails, the message is displayed.

- **&&** - Combine Blue and Green highlighted commands – If the blue command succeeds, then run the green command. If the blue command fails, do **not** run the green command.

```
#! /bin/bash
mkdir scripts || echo "The scripts directory could not be created."
&&
cp *.sh scripts || echo "The files were not copied to the scripts
directory."
```

***Figure 3-17.*** ***&&*** *and || chaining operator combined*

Another way of saying that:

- If the **mkdir** command fails:

    - "The scripts directory could not be created" message is displayed

    - **cp** command does not execute

- If the **mkdir** command executes

  - **cp** command is executed

- If the **mkdir** command executes and **cp** command fails

  - "The files were not copied to the scripts directory" message is displayed

# Repetition Construct

In Figure 3-18, the Welcome message will be displayed five times. The **for i** statement will use **i = 1** in the Welcome message, then it will use i = 2 in the Welcome message, and so on, until it reaches 5, and the script will end. The variable after **for**, in this case, **i**, is called the indexing variable. In Figure 3-18, **i** is in a list of numbers. Note there are NO commas between the numbers.

In Figure 3-19, **i** acts as a counter. When done is reached, **i** takes on the value of i+1. When **i** exceeds the terminal value, in this case 5, the loop terminates and control is passed to the next command in the script.

Figure 3-19 has the same output as Figure 3-18, but you do not have to list all the numbers. Here, you list the first and last numbers, two dots, and use curly braces.

```
#! /bin/bash
#JH-03-27-2023-forcon.sh
for i in 1 2 3 4 5
do
    echo "Welcome $i times."
done
```

***Figure 3-18.*** *for statement using a list of values*

```
#! /bin/bash
#JH-03-27-2023-forcon2.sh
for i in {1..5}
do
    echo "Welcome $i times."
done
```

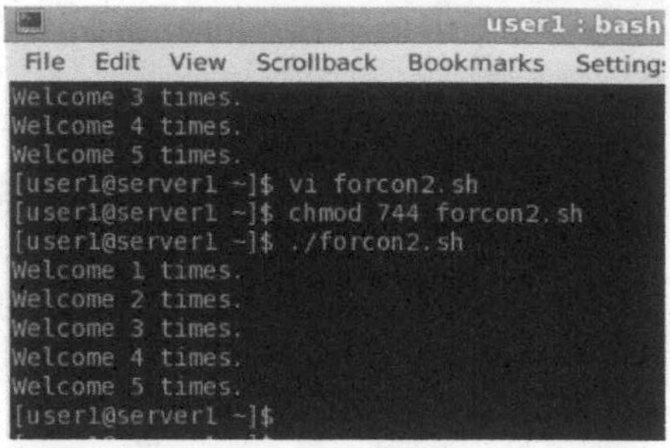

***Figure 3-19.*** *for statement showing the initial and terminal values*

In Figure 3-20, the **seq** (sequence) command is used in this example only to show you how it could be used. The **seq** command supplies a sequence of numbers using this syntax – FIRST INCREMENT LAST. Therefore, this example starts with 1, then uses 3 (increments by 2), then 5 (again by 2), up to 20 (actually stops at 19).

In Figure 3-21, the script is the equivalent of the **seq** example. The format of this is FIRST LAST INCREMENT.

In **for**, the set of statements is ALWAYS done once, as the condition is tested at the end. The indexing variable (**i**) is set IN the **for** statement.

```
#! /bin/bash
#JH-03-27-2023-forseq.sh
for i in $(seq 1 2 20)
do
    echo "Increments by 2-$i."
done
```

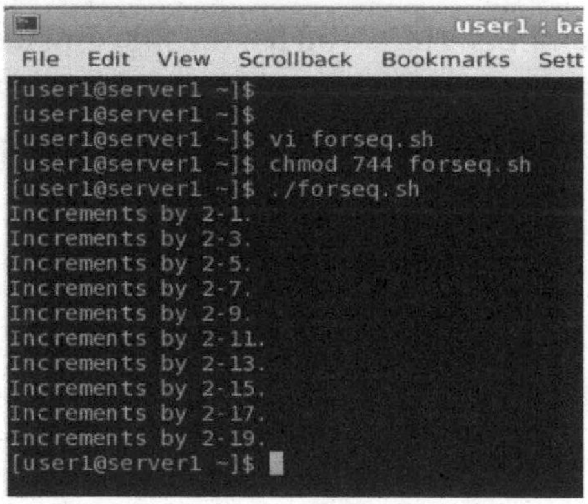

***Figure 3-20.*** *for statement with seq()*

```
#! /bin/bash
#JH-03-27-2023-forseq2.sh
for i in {0..10..2}
do
    echo "Increments by 2-$i."
done
```

*Figure 3-21.* *for statement with seq{}*

## Key Fact

## Repetition

- **in 1 2 3 4 5** – every number from 1 to 5

- **in {1..5}** – every number between and including 1 and 5

- **in $(seq 1 2 20)** – (<first> <increment> <last>) – starts with 1, increments to 3, then to 5, then to 7, etc., to 19

- **in {0..10..2}** – {<first> < last> <increment>} – starts with – 0, then 2, then 4, etc., to 10

# while Statements

A while statement is a control flow statement in Bash scripting that permits the repeated execution of a certain block of code as long as a specified condition remains true. The **while** statement is much like the **for** construct except it starts with a condition or test statement. The commands within the do statement will be executed until the while condition is satisfied (Figure 3-22 and 3-23).

```
#! /bin/bash
#JH-03-27-23-Displays message
#5 times - dowhile.sh
i=1
while [ $i -le 5 ]
do
    echo "Hello $i times."
    i=$(( $i + 1 ))
    #stops infinite loop
    exit
done
```

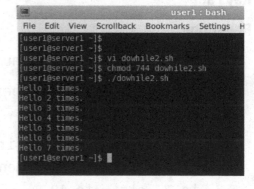

*Figure 3-22.* **while** *statement using less than operator*

```
#! /bin/bash
#JH-03-27-23-Displays message
5 #times - dowhile2.sh
i=1
while [ $i != 8 ]
do
    echo "Hello $i times."
    i=$(( $i + 1 ))
    #stops infinite loop
done
```

*Figure 3-23.* **while** *statement using NOT operator*

In **while**, the set of statements may never be done, as the condition is tested at the beginning of the loop and may be false before you start. The indexing variable (**i**) is initialized before the loop starts, then incremented inside the loop. If the indexing variable never changes because there is no incrementing statement inside the loop, then there will be an infinite loop. This will require operator intervention to interrupt the processing.

The done statement tells the script where the while loop ends. Thus, the set of statements that are repeated (the loop) are the statements between do and done.

The **while** statement is similar to the **if** statement – **if i=5 then exit**.

# Status of Script

When a command is executed, it returns an exit status or exit code. It is good practice and informative to check the exit status code in the script. In the script below, you will learn how to use return error messages and exit a script if a command fails.

The last command – **exit** – reports that the script was executed successfully. The exit command is most commonly used after each task is performed in a script. If that task fails, the entire script will be stopped and an error message stating what the error is will be displayed. If you do not check for errors as the script is executed and return an exit code, you don't know if, or where, the script failed.

Figure 3-24 is an example of why an exit code should be included. A simple shell script was created that an employee would execute before leaving for the day. The purpose of the script is to back up some critical data to tape and print to paper that the task had been completed. The hard drive failed, and the previous day's backup had to be used to restore the data. Guess what! The tape was blank! The printout was there so what happened? We executed the commands by hand, one at the time and saw that the backup command failed. Since there was no exit code in the script, the next commands were then executed which indicated that the backup was successful. If the exit code had been included, it would have been obvious that the backups were not correctly created.

On the test statement to see if the $BAK directory exists, the echo statement ends with a semicolon and is followed by an exit command. The semicolon tells the system that another command is coming on the same line. It acts as a separator. Both those commands are enclosed in curly braces. The curly braces indicate what is inside them are to be executed together – as in a subshell. A set of parentheses mean the same thing.

The **$?** returns a status. If $BAK and $TAPE both exist but the backup fails, the **$?** will not return the success code of 0. **If [ $? –ne 0 ]** is true, then the status of the backup command was not equal to 0; therefore, the backup failed.

```
#! /bin/bash
#JH-03-27-23-Backup dir to tape - backup.sh
BAK=data2
TAPE=dev/st0
echo "Backing up the $BAK directory to tape device $TAPE"
   #Test if $BAK exists else script stops
[ ! -d $BAK ] && { echo "Source backup directory $BAK does not
exist."; exit 1; }
   #Test if $TAPE exists else script stops
[ ! -b $TAPE ] && { echo "Tape drive $TAPE not found."; exit 2; }
tar cvf $TAPE $BAK 2> /tmp/error.log
   #Using the tar command, backup is attempted with result going
   #to the file error.log
if [ $? -ne 0 ]
   then
   echo "An error occurred during the backup."
   exit 3
fi
echo "Backup complete."
exit 0
```

*Figure 3-24.* *Working with **exit** codes*

The following script (Figure 3-25) uses the same script as before, with the addition of the **mail** command. Notice that the error message was sent as the body of the mail. The syntax for the mail command is **mail -s <subject> <recipient's e-mail>**. If the recipient is at the same location (same domain), you don't have to put the @domain name.

To view this mail, log in as root and change to the /var/spool/mail directory. Use the **cat** command to display all mail that has not been removed. You can also type **mail** to see all mail. The **<enter>** key scrolls you through the mail. Use **^Z** to escape from this option.

To delete all mail in a user's directory, use the command

**rm -f /var/spool/mail/ <user>**

```
#! /bin/bash
#JH-03-27-23-Backup data - backupdata.sh
BAK=data2
TAPE=dev/st0
echo "Backing up the $BAK directory to tape device $TAPE"
[ ! -d $BAK ] && { echo "Source backup directory $BAK does not
exist." | mail -s "Backup Error" root; exit 1; }
    #Test if $BAK exists else script stops
 [ ! -b $TAPE ] && { echo "Tape drive $TAPE not found." | mail -s
"Backup Error" root; exit 2; }
    #See if $TAPE exists else script stops
tar cvf $TAPE $BAK 2> /tmp/error.log
    #Using the tar command, backup is attempted with result going
    #to the file error.log
if [ $? -ne 0 ]
    then
    echo "An error occurred during the backup." | mail -s "Backup
Error" root
    exit 3
fi
echo "Backup complete."
exit
```

***Figure 3-25.*** *Conditional mailing to the superuser*

# Databases & SQL Commands

## Database Services

A database is a container for information that can be updated and put into reports in a meaningful way. Each database is made up of one or more tables. Each table is made up of records. Each record is made up of fields. You can think of a spreadsheet as a table. It has rows and columns. Each row is a record; each column is a field. A cell contains a value.

Structured Query Language or SQL (pronounced sequel) is a language that allows you to manage and manipulate the data stored in a database.

What is a relational database?

- Collection of information stored in tables that are linked together by a common field.

- Each table has one theme.

- Tables are made up of records.

- Records are made up of fields.

- Fields are attributes.

What is SQL?

- Structured Query Language (SQL) is a programming language used to manage information in a database.

- SQL statements allow you to create, update, and query the data in a database.

Figure 3-26 shows you the various parts of a database. You can see from this why a table is often compared to a spreadsheet. They look similar, but well-designed databases have many powerful features not available in spreadsheets.

| Emp# | F_name | L_name | Address | City | St | Zip |
|------|--------|--------|---------|------|-----|-----|
| 0001 | Joe | Biwe | 200 S. Second St. | Nacogdoches | TX | 75039 |
| 0002 | Susie | Smuel | 215 House St. | Dallas | TX | 75209 |
| 0003 | Anna | Jonathan | 324 College Rd. | Denton | TX | 75442 |
| 0004 | Mark | Rodger | 1000 Knob Ave. | Mesquite | TX | 75142 |

Common Field

Attribute or Field (Column)
(Column)

| Emp# | Job# | Hrs | Wk_Start |
|------|------|-----|----------|
| 0001 | 99765 | 40 | 03/27/2023 |
| 0004 | 84332 | 35 | 03/27/2023 |
| 0001 | 38776 | 20 | 03/27/2023 |
| 0002 | 88765 | 25 | 03/27/2023 |

Field Name

Record (Row)

**Figure 3-26.** *Design of a database*

# Client/Server Model

Databases have what is called a client/server model. The database acts as the server, and there is a client that can pull and/or manipulate data in the database.

MySQL is an open-source relational database management system (RDBMS) built upon Structured Query Language (SQL). It is compatible with various platforms, such as Linux, UNIX, and Windows. The client side can be in the form of commands executed in a terminal session or as a GUI utility.

Note – MySQL is pronounced My S Q L – not MySequel.

Client/Server Model

- Server – stores information

    - The most common SQL Servers used by Linux are PostgreSQL and MySQL.

- Client – accesses and manages information

    - Command line or GUI utilities.

# SQL Commands

Table 3-7 details the use of various SQL commands and their descriptions as well as how they are used.

***Table 3-7.*** *SQL Commands and Descriptions*

| Command | Syntax | Description |
|---|---|---|
| CREATE DATABASE | CREATE DATABASE Movies; | Creates a new database |
| CREATE TABLE | CREATE TABLE Movie (name VARCHAR(50), yr INT(4), genre VARCHAR(12),seen ENUM("y","n")); | Creates the table named Movie with fields: name, yr, genre, and seen |
| SHOW TABLES | SHOW TABLES Movies; | Lists all tables in the Movies database; there will probably be more tables than just Movies such as Actors, Directors, and Producers |
| USE | USE Movies; | Specified the database to work in |
| DESCRIBE | DESCRIBE Movies; DESCRIBE Movie; | Displays information about the database Movies Displays information about the table Movie |
| INSERT INTO | INSERT INTO Movie VALUES ("The Hulk",1973,"fantasy",yes) | Add records to a table |
| DROP TABLE | DROP TABLE Movie | Deletes the table Movie |

*(continued)*

***Table 3-7.*** (*continued*)

| Command | Syntax | Description |
|---------|--------|-------------|
| ALTER TABLE | ALTER TABLE Movie ADD COLUMN rate ENUM('G','R','X'); | Adds a field or attribute to the table Movie |
| | ALTER TABLE Movie ALTER COLUMN rate rating; | Changes the field named rate in the table Movie to have the name rating |
| | ALTER TABLE Movie DROP COLUMN seen | Drops the field seen |
| SELECT | SELECT FROM Movie WHERE yr=1973 GROUP BY genre SORT BY yr; | Select all the information from table movie if yr=1973, group it by genre, and sort that by year |
| DELETE FROM | DELETE FROM Movie WHERE rating="X"; | Deletes all records in the Movie table for all X rated movies |
| UPDATE | UPDATE Movies SET genre="comic fantasy" WHERE genre="fantasy" | Updates/replaces values in records |
| JOIN | SELECT Movie.name, Movie.yr, Actor. fname, Actor.lname FROM Movie JOIN Actor ON Movie.name=Actor.movie | Joins the tables Movie and Actor to display the Movie's name and year and the Actor's first and last name |

# Verifying MySQL Is Installed

This is how you can tell if MySQL is installed, and how to install it if it is not there already.

To determine if MySQL is installed:

- **su –** # change to root

- **rpm –qi mysql** # using rpm, query MySQL

To install MySQL:

- **yum install mysql**

# Summary

- The shell is the user interface that accepts input and passes it to the kernel for processing. Its appearance is set when the shell is configured, and can be customized. Environment variables modify the way the shell functions.

- Functions are mini-scripts that can be stored and used by multiple scripts. Functions can be called from a library or from within a script.

- A script is a collection of commands that can be saved and used on a scheduled or as-needed basis. Scripts are lines of code. All code can be classified as being part of one of three structures: sequence, decision, and repetition. Decision statements are **if** and **case**; repetition statements are **for** and **while**. Specific syntax rules must be followed to avoid errors. The chaining operators **||** and **&&** can be used in scripts to execute more complex logic.

- After a command is executed, it returns an exit status that can be queried to determine if another line of code should be executed or not. Adding an exit command at the end of a script is good programming practice.

- A database "keeps track of things." SQL is a language that allows you to manage and manipulate data stored in a database. My SQL is an open source database engine commonly used with Linux. Simple scripts allow you to determine if MySQL is installed, or to install it on your machine.

# CHAPTER 4

# Boot Process and Shutdown

In this chapter, you will learn about installing boot loaders and identifying the initialization phase, and ways to shut down Linux.

By the end of this chapter, you will be able to

1. Identify the steps needed to boot a Linux system

2. Install boot loaders

3. Identify the Initialization phase

4. Identify ways to shut down Linux.

## Boot Process
### Fedora Boot Process

Figure 4-1 shows the boot process used by Fedora. When a host first starts, the BIOS takes over, and it does what is called a POST (power-on self-test) where it checks all the hardware and makes sure everything is running properly. Then, it kicks everything over to the Master Boot Record (MBR)/GUID Partition Table (GPT), which looks to see if an operating system should be loaded or if there is a boot loader (as there usually is with Linux). The boot loader loads the kernel, which in turn loads the initialization (init) process. Then the init process starts all the daemons or services.

Each one of these will be covered in a little more detail within the chapter.

© Ahmed F. Sheikh 2024
A. F. Sheikh, *CompTIA Linux+ Certification Companion*, Certification Study Companion Series,
https://doi.org/10.1007/979-8-8688-0128-0_4

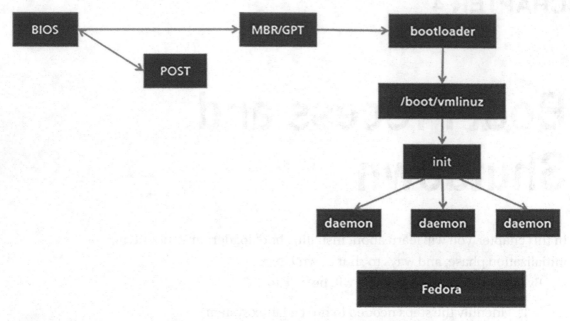

**Figure 4-1.** *This diagram demonstrates Fedora's boot process*

# BIOS

The term BIOS stands for *basic input/output system*. Instructions are stored in a nonvolatile, read-only memory (ROM) chip that is on the motherboard of every host. That means these instructions are stored on this chip and is not changed when the system is rebooted. It stores low-level instructions that tell the CPU what hardware is on the host and how it is supposed to talk to the CPU. In past years, the BIOS was not upgradeable, but the newer chips can be upgraded by a program, which is known as flashing the BIOS.

The first process that runs when you turn on your host is called the POST (power-on self-test). It is an operation triggered by a computer once it is powered on but before it proceeds to boot up the operating system. It initializes and tests each piece of hardware that the BIOS knows about.

Now you will learn about the volatile information the BIOS reads from the CMOS (complementary metal-oxide semiconductor chip), which is also located on the motherboard of each host.

Normally, when you first turn on your machine, you get a message that says hit F2, F10, or escape to get into the BIOS setup program. That program is where you would make any changes to the configuration used by the BIOS and is saved in the CMOS chip.

After the BIOS does its POST and gets all its information from CMOS, then it goes to the MBR (Master Boot Record) or the GPT (GUID Partition Table). The GPT is a table like the MBR, except it works with larger hard drives. Both of these are located in the boot sector, which is usually in the first or second sector of the boot partition. This tells the boot loader where the boot files are located.

# Boot Loader

A boot loader is a piece of software that is used to determine from which operating system you are going to boot. You may have created a dual-boot system where you can boot from one of several operating systems, such as Windows XP, Windows 7, or Linux. Linux boots from a boot loader, which brings up a menu that lists all the operating systems that are available to run on that host. Normally one of these operating systems is set to boot by default if you do not make another selection.

For Linux installations, the boot loader will first create what is called a RAM disk. This is a virtual disk that is created in the RAM of your host, and it will load an image called *initrd*. The initrd image is a small, very basic Linux operating system (OS) that contains all the start-up processes that you need and sets up the locations of where your root system files are.

One of the nice things about Linux is you can boot from several different locations. You can boot from the local hard drive; you can boot from a local USB device; or you can boot from a completely different machine. This image allows you to set up and load any device drivers that are needed to be able to load the boot process. Then it loads the kernel.

# Kernel

The kernel, which is the core of the operating system, is loaded into RAM by the boot loader. The boot files are located in the /boot directory. It initializes the hardware that it learns about from the BIOS and CMOS settings. It then searches in the initrd file system and runs a program called *linuxrc* that is used to set up the rest of the tasks that load the system. At that point, the initrd file system is dismounted and the RAM disk is destroyed.

The kernel then searches for any new hardware and loads the appropriate device drivers. The init process then runs from the /etc/inittab directory. Note that Ubuntu has a little different process. It uses .conf files that are located in the /etc/init directory. Init spawns everything including processes that start other processes. All services or daemons are now loaded, and you have a fully operating Linux system.

## Common Boot Loaders

If you are familiar with the Windows boot.ini file, you know Windows can boot from a list of different OSs also. You are able to specify which OS you are going to boot, what the default will be, how long before it automatically picks that default, and a few other options. In other words, it can be configured to load one of several different distros of Linux or even Windows. The most common of the boot loaders are LILO and GRUB.

Experiment with both to see which option works best for you and your environment. Before you start to make actual changes to your boot loader, make a boot disk and create a copy of the files that will be modified. You could mess your system up to the point that it will not boot. Better safe than sorry!

## LILO

The oldest of these two boot loaders is LILO (LInux LOader.) It was the original boot loader used by Linux. Because no improvements were made to LILO for a long time, the GRUB boot loader was created. Since that time, it has been upgraded to meet all the features available in GRUB. Its configuration file, lilo.conf, is located in the /etc directory. You will find there are mixed feelings about LILO. Some people love it and prefer to use it over GRUB.

## GRUB

GRUB is the boot loader that is normally used with Linux installations. GRUB stands for Grand Unified Boot loader. The boot loader is installed at the beginning of a Linux installation. Be aware that it does have to be installed before a Linux OS can be installed. Its configuration file, grub.conf, is located in the /boot/grub directory. This grub.conf file is not used by every distribution of Linux. For instance, Suse Linux uses the menu.lst.

Be aware there are log files being created by the syslogd or klogd daemons as your system boots. These can be very helpful if problems occur during your boot process. After syslogd or klogd have been started, contents of the kernel ring buffer will be sent to the /var/log/messages log. If you need to capture that same content before syslogd or klogd have been loaded, you can use dmesg > boot.message command at boot up. This should be typed just after the initialization phase of your system's boot process. There are numerous log files that are stored under the /var/log directory that can be opened with any simple text editor.

If for some reason you want to install GRUB before you start the Linux installation, the command to do that is grub-install. Then you list the partition on which you will put it – for example, /dev/hd0,0. That is a little different from the labeling for partitioning. Instead of doing hda1, GRUB uses hd and the number of the drive, a comma, and then the number of the partition. Remember 0 is like 1 to a computer.

During the installation, GRUB creates a root directory under the /boot directory. This root contains all the files that will be used in the next step. If you created a /boot directory on a separate partition, which is recommended, the /boot is dropped from the path.

GRUB loads in two parts. The first part looks at the MBR/GPT and looks for the location of part two, and that is all it does. When it goes to part two, it displays a menu so you can pick the OS you want to load. This menu contains several configurable parameters. Later in this chapter, you will see a demonstration of how you work with the GRUB boot loader, how you make modifications to it, and what it can do for you.

# GRUB Parameters

Table 4-1 lists the most common configuration parameters used in the GRUB boot loader.

***Table 4-1.*** *Common Configuration Parameters in the GRUB Boot Loader*

| Parameter | Description |
|---|---|
| default | Indicates which OS will boot by default |
| timeout | Shows how many seconds GRUB waits before the default is selected |
| gfxmenu splashimage | Shows the image file the GUI will display |
| hiddenmenu | Enables or disables the menu when GRUB starts |
| title | Displays name on menu |
| root | Indicates the location of the root file system |
| kernel | Specifies the kernel to load along with any options |
| initrd | Specifies the initrd image file that builds the RAM disk |
| chainloader | Indicates the number of sectors that GRUB should read |
| password | Sets a password, which is required for authentication; should be encrypted |
| lock | Requires that the password be provided before entering the GRUB menu |
| quiet | A configuration option to hide system-related output while the system is booting up. |

# GRUB2

As with most programs, GRUB has been updated and is now known as GRUB2 (Table 4-2). It comes with the most current Linux distributions. It is important to know that these two versions are totally different in the configuration and files used. GRUB2 uses scripting and different configuration files. If you are not sure which version your distro is using, you can check by using the grub-install -v or grub2-install -v commands from a terminal session. GRUB2 is v1.98 and higher.

The way GRUB2 works is totally different from its predecessor, GRUB. Instead of one file that is configurable, three files work together to make GRUB2 work.

*Table 4-2.* *GRUB2*

| File/Directory | Description |
|---|---|
| ./boot/grub/grub.cfg | • Similar to menu.lst or grub.conf in the older version |
| | • Should not be edited directly |
| | • Updated with update-grub |
| | • Contains menu information |
| | • Sections start with ###BEGIN |
| ./etc/grub.d | • Directory holding script files |
| | • Scripts read by update-grub and pushed to grub.cfg |
| | • Most script files start with ##_ ; loads in numerical order with 00_ having the highest priority |
| | • Script files not starting with ##_ executed last |
| ./etc/default/grub | • Controls how the system appears and functions |
| | • Changes to this file are pushed to grub.cfg by the update-grub command |

- The **/boot/grub/grub.cfg** file is similar to the older /boot/grub/
  menu.lst file but should never be modified. The update-grub
  command takes information from /etc/default/grub and /etc/grub.d
  and creates or updates the /boot/grub/grub.cfg file.

- The **/etc/grub.d** directory contains executable script files that
  start with two numbers and an underscore such as 00_header. The
  numbers control the order in which these scripts execute. Changes
  to these files are pushed to the /boot/grub/grub.cfg file when the
  update-grub command is executed. There can be scripts that do not
  start with numbers, and they are executed after all the numbered
  scripts are run.

- The **/etc/default/grub** file controls how the GRUB2 menu looks and
  acts. Edits to this file are also pushed to the /boot/grub/grub.cfg file.

Another big change in GRUB2 is the numbering of the partitions. Previously, h0,0
was used for the first hard drive and the first partition. In GRUB2, it is now h0,1.

Be sure to run the update-grub command after any changes are made to the script files in the /etc/grub.d directory or to the /etc/default/grub file. Otherwise, your changes will never be used by the /boot/grub/grub.cfg file.

Table 4-3 includes the most common script files used with GRUB2 which are located in the /etc/grub.d directory.

***Table 4-3.*** *Common GRUB2 Script Files*

| Script File | Description |
| --- | --- |
| 00_header | Sets up the original items in the menu – imported from /etc/default/grub |
| 05_debian_theme | Sets the theme – colors and background image |
| 10_linux | Identifies kernels on root device and creates menu items |
| 20_linux_xen | Script that enables Xen to load (hypervisor) |
| 20_memtest86+ | Open-source memory test software that tests RAM for errors |
| 30_os-prober | Searches for other OSs and creates menu items |
| 40_custom | Sets custom menu entries that go into /boot/grub/grub.cfg |

# Common Options Used in the /etc/default/grub File

Many of the options in Table 4-4 are similar to the parameters used with the original GRUB and are self-explanatory.

The GRUB_HIDDEN_TIMEOUT and the GRUB_TIMEOUT option can be confusing. The GRUB_TIMEOUT is like the original timeout; it sets how many seconds before the default OS is selected and loaded. In GRUB2 you can choose to hide the menu and only display a blank screen. You can even hide the counter if you want. This can be used to hide the menu from all users that do not know what operating systems are available to run on this host and their order in the menu.

A new option added in GRUB2 is the GRUB_INIT_TUNE, which sounds a beep warning you that the GRUB2 menu is about to open.

*Table 4-4. Common Options in /etc/default/grub File*

| Option | Description |
| --- | --- |
| GRUB_DEFAULT | Defines the default menu option |
| GRUB_SAVEDEFAULT | Saves the last menu option that was selected as the default |
| GRUB_HIDDEN_TIMEOUT | Sets how long GRUB2 will pause and wait for user interaction before booting into the default OS |
| GRUB_HIDDEN_TIMEOUT_QUIET | Determines if a counter will display |
| GRUB_TIMEOUT | Sets how long the system will wait for user interaction before starting the default menu selection |
| GRUB_CMDLINE_LINUX | Add items for a command line for normal and recovery modes |
| GRUB_GFXMODE | Sets the resolution of the menu |
| GRUB_INIT_TUNE | Sounds a single beep prior to GRUB2 menu displaying |
| GRUB_BACKGROUND | Determines the background image to be used by GRUB2 |
| GRUB_DISABLE_OS_PROBER | Disables probing for OSs not already listed on the menu |

# Runlevels

If you have ever done any troubleshooting in Windows, you know that if you press F8 when booting your system, you will get a special menu that allows you to boot into safe mode or safe mode with networking. You can use a runlevel to do the same thing (although you would not press F8). Changing the runlevel allows you to boot into a different mode, such as with a GUI or without a GUI.

In Unix and Linux, there are seven runlevels, ranging from zero to six, each serving a distinct purpose. Runlevels 1 through 6 typically correspond to single-user mode, multiuser mode with and without network services initiated, system shutdown, and system reboot.

Using Runlevels in Linux gives you similar options on how you want to boot your Linux system (Table 3-5) – in GUI mode, in single user mode with no GUI, etc.

# Runlevels on Fedora

In Fedora, you will find an init script in the /etc directory that sets the mode in which you can boot your system. The default runlevel is defined in the /etc/inittab file during the initialization phase of bootup (Table 4-5).

***Table 4-5.*** *Fedora*

| Runlevel | Directory | State |
| --- | --- | --- |
| 0 | /etc/rc.d/rc0.d | Shutdown/halt system (init 0) |
| 1 | /etc/rc.d/rc1.d | Single user mode – no GUI |
| 2 | /etc/rc.d/rc2.d | Multiuser mode with no network services – no GUI |
| 3 | /etc/rc.d/rc3.d | Text/console only – full multiuser mode-Server |
| 4 | /etc/rc.d/rc4.d | Reserved for local use – also X-windows |
| 5 | /etc/rc.d/rc5.d | XDM X-windows GUI mode-Desktop |
| 6 | /etc/rc.d/rc6.d | Reboot  (init 6) |

Notice on 0 and 6, the commands "init 0" and "init 6" were added. The init command with any of the runlevels can be executed from a terminal session which causes the system to reboot into that mode. Do not set your default to runlevel 0. This will cause your system to automatically shut down during reboot.

# Runlevels in Ubuntu

Runlevels in Ubuntu are almost the same as in Fedora; however, there are not as many options (Table 4-6). The default runlevel is set in the upstart files (rather than the /etc/inittab for Fedora).

***Table 4-6.*** *Ubuntu*

| Runlevel | State |
| --- | --- |
| 0 | Shutdown/halt system |
| 1 | Single user mode (administrative) |
| 2-5 | Multiuser mode |
| 6 | Reboots system |

# Runlevel Commands

***Table 4-7.*** *Commands Used with Runlevels*

| Command | Description |
| --- | --- |
| runlevel | Displays the previous and current runlevels |
| init # or telinit # | Changes the runlevel (mode) to the # |
| init q or init Q | Directs init to examine the inittab file immediately |

The runlevel command will display the previously set runlevel and the current one. If the runlevel has never been changed, the first character will be "N."

Init and the runlevel number (#) will reboot the system and boot into that runlevel (Table 4-7).

The init q or init Q causes the /etc/inittab file to be re-read immediately.

# Kernel Options

Kernel options (Table 4-8) give you more control over how a system boots when troubleshooting is required. The options listed in the table can cause failures that will stop a system from booting properly. By making these changes, a sysadmin can determine what is causing the problem.

You would make these changes from the GRUB boot loader using the "a" or "e" keys.

***Table 4-8.*** *Kernel Options*

| Command | Description |
| --- | --- |
| Runlevel_number | Boots to the specified runlevel |
| vga | Changes the monitor settings |
| init | Changes the shell started at boot up |
| acpi | Enables/disables Advanced Configuration and Power Interface (ACPI) |
| apm | Enables/disables Advanced Power Management (API) |

# Init Scripts

Earlier when reviewing the boot process, you learned about the init process and services or daemons. Now, you will look at the init scripts in a little more depth.

The init scripts are used to start and stop services in Linux. Windows has the services app that lists all the services and allows you to control the action of each script.

Linux uses init scripts. These init scripts are stored in different locations based on the distribution. An example is System V (Fedora), Red Hat, BSD (Suse), and more.

## System V Distros

In System V distros, all the init scripts are located in the /etc/rc.d directory. The /etc/inittab sets the runlevel used on the system, and the boot process goes to that runlevel directory.

For example, if the runlevel is set to five, then the process looks in the /etc/rc.d/rc5.d directory for the init scripts that need to run. This directory contains symbolic links that are like shortcuts in Windows. These links point to the actual init scripts that are located in the /etc/rc.d/init.d directory.

When you look in each /rc#.d directory, you will see file types. Files that start with K are the scripts that kill or stop a service; files that start with an S are the scripts that start a service. The two numbers after that set the order in which the scripts will run. Some services require that other services be started so they can start properly.

Each runlevel can stop running services and start new ones depending on the services required at that runlevel. The directories outlined in the following table contain symbolic links to the actual init scripts in /etc/rc.d/init.d needed for runlevel "#". The symbolic links start with either S for start or K for kill and ##. These scripts are executed in order.

**The /rc#.d Directory**

| Directory | Number |
|---|---|
| /etc/rc.d/rc0.d | 0 |
| /etc/rc.d/rc1.d | 1 |
| /etc/rc.d/rc2.d | 2 |
| /etc/rc.d/rc3.d | 3 |
| /etc/rc.d/rc4.d | 4 |
| /etc/rc.d/rc5.d | 5 |
| /etc/rc.d/rc6.d | 6 |

# BSD Distros

The same process is true for BSD distributions, except there is no rc.d directory. The init scripts and the runlevel directories (rc0.d, etc.) are all located under the /etc/init.d directory. The runlevel directories still contain symbolic links to the actual script files as with System V.

- /etc/init.d directory contains all init scripts used to start and stop services depending on the system's default runlevel.

- /etc/init.d directory also contains rc0.d through rc6.d directories which contain symbolic links (like shortcuts) to the appropriate init scripts that should be run for that runlevel.

# Managing Init Scripts

To manage the init scripts, you have to be logged in as the root user. Then you can use the name of the script and the appropriate parameter (Table 4-9). In the provided example, you would type the name of the init script - ntpd and restart as the parameter.

You can stop, start, or restart a service this way and check the status of the services using the status parameter. The reload is much like the restart parameter, except it does not stop the service – it only reloads any configurations for that service. If you have a production web server running that you cannot take down long enough to restart the service, you can reload its configuration. To restart the ntpd service, use the command */etc/rc.d/init.d/ntpd restart.*

***Table 4-9.*** *Service Parameters*

| Parameters |
| --- |
| start |
| stop |
| status |
| restart |
| reload |

# Configuring Init Scripts

There are two commands used to configure services – insserv and chkconfig
(Table 4-10). The insserv only works on BSD systems and chkconfig works on BSD and
System V.

The command insserv <script> starts a service on the runlevels listed in the INIT
INFO block of the service's script. For example, if the INIT INFO shows Default-Start:
3 5 in the ntpd script, the insserv ./ntpd command sets the ntp service to start if the
system's run level is 5. Adding the -r stops the service from starting at any runlevel and -d
restores its runlevels.

The ###BEGIN INIT INFO block also lists:

- Default-Stop: 0 1 2 6 (separated by a space)

- Required-Start: and Required-Stop: lists services that have to be
  started or stopped before this service can start.

- Should-Start: and Should-Stop: list recommended services that
  should be stopped or started.

You can type the command less ./ntpd from the directory where the script is located
to see the INIT INFO block.

The chkconfig command is more powerful than insserv. It manages all services
running on a Linux system:

- chkconfig --add <service> will tell chkconfig it is supposed to manage
  that service and will set up the symbolic links in the appropriate
  runlevel directories (rc#.d).

- chkconfig --del <service> deletes the service and all its
  symbolic links.

***Table 4-10.*** *Configuring Init Scripts*

| Command | BSD | System V | Description |
| --- | --- | --- | --- |
| insserv | <script> | n/a | Starts the runlevels on a service |
| | -r <script> | n/a | Stops service from starting at any runlevel |
| | -d <script> | n/a | Restores service to start at default runlevels in scripts |
| chkconfig | -l <service> | --list <service> | Shows current service's config |
| | | --add <service> | Service added and links created in rc#.d directories |
| | | --del <service> | Service removed and  links removed from rc#.d directories |
| | -s <service>  35 | --level <level> <service> | Sets the runlevels for a service (--level 35 ntp) – 3 and 5 |
| | <service> on\|off | --level <level> <service>  on\|off | Enables/disables service |
| service | <service> start\|stop\|status\| restart\|... | <service> start\|stop\|status\| restart\|... | Starts a service |

To see the current runlevels set on a service, use the chkconfig --list <service> command. To see all the services controlled by chkconfig, leave off the <service> in the --list command. The chkconfig --level <runlevel> <service> on|off enables or disables the service at the specified level. For example, chkconfig --level 35 ntp on will enable runlevels 3 and 5 for the ntp service. There is no space used between the runlevels with this option. You can also use the service command to start and stop services or daemons.

The more you review this process, the more intuitive it will become.

# Additional Scripts

***Table 4-11.*** *Scripts in the init.d Directory*

| Scripts | Description |
|---------|-------------|
| halt | Stops or restarts the system (BSD only) |
| rc | Switches between runlevels |
| boot | Init script runs at boot up (BSD only) |
| rc.sysinit | Similar to boot script (System V) |
| boot.local | Runs with boot (BSD only). Additional commands to execute at boot before transitioning to a runlevel. |
| rc.local | Similar to boot.local script (System V) |

There are other scripts used during the init process in addition to the init scripts found in the init.d directory (Table 4-11).

- The halt script is used to shutdown or reboot a system.

- The rc script is used to switch between runlevels.

- The boot script is actually in the init.d/boot.d directory and runs the script that checks the system, sets the clock, and loads kernel modules.

- The rc.sysinit is very similar to the boot script, but it runs on the System V distros.

- The boot.local runs additional scripts after the boot script is finished. This is a good place to put any additional services you want started automatically each time you boot a system.

- The rc.local is the System V version of boot.local.

To summarize the processes followed by the two categories of distributions,

- In BSD, the boot scripts run, the inittab determines the runlevel and those scripts are run, and last the boot.local script runs.

- The System V process runs the rc.sysinit, then the inittab determines the runlevel and those scripts are run, and next the rc.local script runs.

# Upstart

Upstart is an event driven by a process that was originally created for Ubuntu to replace the init process. The init processes its scripts synchronously, which means it runs one command after the other. Tasks must be defined and put in the order they should be run. They also only worked when a runlevel was changed.

Per Figure 4-2, the runlevels are different and only 0, 1, 2, and 6 are used in upstart. Runlevel 2 is the default instead of 5.

The upstart process works asynchronously, which means that multiple processes can run at the same time – allowing the system to load much faster. Also, init did not know when there was a hardware change, such as when a USB drive was added to the host. The system would recognize it, but the init processes did not know anything about it. The proper way to shut down any external device is to unmount it. The init system did not know it had to run this process at shutdown.

Upstart will listen for events and dynamically manage the service. For example, if a required service stops unexpectedly, upstart will attempt to restart the service.

As Figure 4-2 shows, a process generates an event and upstart captures that event, and it performs a job.

You may recognize many of the commands used with upstart, which are listed in Figure 4-2. One command that may be new to you is telinit. Instead of using init 6 to reboot your system, use telinit 6 when your host is using the upstart process.

Changes to the default runlevel are done on the environment variable DEFAULT_RUNLEVEL in the /etc/init/rc-sysinit.conf file.

**Upstart**

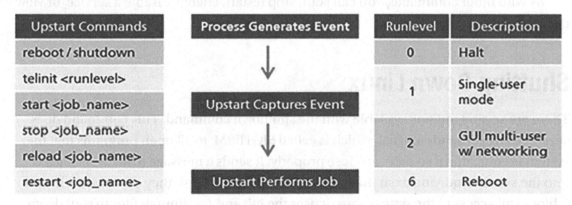

| Upstart Commands | Process Generates Event | Runlevel | Description |
|---|---|---|---|
| reboot / shutdown | | 0 | Halt |
| telinit <runlevel> | | 1 | Single-user mode |
| start <job_name> | Upstart Captures Event | | |
| stop <job_name> | | 2 | GUI multi-user w/ networking |
| reload <job_name> | | | |
| restart <job_name> | Upstart Performs Job | 6 | Reboot |

*Figure 4-2.* *This diagram displays Upstart commands, the Upstart process, and runlevels with associated descriptions*

# Systemd

Systemd is a replacement for the original init and upstart processes. Interestingly, many of the distributions that went to the upstart process are now going to the systemd process.

It is also asynchronous, which helps the system complete the boot-up process faster. Systemd is compatible with most init scripts and has the same runlevels. If you are already familiar with the init process, it is relatively easy to change to systemd. It supports snapshotting, which is a process that allows you to take an exact copy of your system at a single point in time. You can restore the system to where it was before an event if necessary. This term comes from photography, which is taking a snapshot or picture of something.

Sockets and D-Bus activation are an easy, simple way for applications to talk to each other and for interprocess communications to occur. They help services to start on demand as needed.

Systemd uses control groups, or cgroups, to track and control processes. A cgroup ties a set of tasks to a set of parameters. They utilize what is referred to as a parent–child relationship or hierarchy. A cgroup that is a child or another cgroup will inherit all processes included in the parent cgroup.

Managing runlevels and services is done with the systemctl command rather than the chkconfig and service commands. Systemctl uses targets to process the runlevel. You can change the runlevel after your system is booted, or you can change the default runlevel that is selected at boot up by modifying the /etc/systemd/system/default.target file. You can change the default target to muti-user.target, graphical.target, or runlevel and the number of the runlevel.target.

As with other commands, you can start, stop restart, enable, disable a service, or view the status of a service.

# Shutting Down Linux

There are several options available with the shutdown command. This command does several things. It sends a signal, which is called SIGTERM, to all open programs that the system is going down so they can close properly. It sends a message to all users logged into the system notifying them that the system is going down so they can save their work. It blocks all access to the system. Last, it uses the init and /etc/inittab files to shut down all running processes before the system shuts off completely.

The -h now option will shut down the system immediately. Poweroff, half, and init 0 will do the same thing. The -h +10 option will shut down the system in 10 minutes with a warning message.

Using the -r now option will reboot the system right away. Reboot and init 6 will also reboot the host.

Adding a number (in minutes) will cause the shutdown or reboot to wait that length of time. For example, +4 causes a time delay of 4 minutes.

The -c option cancels the shutdown. This one can come in handy if you have to stop a shutdown action. Maybe you used the -h rather than -r option, and you are not physically at the boot to turn it back on.

If you want to send a message to all users that are logged onto the host, you can use the -k <message> option. You might need to make configuration changes to the host that do not require a reboot; however, you want all users off the host to make sure you do not interfere with their work or that they do not lock a process that you need to use.

The last option, the -a, is added to the /etc/inittab file and causes the shutdown command to read the /etc/shutdown.allow file. This file contains a list of users who are allowed to shut down the host.

Of course, you can always shut down the system from the GUI. You will soon realize that most things a system administrator does is initiated from the command line or in scripts.

# Summary

In this chapter, you learned important concepts relating to installing Linux. Keep the following in mind:

- The Boot Process flows through the BIOS ➤ POST ➤ MBR/GPT ➤ Boot Loader that loads the kernel ➤ Initialization process, which starts all required services.

- The two most commonly used boot loaders in Linux are LILO and GRUB.

- The Initialization Phase loads all the required daemons (services) and sets the runlevel.

- In addition to the option from the GUI, there are numerous ways to shut down Linux from a terminal window.

# CHAPTER 5

# Desktop and User Interface

This chapter introduces you to the various components that make up a Linux host. You have more options in Linux than in Windows. You will learn how to set Accessibility options which can make your experience with Linux better.

By the end of this chapter, you will be able to

1. Configure components that make up the X Window System

2. Configure the Display Manager

3. Configure accessibility features available in Linux

## X Window System

There are several components that make up the Linux GUI (Figure 5-1). Linux's GUI was created in a modular fashion so each part could be modified and not affect the other parts. Each module plays a different part and is important to make the GUI functional. You will learn that Fedora and Ubuntu both use X Window.

77

© Ahmed F. Sheikh 2024
A. F. Sheikh, *CompTIA Linux+ Certification Companion*, Certification Study Companion Series,
https://doi.org/10.1007/979-8-8688-0128-0_5

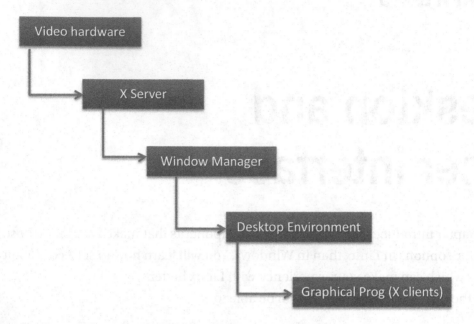

**Figure 5-1.**  *Components of the Linux Operating System*

When the X Window System was first created, the developers intended for the X to be replaced with a name that was to be selected later. It grew in popularity so quickly that it went into production before that could happen. As a result, it is still called X Window System. X provides the fundamental framework for a GUI environment, encompassing tasks such as drawing and moving windows on the display device, along with interactions using a mouse and keyboard.

# Video Hardware

Most Linux applications are written to be hardware independent so they can run on multiple platforms. A hardware abstraction layer (HAL) is created so software can be written to use a generic set of commands called API (Application Programming Interface). An API serves as a means for two or more computer components to communicate with one another. The application talks to the special commands that then talk to the hardware. Each Linux host is configured to know the details of all of its installed hardware. Hardware can be damaged if it is not properly configured so it is critical that it be done properly.

**Key Facts**

**Video Hardware**

- Most graphical programs are written so they are hardware independent.

- Uses hardware abstraction layer (HAL) to make calls to installed hardware.

- Check the Hardware Compatibility List for the version of Linux you are running.

# X Server

The next, and probably the most important, component of the X Window System is X Server. It is the core of this system. The most commonly used versions are X Window and XFree86. X Window is also known as X.org or X11 or simply X. Both are now open source software; however, XFree86 was created because X Window was not originally free.

X Server can be run from a local machine or from a machine on a network. In an enterprise environment, you may find a powerful machine set up specifically to provide X Window or XFree86 to older hardware that cannot run it locally.

You can modify your DISPLAY environment variable to change the location of X Window. DISPLAY = 0 indicates you are working with a local version of X Server.

# Window Manager

Window Manager controls how windows on your screen will look and act. There are numerous Window Managers that can be used in Linux. You can install any or all of them and experiment with each until you decide which one you like the best.

Whichever Window Manager you select works with the Desktop Environment you install to change the way your desktop looks and feels. The following lists several types of Window Managers:

- Enlightenment

- Sawfish

- Fluxbox

- Matchbox

- Metacity

- KDE Windows Manager (kwin)

- Mutter

- Window Maker (wmaker)

- Tab Window Manager (twm)

- Flexible Virtual Window Manager (fvwm)

# Desktop Environment

The desktop environment controls how your desktop looks including backgrounds, screensavers, icons, and menus. Windows does not give you a choice of desktops; you can change the way they look and feel but not completely change the desktop environments as Linux does. Each environment comes with what is known as a "toolkit" which includes a development tool, programming language, and a Window Manager.

The most common desktop environments (Table 5-1) are GNOME and KDE. GNOME stands for GNU Network Object Model Environment; KDE is short for K Desktop Environment. KDE was originally known as Kool Desktop Environment, but Kool was shortened to just K years ago.

---

**Note**   There are two Window Managers listed for GNOME. Mutter became the default Window Manager in version 3 of GNOME. Previous versions used metacity.

---

## Key Facts

## Desktop Environment

- Set of GUI tools and desktop features

  - Screensavers, wallpapers, taskbars, icons, menus, etc.

- Most common desktop environments

    - KDE – K Desktop Environment (kwin) – Stylish look and very customizable but not as stable

    - GNOME (pronounced gəˈnoʊm ) – GNU Network Object Model Environment (metacity/mutter) – Focuses more on stability and productivity than look

- Usually comes with development tools – toolkit

**Table 5-1.** *Desktop Environments*

| Desktop Environment | Development Tool / Programming Language | Window Manager |
|---|---|---|
| KDE | Qt toolkit for C++ | kwin |
| GNOME | GTK+ for C | metacity/ mutter |

# Gnome Desktop Example

In Figure 5-2, the GNOME desktop example shows how you can switch to the KDE desktop environment before you log in. Before you can see this option, you have to select a user from the list. The commands listed are how you can switch environments from a terminal session after you have already logged into GNOME.

The KDE desktop example in Figure 5-3 shows the Kickoff Application Launcher where you would expect the Start button in Windows. You can immediately see that KDE has a much softer look to its design.

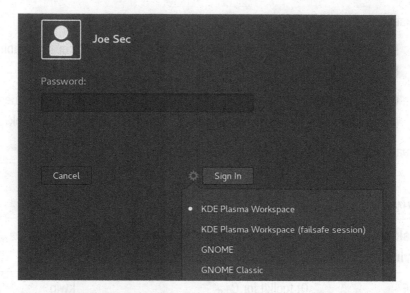

***Figure 5-2.*** *Change Desktop from Gnome to KDE*

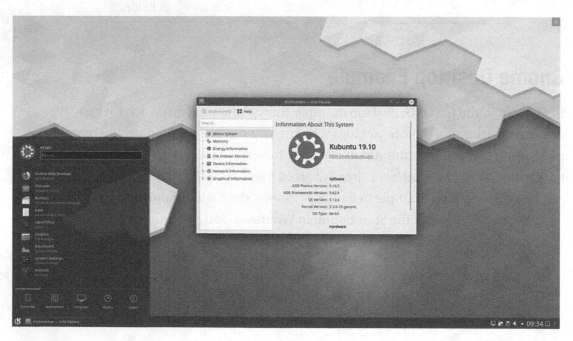

***Figure 5-3.*** *KDE Desktop*

Syntax:

- <prompt>$ **switchdesk kde**

- <prompt>$ **startkde**

# X Client

The X client is basically any graphical application written to run in a local desktop environment or across the network.

---

## Key Facts

### Graphical programs that draw display (X client)

- An application program that runs on the local machine or on a remote machine.

- Almost any program that can run in the GUI is an X client.

---

# X Font Server

It was originally used to provide fonts to the local system or to systems across a network. The processing power used to manage fonts takes more resources than were available to most computers when X Font Servers were popular.

---

## Key Facts

### X Font Server (optional)

- Legacy server

  - Required processing power that older hardware did not have

- Provides fonts to local or remote computers

---

# Configuring X Server

Since X Window works directly with the video card and monitor, it is extremely important that you know certain details about this hardware. If X Window is not configured correctly, you can damage the hardware.

Before configuring X Server, know the following about your system:

- The manufacturer and model of the video card and the monitor

- The amount of memory that is on the video card

- Its maximum resolution and color depth

- Its chipset

The maximum sync rate for the monitor is critical; if you select a sync rate that is too fast for your monitor, you can literally burn it up.

---

### Key Facts

Configuring X Server (X Window)

- Know the specifications of your video card and monitor.

- Files containing configuration information.

  - X Window – /etc/X11/xorg.conf

  - xFree86 – /etc/X11/XF86Config

---

Both the xorg.conf and XF86Config files are made up of several sections (Table 5-2) where you configure devices such as your keyboard, mouse, monitor, video card, and how it all ties together.

**Table 5-2.** *Sections of Configuration Files*

| Name | Description |
|------|-------------|
| Files | Details the files the server needs to function properly |
| ServerFlags | Lists global server options used in debugging and advanced configuration |
| Module | Indicates which server modules to load |
| InputDevice | Provides required information on each input device |
| Device | Contains information on the video card |
| VideoAdaptor | Contains details for the X video |
| Monitor | Includes specifications on the monitor |
| Mode | Holds different monitor mode settings when required |
| Screen | Proves selections for resolution, color depth, etc. |
| ServerLayout | Ties all other configuration details together |
| DRI | Contains details for video rending and 3D acceleration |
| Vendor | Includes any available vendor-specific settings |

# Editing xorg.conf Files in Fedora

Even though you can edit the configuration files with a text editor, it is not recommended. If you configure something wrong, you can damage your card, your monitor, or both. If you must make your changes manually, make a copy of the configuration file in case you need to restore it.

The utilities shown in Table 5-3 are recommended for use on Fedora. The last three tools are used specifically on Fedora; the others depend on the distribution of Linux. Two tools that are not listed here are **YaST** and **SaX** which are used with Suse Linux. Those do not work with Fedora or Red Hat.

The top three tools are very helpful since they actually look at the hardware in your system. They take a "best guess" and configure the file. Both the **xorg –configure** and **xorgcfg** commands create a xorg.conf.new file after their scan completes. You can take a look at the contents of the .new file and make sure it is consistent with the information you gathered before starting the utility. Then all you have to do is remove the .new file extension.

Another tool that can be used to tweak the monitor settings for xorg.conf is **xvidtune**. It is described in Table 5-3.

***Table 5-3.*** *Editing xorg.conf configuration file in Fedora*

| Utility | Description |
| --- | --- |
| Xorg  (Xorg -configure) | Creates the xorg.conf file after probing hardware – use when there is no GUI |
| xorgconfig | Scans hardware and creates the xorg.conf file when no GUI is available – can also be used to edit this file |
| xorgcfg | Used to edit xorg.conf when a GUI is already installed |
| System-config-mouse | Configures mouse settings |
| System-config-display | Configures video card and monitor settings |
| System-config-keyboard | Configures keyboard settings |

**Note**    If you HAVE TO edit xorg.conf manually, be sure to make a backup copy of the files in case you do something wrong.

# Editing XF86Conf File in Fedora

As with some of the utilities already discussed, Table 5-4 lists tools that can be used with XFree86 to configure its XF86Conf file. You will notice the same functionality in these utilities as you saw previously. The XFree-86 and the xf86config utilities also create the configuration file ending with .new. The xf86cfg tool is used to make changes if the GUI already exists. The monitor can be fine-tuned or tweaked with the **xvidtune** tool.

*Table 5-4.* *Editing XF86Conf configuration file in Fedora*

| Utility | Description |
| --- | --- |
| XFree-86 (Xfree-86 -configure) | Used when no GUI exists; probes hardware and creates the XF86Conf file |
| xf86config | Proves hardware and creates the XF86Conf file with no GUI exists; also used to change this file |
| xf86cfg | Used when GUI is already set up; makes changes to XF86Config |
| xvidtune | Can be used to make changes to monitor settings |
| Xconfigurator | Creates configuration file and links |

**Note**   Test the configuration file after changes have been made before saving it. This is similar to testing changes made to screen settings in Windows.

# Restart X Server

After saving changes to your X Server, restart the PC in order to implement the changes. Use one of these methods to reboot the system:

- Reboot the system if X Server was not running yet or if it was already running, reboot the system.

- Logout and back in.

- Use Ctrl+Alt+Backspace. This key combination stops and restarts X Server.

### Key Facts

### Restart X Server

- Restart X Server after changes using one of the following:

    - Reboot system.

    - Press Ctrl+Alt+Backspace.

    - Log out and back in.

- Start the GUI from text mode (boot using runlevel 3).

# Configuring Window Manager and Desktop Environment

You can change the default Window Manager or the Desktop Environment by downloading and installing the appropriate package. After starting the new manager or environment, take time to play with it to make sure it is what you would like to have each time your system reboots.

If you made changes you do not want to keep, simply reboot your system. You will then be back to your original setup. If you wish to make this your default, changes have to be made to a file so the new configuration will be saved.

To make the change permanent, locate **$WINDOWMANAGER** in the appropriate file, and replace it with your new selection. Table 5-5 shows a small sample of what can be added to the appropriate configuration files.

If you are starting the GUI from text mode or **runlevel 3**, configure the hidden file .xinitrc in the home directory. Find the line that reads **exec $WINDOWMANAGER**, and replace the value with the Window Manager or Desktop Environment you want to use – for example, **startkde** or **gnome-session** or **sawfish**. Exit the GUI, and run **startx** to load the change.

If you are starting from **runlevel 5**, make the same change but do it in the .Xsession, Xdefaults, or .Xclients depending on distribution.

Use the **–a** option with the **ls** command in order to see hidden files.

***Table 5-5.*** *Runlevels*

|  | File(s) in Home Dir |
|---|---|
| Runlevel 3 | .xinitrc |
| Runlevel 5 | .Xsession, .Xdefaults, or .Xclients |
| startkde | KDE Desktop |
| gnome-session | gnome Desktop |
| enlightenment | window manager |
| sawfish | window manager |
| twm | Tab window manager |

# GUI Problem-Solving Utilities

If you have problems with your GUI loading, use the **xwininfo** or **xdpyinfo** commands (Table 5-6) or view the /var/log/Xorg.0.log file.

To get detailed information about a window or all windows, use the **xwininfo** command with its many options. The **xdpyinfo** command gives you details about the X server.

***Table 5-6.*** *Utilities to Help Solve Problems with GUI Configurations*

| Command | Purpose |
|---|---|
| xwininfo | Provides information on windows |
| xdpyinfo | Provides information on X Server |

# Display Manager

An important part of the Desktop Environment is the Display Manager. It manages the GUI. Commonly used Display Managers include X Display Manager, Gnome Display Manager, and KDE Display Manager. Windows users may find this confusing since there is not a choice regarding Display Managers – there is only one. Each display manager has specific configuration settings that need to be specified.

For Windows users, having multiple options for Display Managers is a new concept, since Windows only has one.

---

### Key Facts

### Display Manager

- Manages the login screen

- Most commonly used Display Managers

    - XDM – X Display Manager – Suse

    - KDM – KDE Display Manager – Fedora and Ubuntu

    - GDM – Gnome Display Manager – Fedora and Ubuntu (default)

---

# Configuring Display Manager

After you select a Display Manager (DM), you need to change a setting – which one depends on the distribution you are using. If your distribution uses init.d scripts, you will replace the existing one with the appropriate script that matches the manager you selected.

Next if you want the selected DM to run at startup, use **chkconfig on|off**. If your system boots into **runlevel 3** or text mode, you can manually start it with Display Manager's abbreviation with the **start** or **stop** command while logged in as root.

One last general item is setting the color depth. If you want to speed up your application, use a lower color depth. If you want the best quality picture, use 24 bit which is considered "truecolor."

**Key Facts**

**Configuring Display Manager**

- Replace current Display Manager's script with new one in /etc/init.d or /etc/rc.d/init.d directory.

- Manually start or stop.

  - **/etc/init.d/<xxx> <start|stop>**

- Make change persistent at startup.

  - **chkconfig <xxx> <on|off>**

- Modify color depth.

  - **startx –depth <8|16|24|32>**

**Note – xxx = xdm, gdm, or kdm**

# X Terminal or X Station Support

A machine with very few resources, perhaps not even a hard drive, is known as a "dumb terminal." In the 1960s and 1970s, the machines on our desks were connected remotely to a computer with many more resources which would do all the processing and simply supply the display to the terminals. Those dumb terminals were configured to look for this server when they booted.

An X terminal or X station has the same function in Linux. In a large environment, a high-end machine can be configured to act as an X Server and provide a Display Manager and a Desktop Environment to a low-end machine. Older equipment is often used for this type system. Either way, a company can see a great cost reduction. X terminals gained popularity in the early 1990s by providing a more cost-effective alternative to a complete Unix workstation, contributing to their widespread use during that period.

## Key Facts

### X Terminal or X Station Support

- Uses low-end and/or older hardware that runs a display manager.

- Looks for X Server when booted.

- The X Server and X Terminal both run the XDMCP (X Display Manager Control Protocol) to send and received an XDM login screen.

# Configuration Steps on X Server

A few changes have to be made on the host that will be delivering the display to the X terminal. Depending on the distribution, you need to allow the host to listen for Transmission Control Protocol (TCP) requests. Open port 177 so the XDMCP protocol can use it. Last, add a line for each host or for a domain that can access this host to get their displays. If you want to block a host, use an exclamation mark. After this or any change to a configuration file, either reboot the system or use the **ifdown** and **ifup** commands to reset the interface.

## Key Facts

### Configuration steps on X Server (not the same for all distributions)

- Edit /etc/X11/Xservers (for xdm and kdm).

    - Remove  **-no listen tcp.**

- Edit /etc/X11/gdm/gdm.conf (for gdm).

    - Set **disallowTCP=False.**

- Reboot or use the **ifdown/ifup** command.

- Open port 177 that is used by XDMCP.

- Edit /etc/X11/Xaccess.

    - Add line for each host (host1) or for a domain (*.mydomain.com) that will access this host.

    - To block a host – !<hostname>.

# X Display Manager (XDM)

XDM or X Display Manager was the original and is still used by Suse Linux and by X terminals. Different distributions will have their configuration files in different locations. You will need to find where these files are located.

## Key Facts

## XDM

- Original Display Manager.

- Used by Suse Linux and X Terminals/Stations.

- Configuration files are usually in one of the following directories:

  - /etc/X11/xdm

  - /usr/X11R6/lib/X11/xdm

# XDM Configuration Files

There are several configuration files used by XDM.

- Xresources file

- Xservers file

- xdm-config

- Xaccess

Xresources – Settings used for the login screen are stored in the Xresources file and contain the options shown in Table 5-7. The names explain the function.

*Table 5-7.* *Xresources File Options*

| Xresources | Xresources |
|---|---|
| xlogin*Foreground | xlogin*login.promptFont |
| xlogin*Background | xlogin*login.promtFont |
| xlogin*greetColor | xlogin*login.failFont |
| xlogin*failColor | xlogin*greeting |
| xlogin*login.Font | xlogin*namePrompt |
| xlogin*login.greetFont | xlogin*fail |

Xservers – The Xservers file lists the location of the server. You can also use the –**nolisten tcp** option to block the server from listening on TCP ports. The **:0 local** line shown in the following command sets the color depth to 24 bits. The –bpp stands for bits per pixel.

**:0 local /usr/bin/X11/X ft7 –bpp 24**

Xaccess – This file lists machines that can make requests and ones that can see chooser broadcasts.

Xdm-config – It contains the name and location of other configuration files plus basic access permissions

---

**Warning**    Because XDM runs as root, it is not as secure as other X Display Managers.

---

# Remote X Window

Recall that X Window is a network application. X Window clients listen on port 0 for traffic generated by the server part of X Window. After a minor change to the Display Manager configuration file on the client and the server, an authorized user can take control of a remote Linux box to perform any task that the remote system can do. Basic administration as well as troubleshooting can be done using this utility.

There are several ways to set up a Remote X Window connection. This example works for Fedora running gnome.

1. Allow TCP connections on both systems.

2. The xhost + command adds information to a type of access control list which allows a connection to be made with the IP address provided or with any host if no address is provided.

3. The **ssh** command creates a secure TCP connection to the remote host. You can use **telnet**, but it is not as secure as **ssh**.

4. Tell the remote host that you want its display or screen to display on the local host rather than on the remote host. The 0.0 indicates port 0 and the first display.

5. If you want to remove the remote host from your local list, use a minus instead of a plus after xhost.

Now you will see the remote host's display, and you can execute any command.

---

### Key Facts

### Remote X Window

- Utility used to securely access and control a remote computer.

- Add **DisallowTCP=false** to /etc/gdm/custom.conf to client and server systems.

- From local host – **xhost + <remote host's IP address>.**

- From local host – **ssh root@<remote host's IP address>.**

- In remote host shell – **export DISPLAY = <local host's IP address>:0.0.**

- From local host – **xhost - <remote host's IP address>** (optional).

Local host – Computer where you are sitting.

Remote host – Computer you want to work on across the network.

---

# KDM

KDM is very similar to XDM in several ways. Similarities include support for XDMCP, its configuration files which are usually the same as XDM files, and sections that control how KDM functions. See Table 5-8 for a description of the main sections of the KDM configuration file.

## Key Facts

### KDM

- Login Manager for KDE.

- Configuration files are usually the same as XDM files.

- Supports XDMCP.

- Some control options are in /etc/kde/kdm/kdmrc file.

- Other distros have files in the /etc/X11/kdm directory.

***Table 5-8.***  *Sections of KDM*

| Section | Description |
| --- | --- |
| General | Contains general settings |
| XDMCP | Controls how users access remote computers using KDM |
| Xgreeter | Controls what you see on the login screen |

# GDM

The GDM Display Manager is normally used with Gnome. It was a replacement for XDM and was written completely from scratch.

As with XDM and KDM, you can configure it to start automatically when booting into **runlevel 5** or the GUI, or you can start it from **runlevel 3**. It also allows you to open another desktop such as KDE.

**Key Facts**

**GDM**

- Manages the login functions on some distributions of Linux

- Gnome Display Manager (GDM) automatically starts with **runlevel 5** in Fedora.

- GDM can be started by root user from **runlevel 3** using the **gdm** command.

- Allows loading of GNOME or KDE desktop at login.

- **gmdsetup** – GUI based configuration tool.

The actual location of any of the Display Managers' configuration files can vary depending on the Linux distribution. Notice that most of the sections in the GDM configuration file look much like the KDM one. Table 5-9 lists sections of the GDM configuration file.

- Configuration file – /etc/X11/gdm/gdm.conf or /etc/gdm/custom. conf – depends on distribution.

*Table 5-9.* *Sections of the gdm.conf File*

| Section | Description |
| --- | --- |
| Security | Used to increase or decrease security based on system's function |
| Greeter | Sets the look and feel of the login screen |
| XDMCP | Controls how users access remote computers using GDM |
| XDMCP Chooser | Controls who can see XDMCP broadcasts |
| Other | Could be other sections depending on distribution |

# Accessibility

A common request is to set up one or more accessibility options for a user. Most operating systems are now including numerous options that will help people with a variety of disabilities so they can use a computer or phone. Other users opt to use some of these features including the magnifier and toggle key (sound option for Caps Lock and Num Lock)!

## Key Facts

### Accessibility – also known as Assistive Technologies (AT)

- Technology that helps people to use a computer

  - Visual

  - Physical (Tactile)

  - Auditory

Different flavors of Linux have accessibility tools in various places. We will explore what is available in Fedora. AccessX is included with X Window and includes several options that can help people who have physical and visual disabilities. To get to this tool, select System, Preferences, and then Assistive Technologies. The window appears as shown in Figure 5-4.

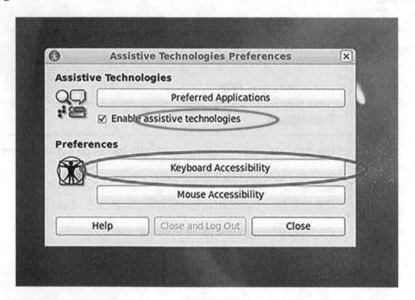

***Figure 5-4.*** *System ➤ Preferences ➤ Assistive Technologies*

First, let's look at two of the keyboard preferences. Several of the tabs allow you to make modifications to the behavior of the keyboard. Figures 5-5, 5-6, and 5-7 show you the features available on the General, Mouse Keys, and Accessibility tabs. Figure 5-7 shows the Audio options available by clicking on the Audio Feedback button on the Accessibility screen.

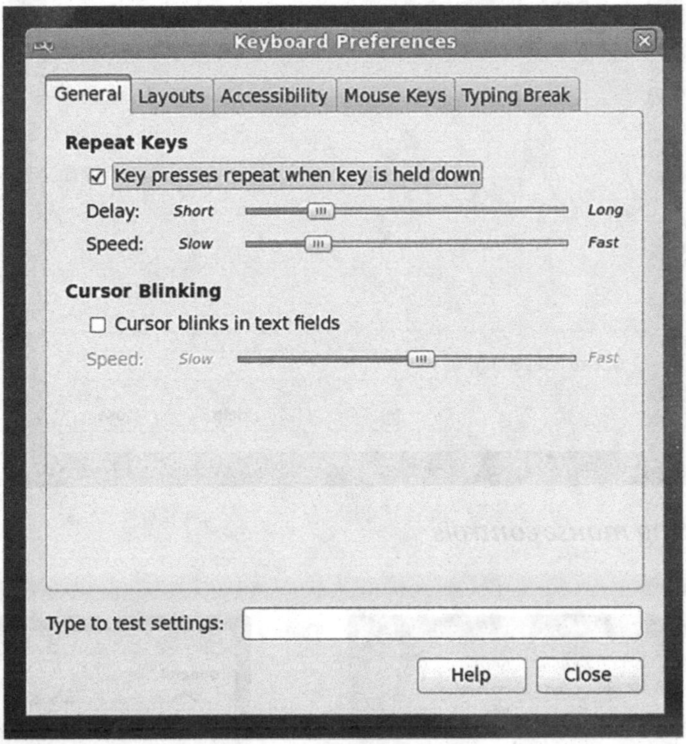

*Figure 5-5.* *Setting repeat keys*

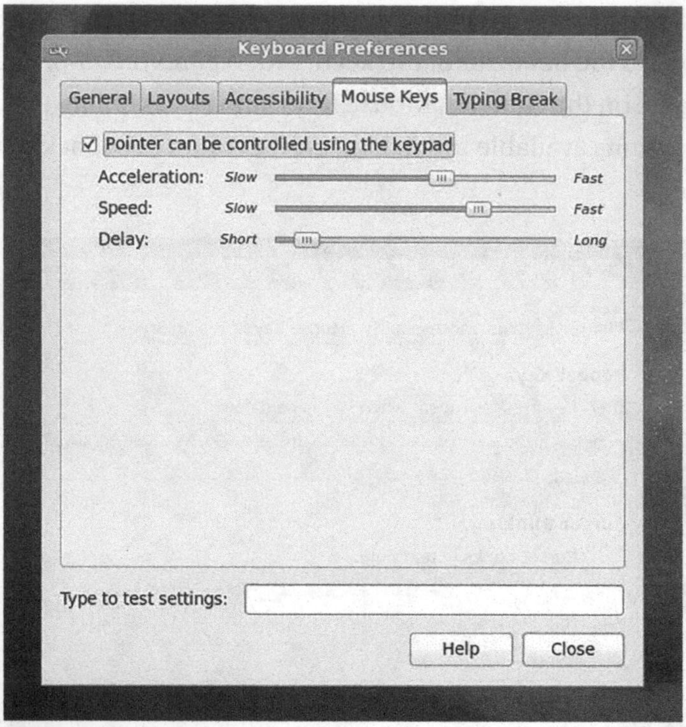

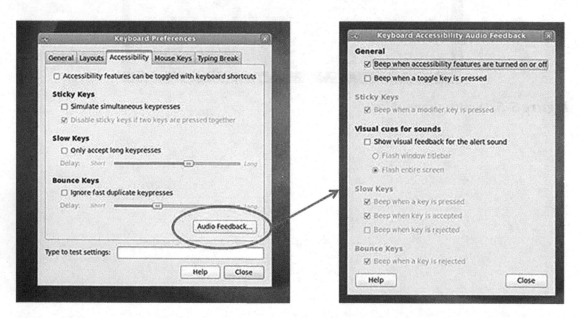

**Figure 5-6.**  *Setting mouse controls*

**Figure 5-7.**  *From Keyboard Preferences, select Accessibility and click on Audio Feedback to view the audio settings*

*Table 5-10.* *Accessibility Key Controls*

| Task | Description |
|------|-------------|
| Sticky keys | Causes the Ctrl, Alt or Shift keys to "stick" when pressed – helps users who can't press multiple keys at the same time |
| Slow keys | Controls how long a key should be pressed before it is accepted by the system – prevents accidentally pressing keys |
| Bounce keys (Delay keys) | Ignores a key pressed several times very quickly – assuming a single key press was intended |
| Mouse keys | Controls the mouse with keys from your key pad |
| Toggle keys | Creates a sound when Caps Lock or Num Lock is on |
| Repeat rate | Determines how quickly a key is repeated when pressed – prevents unintended key duplication |

By selecting Keyboard Accessibility from the AT screen, you get two tabs which aid in changing the action of your keyboard and mouse.

Sticky keys (Table 5-10) allow you to lock or "stick" what is called a "modifier key." The most common of these special keys are Fn (Function), Windows logo, Ctrl, Alt, and Shift keys. A user may not be able to press two or more keys at the same time. What if a user had to press the Ctrl + Alt + Del keys as we do in Windows? By using the sticky key function, you can select and the Ctrl key, then the Alt key, and then the Del key, in that sequence, and they will react as though they were all pressed at the same time.

Slow keys require a user hold down a key for a specific amount of time before the system will acknowledge the key has been pressed. The bounce key, which is also known as the delay key, ignores a key that is pressed several times in quick succession. It is very easy to "stutter" on a key that was intended to be a single key stroke. By setting the amount of delay time between key strokes, this effect can be stopped.

Mouse keys allow you to control the mouse with keys or a combination of keys issued from your keyboard. You may still have to know how to move around in the system using only your keyboard and these special option keys.

Toggle keys allow you to create a sound when a key that toggles between one function to another has been pressed. Two examples are Caps Lock and Num Lock. When moving between typing with Caps Lock turned on and using regular sized fonts, this is a great feature for anyone.

Repeat rate sets how long a key has to be pressed before it will start repeating. Have you ever stopped to think what you are going to type next only to look up and find that your finger was resting on the last key you typed?

# Mouse Accessibility

Mouse Accessibility (Figure 5-8) offers useful customization options (Table 5-11).

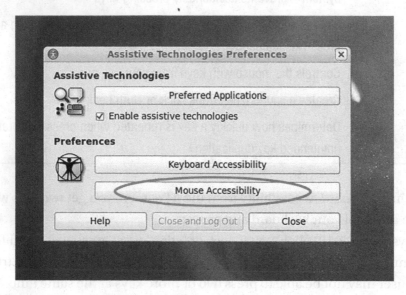

***Figure 5-8.*** *Mouse Accessibility options*

***Table 5-11.*** *Mouse Accessibility Options*

| Task | Description |
| --- | --- |
| Simulated Secondary Click | Mouse issues a double click to the system when the primary button is held down |
| Mouse gesture (Dwell Click) | Configures a certain mouse movement to perform a specific task <br>• Requires Mouse Tweaks be installed <br>• Assistive Technology support must be enabled |

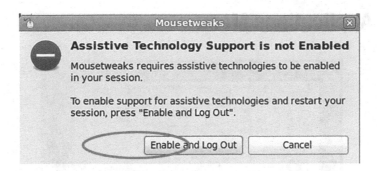

**Figure 5-9.**  *Enabling AT Support*

When you select the Simulated Secondary Click, you can simply hold down the primary mouse button (usually the left one) and the system is told to perform a double click. Some mouse devices have a very sensitive left button, so most of the time the double click doesn't work the first time a user tries to execute it. An alternative is to do a right click and select Open. This has been the case with a small "travel" Bluetooth mouse. If this were the case with your primary mouse, setting Assistive Technology device settings could make the use of this mouse easier (Figure 5-9).

If the Dwell Click option is used, you can set certain "mouse gestures" to indicate an action you want performed. Before this option can be set, your system has to have the package Mousetweaks installed and Assistive Technology support must be enabled. Note that you are logged out when this support is enabled.

Before logging in, you will now see an icon drawing of a little person with outstretched arms. By clicking that icon, you get a menu of general accessibility options you can turn on without having to go into the Assistive Technology menu and turning on the required option.

# Preferred Applications Menu

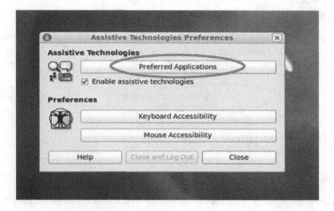

**Figure 5-10.**  *AT Preferred Applications*

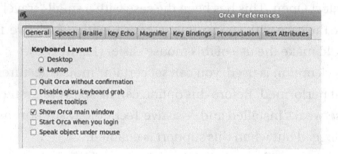

**Figure 5-11.**  *Options in Orca Application*

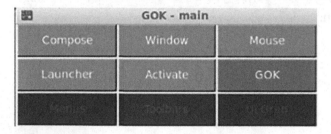

**Figure 5-12.**  *GOK Main Menu*

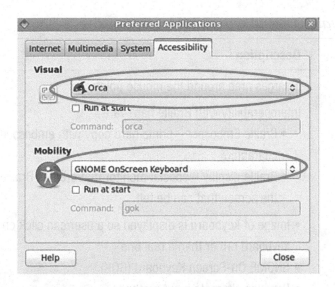

***Figure 5-13.*** *Visual and Mobility accessibility options*

The Preferred Applications menu (Figure 5-10) has more options. Here we can set applications that help people who have a visual or physical disability. In Figure 5-13, under Visual, you see the application Orca selected. This is a widely used application that can act as a screen reader and a magnifier. Notice just under the Run at start option, there is a Command window. Orca's screen reader can be started from a terminal session with the command **orca**. To use the screen reader AND the magnifier, use **orca –e magnifier**. Look at all the tabs in the Orca Preferences window (Figure 5-11) to see all its functionality. Note that it can help with Braille accessibility also.

The mobility section allows you to use an on-screen keyboard. The most well-known one is GOK – GNOME OnScreen Keyboard. This application can be started with the command **gok**. When GOK first loads (Figure 5-12), you are asked if you want to deactivate Sticky Keys because it can affect the way the keyboard works.

In the same way as Mouse Keys were helpful when there is no mouse available on a Linux box, GOK is helpful if you don't have a keyboard.

***Table 5-12.*** *Visual Accessibility Technology Options*

| Task | Description |
| --- | --- |
| Screen magnifier | Enlarges area around the mouse pointer |
| Braille device | Interoperability with Braille hardware<br>• Braille Embosser – prints hard copy with embossed Braille characters<br>• Braille display – special monitor that creates Braille characters on the screen that can be felt |
| Onscreen keyboard | • Image of keyboard is displayed so a user can click on the onscreen keyboard rather than a real one<br>• GNOME On-Screen Keyboard (GOK)<br>• Provides alternate input methods<br>  • Moving of head<br>  • Moving limbs<br>  • Contracting muscles<br>  • Blink an eye<br>  • Blowing or sipping |
| Screen reader | Reads on-screen text, menus, and button labels – common Linux screen readers<br>• Emacspeak – usually provided with text editors – free<br>• Orca – works with GNOME – free |

Table 5-12 lists and describes four options in Assistive Technology.

Screen magnifier does as its name implies – increases the size of type and images on the screen.

Applications such as Orca provide the interoperability needed to make braille devices function. Text can be sent to a printer that will emboss the characters on the paper. A braille display will allow the user to touch the special screen to feel the braille characters.

Onscreen keyboards can also be configured to work with special gestures or actions performed by a user. Consider Christopher Reeve, the actor who played Superman in several movies. A riding accident left him paralyzed from the neck down. His wheel chair was enabled with one of the input methods mentioned here known as "blowing or sipping."

Screen readers can read all text, menus, and labels that the reader sees on a screen. The visually impaired are able to work with computers because of this assistive technology. Two frequently used Linux screen readers are Emacspeak and Orca which are both free. If you are reviewing screen readers, make sure they have the capability to read everything on the screen – including a document or an article found in a browser. You will find that issue – not being able to read from a browser – with Window's Narrator. This feature comes in handy for users with normal sight also. When preparing a document that will be shared with others, it is helpful to have an application read it out loud. The user hears how it will "sound" and often catches errors missed when proofreading the document.

## Desktop Themes

Finally, by changing the appearance of your desktop, Desktop Themes (Figure 5-14) can help the users who need help reading the screen. There are at least two built-in Themes that are configured to add higher contrast, making characters and icons easier to see. You can also change the size of your Font (Figure 5-15) so text appears larger. Select: System ➤ Preferences ➤ Appearance.

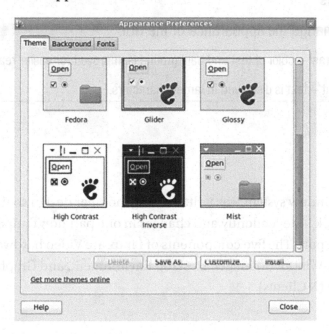

*Figure 5-14.* *Available themes*

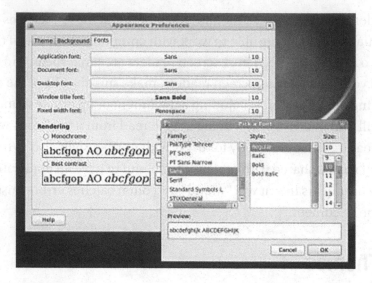

*Figure 5-15.  Font settings*

---

**Key Facts**

**Desktop Themes**

Themes set to change the appearance of the GUI.

- High contrast – color of test and background is improved for easier reading.

- Large print – text is displayed in larger characters.

---

# Summary

- The X Window system was written using modular design so different parts work independently and changes in one part don't impact a different part. The five components of Linux are Video hardware, X Server, Window Manager, Desktop Environment, and Graphical Program (X Clients).

- Linux applications are hardware independent. The core of the system is X Server, which manages access to all input and output devices. Windows Manager controls the look and behavior of windows on the screen. Desktop environment controls backgrounds, screensavers, icons, and menus.

- Configuring X Server requires planning to avoid damage to the hardware. Start by identifying system components, then selecting options that are compatible with the hardware.

- After selecting a Display manager, there are some configuration choices to make, depending on the Linux distribution. When setting color depth, the tradeoffs are between quality of picture and application speed.

- Accessibility options, also known as Assistive Technologies (AT), are included in different versions of Linux. You can specify different options for keyboard accessibility, mouse accessibility, audio settings, and visual options. Free screen readers are available to read words on the screen.

# CHAPTER 6

# Hardware and Process Settings

In this chapter, you will gain an understanding of how to implement device drives and manage kernel modules. You also will be able to describe hotplug and coldplug devices and how to manage processes related to hardware and settings.

By the end of this chapter, you will be able to

1. Describe methods for implementing device drivers

2. Manage kernel modules

3. Describe hotplug and coldplug devices

4. Identify and manage processes

## Device Drivers

A device driver is needed for every piece of hardware installed on a PC. It tells the operating system how to communicate with the hardware. Without this driver, the system may see the hardware, but it has no idea what to do with it.

## Two Ways to Implement

The two ways of implementing device drivers are (1) dynamic kernel modules and (2) compiled into the kernel.

Dynamic kernel modules are loaded dynamically only when needed. They run as though they are part of the kernel. They have an extension of .o or .ko and are found in

© Ahmed F. Sheikh 2024
A. F. Sheikh, *CompTIA Linux+ Certification Companion*, Certification Study Companion Series,
https://doi.org/10.1007/979-8-8688-0128-0_6

the /lib/modules/<kernel_version>/kernel/drivers/<driver> directory. The provided image shows the directories and the files in the power directory.

The driver files are actually compiled into the kernel method. You might ask why this is not how all device drivers are handled. There are several reasons why this is not the best solution. First, the more modules you add to the kernel, the bigger the kernel becomes – meaning additional resources are needed. Why load a device driver if it is not needed? What about when you want to update the driver files? You would have to decompile the kernel, remove the old drivers, add the new ones, and recompile the kernel. As a module implies, it is modular and can be added, changed, or removed as needed. Plus, compiling the kernel is not an easy task. Someone with the knowledge and skills has to be available to do that.

You can see why the recommendation is to only compile into the kernel what you know will be used by the system on a regular basis.

# The /proc Directory

The /proc directory has a wealth of information about the hardware your system uses. This is a virtual directory that is dynamically created when you move to it while in a terminal window. The /proc directory is a great place to get information about the processes that are currently running on your system in addition to the hardware.

Some of the files listed in the /proc directory are listed in the bulleted list. You can view these files as any other text file and glean information about hardware, such as your CPU, hard drives, and modules. Most of these are self-explanatory; however, IRQ (interrupt), I/O address, and DMA channel may be new to you. When earlier PCs had ISA (Industry Standard Architecture) devices, you had to set the interrupt and the IO port that an expansion card would use to talk to the CPU. With the newer plug-and-play devices, those are automatically set for you.

DMA (direct memory access) is a technique used to transfer data from the device to memory without having to go through the CPU, which makes it faster.

Remember, the information found in each of these files is current, because the /proc directory is basically created when you ask for it.

**Information available in files in /proc**

- devices – list of hardware devices
- cpuinfo – information on CPU

- dma - information on DMA channels

- interrupt – lists the interface used by devices to interrupt the CPU

- iomem – details about I/O memory usage

- modules – list of currently running modules

- version – running kernel version

- /scsi/ – information on SCSI devices

- /ide/ – information on IDE devices

- /bus/devices – information on USB devices

# The /sys Directory

The /sys directory is responsible for providing information to all programs that are running on a Linux system. The following information will help you understand for what most of these directories are responsible.

It is normally assumed that all the processes running on Linux need to know how a device works by looking at the driver for that device. The class directory is a little different in that it shows the system's hardware type or class. For example, the system may just need to know that hard drives are attached and not that they are SCSI or ATA.

**/sys directory**

- /sys/block – info on block devices, i.e., hard drives

- /sys/bus – ISA, SCSI, PCI, USB

- /sys/class – device classes

- /sys/devices – hierarchy of hardware

- /sys/modules – kernel modules

# Tools to Manage Device Drivers

There are numerous tools or command line utilities that can be used to gather information about the hardware found on your system. The main ones are listed below.

To see what options you can use with the hwinfo command, use either the man hwinfo command or the hwinfo –h command. Both will tell you more than you wanted to know about this command. You will probably want to limit this report to a specific hardware device, such as USB. Otherwise, you will get a huge report. Again with the lspci command, there are numerous options that can be used to get reports on the PCI buses.

**Tools to manage device drivers**

- lsusb – displays info about all USB devices

- hwinfo <options> – scans all installed hardware and creates a report on the findings

- lspci – scans all PCI buses and reports findings

- lsblk – provides details about the block devices

- inxi – provides details about hardware components in a file system

# Managing Kernel Modules

Each time your system boots, it runs the modprobe command that is covered later in this chapter. This utility looks for a configuration file or files. It is a command-line utility that helps in removing and adding modules from the kernel.

# Configuration Files

The configuration files used to load all required kernel modules at boot up are located in the /etc directory. The modprobe.conf contains three directives: install, alias, and options. The install directive includes the modules that should be started at boot up. The alias directive lists the alias for a module that has a very long path or file name. Creating an alias is almost like creating a nickname for someone who has a hard to pronounce or long name. The last directive, which is options, contains information required for older devices like the IRQ and the I/O port number.

If the /modprobe.conf file does not exist, the modprobe.d directory contains multiple configuration files that can be used at boot up.

Be aware that all distributions of Linux do not use these exact names, but a configuration file(s) do exist.

One more thing on the configuration files: If you want to change what is loaded at boot up, do not make those changes in the etc/modprobe.conf file. Changes should be made in the /etc/modprobe.conf.local

**Configuration files**

- /etc/modprobe.conf

  - install <module>

  - alias <name> <module>

  - options – module <options>

- /etc/modprobe.d/<files>

- /etc/modprobe.conf.local

# Manually Managing Kernel Modules

The commands listed are used when you need to manually manage kernel modules.

The lsmod command lists all loaded modules. To get more information about one of those listed modules, use modinfo <module>. The depmod creates a file, modules.dep, that lists all dependencies for this module. That file is located in the /lib/modules/<kernel_version> directory.

Be careful when using the insmod command. It will install a module, but it does not check for and install dependent modules. It is safer to use the modprobe command, which does look for dependencies and installs them. This utility is run at boot up so that all required modules are loaded. This utility looks for the necessary rules in the /etc/modprobe.conf.

Removing a module with rmmod is simple if you remember you cannot remove a module that is loaded. Also, remember to verify that the module you want to remove is not a dependency of another module. If it is a dependency of another and you remove it, the other module will not function properly.

# Tools to Manually Manage Kernel Modules

- lsmod – lists loaded modules

- modinfo <module> – provides details on module

- depmod <option> – lists module dependencies

- insmod <module> – installs module

- modprobe <option> – loads modules with dependencies

- rmmod <module> – removes module

The lsmod command lists all loaded modules. To get more information about one of those listed modules, use modinfo <module>. The depmod creates a file, modules.dep, that lists all dependencies for this module. That file is located in the /lib/modules/<kernel_version> directory.

You need to be careful when using the insmod command. It will install a module, but it does not check for and install dependent modules. It is safer to use the modprobe command which does look for dependencies and install them. This utility is run at boot up so that all required modules are loaded. This utility looks for the necessary rules in the /etc/modprobe.conf we discussed previously.

Removing a module with rmmod is simple if you remember you cannot remove a module that is loaded. Something else to remember is you should verify the module you want to remove is NOT a dependency of another module. If it is a dependency of another and you remove it, the other module will not function properly, and you will wonder why!

# Hotplug and Coldplug Devices

There are two categories of devices you need to understand when working with hardware – hotplug and coldplug. These are also known as hotswap and coldswap. If you try to add or remove something when the PC is running and you are not working with a hotplug device, you could damage the piece of hardware you are installing and the motherboard as well.

## Hotplug

Hotplug devices are those that use the USB and Firewire ports. Some laptops still use what was called a PCMCIA card (PC card) and a PC-Express card. Those devices can be added and removed while the PC is running without doing any damage. Server-class machines, on the other hand, can have hotplug PCI cards, hard drives, and even RAM. If you have a USB flash drive or thumb drive, you are familiar with this technology. You just did not realize it was called a hotplug device. Printers are now coming with USB plugs.

# Coldplug

Coldplug devices usually come with the PC when you buy it originally. It comes with a CPU, RAM, a hard drive, and a few expansion cards. You may want to upgrade a device, such as a video card, if you are a gamer. You must remember to turn off your PC before making any changes.

If you are not working with a server-class machine, one that has special and expensive hardware, you probably do not have anything that is hotpluggable except for a USB or Firewire port.

Be aware of the hardware you are working with before making any physical changes in hardware devices.

# Components That Manage Devices

You understand that the BIOS and operating system know about the hardware that is installed at the time of bootup. So how does the system know when you plug in a USB device? There are several components that are used in Linux to manage such devices.

The hardware abstraction layer daemon, or hald, provides information about all installed hardware to applications running on the system. This daemon starts when your system boots and is dynamically updated when changes occur.

The next component, sysfs, is a virtual file system that is mounted in /sys and provides applications with information about the hotpluggable devices. Sysfs is the widely used approach for exporting system details from the kernel space to the user space, particularly for specific devices.

The D-Bus daemon, or desktop bus daemon, is a system used for interprocess communication. This communication is used to let other processes know when a hotplug device has been added.

All hardware found during boot up has device driver files located in the /dev directory, but since hotplug devices are normally not available at boot up, no files exist for them. Device files for these hotplug devices are dynamically created and removed by another virtual file system called udev.

It uses two files: the first is /etc/udev/udev.conf and contains the error reporting level for hotplug device errors, while the second is the /etc/udev/rules.d/ file which creates a name for these devices. These two files can be modified, but changes are usually not needed. The udev process normally gets the job done without changes being needed.

# Processes

## What Is a Process?

You have heard the term *process* as it relates to computers, but do you really know what it is? A process is simply any program that is running in memory and on a CPU. It is also known as a task or a job. There are two types of processes – daemons and user executables. A daemon is like a service is to Windows. Many of these daemons start at boot up and run in the background without the user even realizing they are there. They are also known as system processes. A user can start a daemon; however, they are usually started by the system. In most cases, the file name of a daemon ends with .d.

A user process begins when a user starts a program. This could be a built-in command, such as ls, cd, cat, or it could be an application called a binary that was compiled into machine language (like vi) and is started from a terminal session or calculator started from the GUI. It also could be an executable shell script written by a user.

Something to remember about processes is that they do not all actually run at the exact same time unless your CPU has multiple cores. It appears that they do, but in fact, the processing power of the CPU is divided among all the running processes and switches between them; this is called multithreading. This is not the same as multitasking, which means performing multiple tasks at the same time. If the CPU has more than one core, the CPU can perform multitasking.

## Process ID

Each process has a Process ID (PID). This is a unique number that is used to identify the process. When a system boots up, the first thing it does is start its first process called init which has PID of 1. It starts or spawns other processes that are needed to start a Linux system, including the login process. All core processes are low numbers, usually below 100. Each process that is started after the init process will have a Parent Process ID (PPID) as well as a PID. As you might guess, the process with a PID is also called a child process. If needed for troubleshooting, you can draw a family-tree structure starting with the original daemon, init (Figure 6-1).

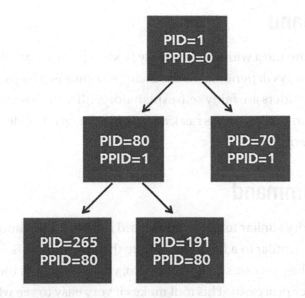

**Figure 6-1.** *This family-tree structure demonstrates relationships between the Process ID (PID) and the Parent Process ID (PPID)*

# Forking and Zombie

Two terms you should know for the Linux+ exam are forking and zombie. Forking, or fork, is when a new process, called a subshell, is created by a parent that has its own PID and its own memory space – it looks just like the parent. An example of when a fork is created is when vi is executed. A separate process actually handles what is done to a file opened by vi. A problem that can occur with forking is that the parent closes before the subshell closes, which causes ghosting.

A zombie process is a child process that is not properly killed when the parent stops. This type of process can unnecessarily use resources.

# The ps Command

The ps command is the most widely used utility to view running processes. It lists the processes in varying ways depending on the included options. The ps is short for *process status*. The column headers are fairly self-explanatory: PID, TTY (where a process started), TIME (how long the process ran), and CMD. The pts/1 under TTY means it was started in a pseudo terminal.

# The pstree Command

A command that is very similar to the ps command is pstree. The running processes are displayed in a format similar to a family tree. Note the first process is init, which then spawned the rest of the processes listed next. Also, you will see that the auditd daemon spawned several other processes. This tool makes it very easy to see what processes have child processes.

# Top Command

The top command is an interactive tool that lists processes in real time and shows the most CPU-intensive processes at the top of the list. You will see much of the same information you did with ps, but the percentage of the CPU being used is extremely helpful. This is much the same as the Processes tab in the Windows Task Manager. This command is interactive, so you will have to use Ctrl-C or Ctrl-Z to stop the utility.

# Process Management

Have you ever started an application, such as gedit, from a shell prompt and noticed you cannot do anything in a terminal session without opening a new one? There is a reason why. When you start vi from a terminal session, a subshell is created. That subshell runs in the foreground, which means you cannot get to the original shell to do anything. When the subshell that is running vi is closed, the original shell is displayed again.

# Foreground Processing

If you want to use that original shell session to do other things after executing gedit, you can use foreground processing by adding a space and the ampersand character. Foreground processes are those that require user initiation or interaction.

**Foreground processing**

- Add space then "&" to the end of a command (gedit &).

- Allows use of original shell.

# Background

What if you forgot to add the ampersand after the command when you wanted to use the original shell? You can switch a process running in the foreground to the background and vice versa. Background processes are those that run independently of user involvement.

Moving a process from the background is easier than the other way around. You only need one command, *fg*, and the job ID. Foreground to background requires an additional step. You must press ctrl+z to stop the process and assign a background ID. Then you use that ID in the bg command.

# The nohup Command

There are times you may want to close a shell but leave a process it started running. By using the nohup command, you can start the process in the background and then close the originating shell.

An example of when you might use this is if you made a remote connection to a host so you can run an application that will take several hours to complete. It is almost the end of the day. You do not want to babysit the process, and you do not want to leave the terminal session open for security reasons. You can start the command in the background using the nohup command (nohup <process> &) and close the original terminal session.

# Prioritizing Processes

Linux is a multitasking system, which means that multiple processes can be running but not concurrently. The CPU gives so much time to each process based on the kernel's priority. There are eight levels of priority, and the higher the priority value, the more CPU time the process gets. So, how do you change a kernel's priority?

## Change Before Process Start

You cannot change the actual priority value, but you can adjust it with a nice value. The nice value is backward from the priority value; a higher number decreases the priority value. This value can be between 0 and +19 if a regular user is using this command; -20 to +19 if you are logged in as root.

The only thing to remember is the command nice and its value must come before the actual command you wish to execute.

## Change After Process Start

You just learned how to change the priority of a process before you start the command, but what if the process is already running? You can use the renice command to do that. If you do not know the process's PID, you will need to look that up using ps. Then type *renice*, the new value, and the PID. Remember, to decrease the priority of a process, you increase the nice value.

It is a good idea to verify that your changes were made. You can use the ps -elf to display the priority and nice values of the process after making your changes both before and after the process has been started.

# Terminating a Process

There will be times when you must terminate a running process that is hung. The only way to reset processes is to reboot the system or to use a utility that has the sole purpose of terminating processes. The most widely used utilities are very appropriately named: kill, killall, and xkill. As a sysadmin, you will be supporting servers and desktops, so you cannot just reboot a server except in a planned time period. These utilities are often the only way you can stop the hung process. Let's explore each termination process in more detail.

# Kill Command

The kill command has a simple syntax – kill <signal> PID. The signal can be one of many, with the most commonly used one shown below. If you do not include a signal, which is the default, the process is terminated with no other action. This command works with Windows and Linux and should be in everyone's arsenal of tools!

- No Kill signal – This is the default and simply stops the process.

- SIGHUP – 1 – Kills and then restarts a process with the same PID.

- SIGHUP – 2 – Kills the process as does ctrl-c.

- SIGHUP – 9 – Kills the process without releasing the resources.

- SIGHUP – 15 – Kills the process after releasing the resources.

The killall command uses the name of the process rather than PID, and it can use kill signals too. If this process has been started more than once, it will kill all the running processes by that name. Another command, pkill, also uses the process name to kill a running process.

The xkill command turns your cursor into a cross-hair character, which allows you to click on the hung window. If you do not know the PID or process's name, this is the easiest way to kill a process from the GUI.

# Summary

In this chapter, you learned about important concepts related to hardware and process settings. Keep the following in mind:

- You learned two methods for implementing device drivers, where they are located, and how to manage them.

- You learned how to manage kernel modules.

- You discovered what hotplug and coldplug devices are and how the system manages them.

# CHAPTER 7

# Users and Groups

There are two types of accounts that can be used to control access to resources on or connected to a server. These are users and groups. In this chapter, you will learn how to manage both.

By the end of this chapter, you will be able to

1. Create and manage user and group accounts

2. Identify and apply best practices when working with user and group accounts

## User Accounts

### Account Locations

There are several locations where user information can be stored. The oldest is a database called Network Information Services (NIS). It has been used, and is still used, by UNIX to supply information about users, groups, and hosts on a network. When a user attempts to login, provided the host is running a NIS client program, the user would be allowed or denied access by the NIS database.

More recently directories have been used for this same purpose. The most well-known directories are eDirectory by Novell (formally known as Novell Directory Services or NDS) and Active Directory by Microsoft. The Lightweight Directory Access Protocol (LDAP) is used to query and even modify these directories. Therefore, any LDAP compliant database or directory can be used to store user information.

Databases can reside on the server or on a local host. The focus of this chapter will be accounts on a local host.

125

© Ahmed F. Sheikh 2024
A. F. Sheikh, *CompTIA Linux+ Certification Companion*, Certification Study Companion Series,
https://doi.org/10.1007/979-8-8688-0128-0_7

# Types of User Accounts

There are two types of user accounts: standard and system users.

Standard user accounts are created by an administrator based on a predetermined naming convention. A home user or an admin working in a company will decide on a standard naming format for your user accounts. The standard could be first initial of the first name followed by last name for company accounts, such as jscott, shernadez, and bchung. For home accounts, the user name could be the first name, such as Julie, Sam, and Brad.

The system assigns each user account a User ID (UID) when it is created. The root user account, created by default at installation, is given a UID of 0. Fedora assigns a UID of 500 to the first user. Suse starts theirs at 1000. This default value can be changed and is often different from distro to distro.

System user accounts are created at installation and cannot be used to authenticate or log into a host. They are used by the system to perform a specific task. Typically, they have a name that tells you what role they play. An example is: system user account "ftp" used to run the ftp services or daemons.

An important distinction between standard user accounts and system user accounts is that only standard user accounts are allowed to log into a host.

# User Account Files

Information used by user accounts is stored in two files, /etc/passwd and /etc/shadow. They each act like a flat file database and are linked together by the account name. Each contains a record (or line of information) that is broken into parts called fields. To function properly they must be synchronized at all times.

---

### Key Facts

### Files on a local host that contain user and password information

- /etc/passwd contains a record for each user account.

- /etc/shadow contains a record for each user account.

- Linked (synchronized) to each other by the "user name" field in each record.

---

# /etc/passwd File

The /etc/passwd file contains information (Table 7-1) that identifies a specific user and some of that user's requirements. With the name passwd, you would assume it contains the user's password. In the past this was true. As tighter security became mandatory, a second file was created to hold the password information. The logic used makes it harder for a hacker to get both files, thus increasing security.

Each record stores the name of the user account that is used to log into the host, the system assigned user ID, the primary group ID, a description of the user (like the user's first and last name), the absolute path to the user's home directory, and the shell the user will use to communicate with the Kernel.

Each record in the /etc/passwd file contains the following fields separated by a colon (":").

- Syntax: name:pw:uid:gid:full_name:home:shell

- Example: jscott:x:500:500:Julie Scott:/home/jscott:/bin/bash

***Table 7-1.*** *Parts of the passwd File*

| Field | Description |
| --- | --- |
| name | User account name – used to login |
| pw | No longer used – defaults to x |
| UID | User ID |
| GID | Group ID |
| Full_name (GECOS) | Description of user – like first/last name |
| home | Absolute path to user's home directory |
| shell | Shell that user will work in |

# /etc/shadow File

The /etc/shadow file enhances the authentication mechanism on Linux systems by implementing stricter access controls at the account level. Within this text file, actual passwords are securely stored in a hashed format, accompanied by supplementary information. The one-way hash function employed in this process converts the plaintext into a hash. The fields listed below are found in the /etc/shadow file which gives you password related information. These fields are also separated by a colon. The fields are similar to those for Windows user accounts and their password requirements.

- name

- password

- lastchanged

- min

- max

- warn

- disable1 (dis)

- disable2 (exp)

The **name** field is the user's account name that is used to log into a host. This field is what links this record to the same user's record in the /etc/passwd file. We then have the actual *password* which has been encrypted. In the example below you will notice this password begins with a "$". That means the password has been encrypted.

The *lastchanged* field is the number of days from 1/1/1970 to when the password was last changed. You may wonder how to calculate that number. Not to worry... There are multiple tools that can do that for you. Use a search engine, such as Google, to search for "Epoch Converter" to find tools that calculate this difference.

The *min* and *max* fields give you control over how soon you can change a password and the number of days before you must change it. The *min* field confuses most people so they ask who cares how soon a password is changed. People get used to a specific password and do not want to remember a new one. They learn to trick the system by making the required change and then immediately changing it back to the one with which they are familiar. If you set a min of 10 days, the user cannot change it back for at least 10 days.

A *warning* can be sent to the user that they have number of days before their password must be changed.

The *disable1* field gives the user a grace period after the *max* setting before the account will actually be disabled. Most distros set this field to -1 so the account is disabled if the password is not changed by the required *max* date.

CHAPTER 7   USERS AND GROUPS

The last field, disable2, is the number of days from 1/1/1970 to the date the account must be disabled. This field is often used on contractors' user accounts. For example, perhaps they are hired for a six month contract which cannot be extended. The *disable2* field allows you to set that six month date so you stay compliant with any regulations.

Each record in the /etc/shadow file contains the following fields separated by a colon.

- Syntax: name:password:lastused:min:max:warn:disable1:disable2

- Example: jscott:$iu048;jajerhad:14823:7:365:3:2:

---

**Key Facts**

- If the password field in the /etc/shadow file starts with a dollar sign, the password is encrypted. If it starts with single or double exclamation marks, you know the account is locked or disabled. An asterisk only indicates the account is a system account.

- Passwords for standard user accounts are always encrypted.

- If you do not want to have to change your password, set the max field to 99999, and it will never expire.

- Fedora's defaults are – min=0, max=99999, warn=7.

---

# Synchronize passwd and shadow Files

The three commands you see below will help you to keep the /etc/passwd and /etc/shadow files synchronized. Recall these two files are linked by the name field. That means you must have a record in both files that contains the account's name in the name field. For example, the first field in a record of both files would contain *susie*. Keep in mind that the password information is in one file and all the other information needed by a user to log into a host is in the other file. Without the information in both files, the user will not be able to login.

- pwck – verifies files are in sync

- pwconv – two functions

  - Fixes these files if they get unsync'd

  - Also used to separate an old /etc/passwd file into two files

If you suspect the files are out of sync, use the **pwck** command to verify your suspicions. It is good practice to run this command periodically to make sure all is good.

If **pwck** finds errors, use the **pwconv** command to resynchronize the files. Another function of the **pwconv** command is to separate an old /etc/passwd file into the /etc/passwd and /etc/shadow files. In the past, only one file was used to store all the user's information, including their password.

There could be a reason that you need to revert to the older format where one file has both user and password data. There is a command for this process **dfdffpwunconv**.

How do they get out of sync? This is usually cause by human error. Hardware failure or damage to a hard drive COULD happen, but that is a lot less likely than an admin making an error. Since these are text files, you can use any text editor to make the needed changes; however, a typo or changing one file and not the other will cause the files to not be synchronized. In Fedora, use the GUI tool, User Manager, designed to manage these files. Ubuntu has a similar tool.

It is important to know these commands for the Linux+ test. However, you should use the GUI tools to make changes to avoid introducing errors.

# Groups

## Group Accounts

Group accounts are typically created for work groups and are containers that hold a group of people. A group can be all the managers, a team, a department, associated by location such as Italy, connected by product type, or be a fundraising group. If Susie is a *manager* and is in the *sales* department and works in *Italy*, Susie's user account would probably be added to all three groups.

Why are they used? Managers usually have access to more information than standard workers. Imagine you have a directory called Manager, and your company has 10 managers. You could grant each user account access to the Manager's directory individually. You could also create a Managers group and add all 10 of the managers to that group. You may be thinking that setting up access on 10 individual user accounts would not take much time. Setting up a group and adding 10 user accounts to it will take as long if not longer than granting the individual access. You haven't saved any time. But what if you had 100 managers? What if they need access to more than just the Managers directory? What if there are six other directories they need to see? Without the group, you would be assigning permissions to those 100 managers in 700 steps versus 7 if you use the group. Which way would be easier? The answer is obvious. You would add all 100 managers to the group and assign permissions to the group!

Here is another twist. Every manager in your company should have access to the same files and directories. Each time a new manager joins your company, you have to grant the new manager the same access as the other managers. Will you remember the list of files and directories and the level of permission? Probably not. You determine what the role "Manager" needs, and grant that access to the group. When there are changes to managers' access requirements, you need only make the change to the group list. Unless you control access with a group, when a manager leaves the company, you have to locate every resource to which he has access and remove it. The easier, more efficient, and safer solution is to remove a specific person as a member of the Managers group.

Using groups allows better management of access to resources.

## Group Account Types

There are two types of Group accounts: primary and secondary groups.

In Fedora, primary groups are created when a standard user account is created in the /home directory. They are usually named the same as the user account. That user is this group's only member. Any file or directory created by that user is automatically owned by that user and that group.

The group ID, or GID, for a user's group is usually the same as their userid (UID). Root's primary group is 0 as is its UID. You can find a user's UID and GID quickly with the **id <name>** command.

Secondary groups (also known as Supplementary Groups) are the ones that can contain one to many user accounts and are usually used to control ownership and permissions for special areas such as a department or a region. Companies typically have secondary groups for departments such as IT, Users, Administrators, Sales, or for locations such as Asia, Europe, Canada, and the USA. These groups are created and maintained by a sysadmin.

You will not need to use groups on your home network unless you have a big family and want to control access.

# Group Account Files

As with the user accounts, group information is stored in two files: /etc/group and /etc/gshadow. Again, each field is separated by a colon. These files are also linked by the group name and must stay synchronized.

## /etc/group

The /etc/group file does not contain as many fields as the /etc/passwd file. One thing you do not see on most groups is a password. If no password is to be used, the password field is left blank. An x in that field indicates there is a password in the /etc/gshadow file.

Just as user's can be members of multiple groups, the user's field can contain multiple user accounts, and each must be separated by a comma.

---

### Key Facts

- /etc/group and /etc/gshadow are linked by group name.

- Each record in the /etc/group file contains the following fields separated by a ":".

  - Syntax: group:password:gid:users:

  - Example: Italy:x:520:jscott, squeue, sspade

---

## /etc/gshadow

The /etc/gshadow file stores the group's password, the user or users that manage the group, and list of users that are members of the group. To list multiple managers and the group's members, separate items with a comma.

A group password serves a different purpose than a user account. The group password allows users to add themselves to a group; the user password allows authentication to a resource.

If the group has a password, any user who knows the password can add themselves to the group using the **newgrp** command. As with the user password, the group password is encrypted.

If the pass field contains an exclamation mark rather than a password, the password cannot be used to access the group account. Two exclamation marks will also block access using the password, but in this case, no password was ever set. Last, if the pass field is empty, only members of the group can access the group account.

By default, when Fedora creates a user account, a group account with the same name is also created. The GID is the same as the UID. That group becomes the user's primary group. You may not see the logic in this process, and it is not used by all distros of Linux. In Windows, a user's primary group is the Users group.

---

### Key Facts

- Each record in the /etc/gshadow file contains the following fields separated by a ":".

    - Syntax: group:pass:group_admins:members

    - Example: Italy:!:jscott:jscott, squeue, sspade

        - Pass field

            - ! – group account can't be accessed by using the **newgrp <password>** command.

            - !! – no password has been set – account can't be accessed with the **newgrp <password>** command.

            - Empty – only group members can access the account.

---

As with the /etc/shadow file, you have to have root privileges to view the contents of the /etc/gshadow file.

# Managing User/Group Accounts

## Default Configurations

Most distros of Linux have default configurations stored in two files that are used when user and group accounts are created. Company policy usually determines the value of each of the defaults. These defaults can be changed or overridden by the **useradd** command.

These files are the /etc/login.defs and /etc/default/useradd. A directory is used along with these "default" files – /etc/skel.

---

### Key Facts

- Default configuration files used with **useradd** command.

  - /etc/login.defs – contains defaults used in /etc/passwd, /etc/shadow, and /etc/group files

  - /etc/default/useradd – contains additional defaults used in /etc/passwd and /etc/shadow files

  - /etc/skel – contains files needed by new users

---

## /etc/login.defs

The /etc/login.defs file contains

- Defaults for the password expiration fields located in the /etc/shadow file

- Hash algorithm used to encrypt the user's password

- Group IDs and user IDs used in the /etc/group and /etc/password files

# add Command

The /etc/default/useradd file is used with the **useradd** command to supply default values. For example, if you use only the **useradd** command with the new user's name, the remaining fields would be completed from this file and the /etc/login.defs file.

---

### Key Facts

- Content of /etc/default/useradd config file

  - Location of home directory

  - Number of days required before disabling user account with expired password

  - Date to disable user accounts

  - Shell used

  - Primary group

  - Directory where default files can be found

---

This file is much smaller than the /etc/login.defs file so it is easier to review the entire file.

# Skeleton Directory

Although it does not hold default values, the /etc/skel directory contains files needed in the new user's home directory like .bashrc, .bash_profile, and .kshrc. One of the default parameters tells the useradd command where to look for this skeleton directory.

The /etc/skel directory holds files and directories that are automatically replicated to a new user's profile when created using the useradd command. This ensures uniform initial settings and environment for all users.

# useradd Command

New user accounts are created with the **useradd** command. The syntax of this command is **useradd <options> <name>**. If no option is used, the default value will be pulled from the .bashrc, .bash_profile, and .kshrc files in the /etc/skel directory. For more detail on each command, use **man <command>** - **man** stands for manual pages.

After the user account is created, a password should be added.

---

### Key Facts

- Command – **useradd <options> <name>**
  - **e <expirydate>** = date account should be disabled.
  - **–f <#>** = # of days before account with expired password will be disabled.
  - **–m** = home directory should be created for account.
  - **–g** = set primary group for the new account.
  - **–c** = includes a description of the new account.

*** Additional options can be found by using the **man useradd** command.

---

# Password

After the user account has been created, a password should be created. The syntax is **passwd <options> <password>**. The account is locked until a password is created, and the /etc/shadow file will have two exclamation marks in the password field.

Use the command **man passwd** to see the available options. Notice the **-l** option which can be used to lock a user account. Two exclamation marks are then placed in the password field in the /etc/shadow file.

This command is also used to change existing passwords. The root user can add or modify any user's password using this command; however, a standard user can change only their own password.

The company's Security Policy usually sets the standard for the format of a password. Many companies require "strong passwords," which have the following characteristics:

- Length: At least 8 characters.

- Complexity: Mixture of lower case, upper case, numbers, and special characters; company policy may require two or three (lower, upper, numbers) and/or specific special characters be used.

- Unique characters: a minimum number of unique characters.

Other guidelines include avoiding

- Dictionary words (too easy to guess, by human or application)

- Family, pet, or friend names

- Personal information, like date of birth or zip code

# Modifying User Accounts

Now we need to learn how to modify an existing user account. The syntax of this command is **usermod <options> <name>**.

It is strongly recommended that you use these commands rather than editing the /etc/passwd and/or /etc/shadow files directly. It is very easy to make an error using that process. These commands help to keep the two files in sync.

There are numerous options that can be used with this command. One of these options – changing the description of the user – can also be done with the **chfn** command.

---

### Key Facts

- Command – **usermod  <options> <username>**
  - Used to modify an existing user account
  - Options
    - **-c <description>** = modify description of user.
    - **-e <expirydate>** = date account should be disabled.

- **-f <#>** = # of days before account with expired password will be disabled.

- **-g <group>** = sets the primary group for an account.

- **-l <name>** = sets a new login name.

\*\*\* Additional options can be found by using the **man usermod** command.

# CHAGE

The command used to make changes to the min, max, and warn fields of the /etc/shadow file is the **chage** command. The syntax is **chage <option> <name>**. No, that is not a typo – it really is spelled c h a g e!

The chage command in Linux serves as a valuable tool for administering password aging policies. It facilitates tasks such as listing current settings, establishing expiration dates, and regulating password lifespan. Regular utilization of the chage command is fundamental for maintaining robust system security practices.

**Key Facts**

- Command – **chage <options> <username>**
  - Used to change password expiry information in /etc/shadow files
  - Options
    - **–l** = displays account aging information
    - **–m** = minimum # of days between password changes
    - **–M** = maximum # of days between password changes
    - **–W** = # of days before user is notified that password should be changed

\*\*\* Additional options can be found by using the **man chage** command.

# Lock/Unlock User Accounts

Earlier in the chapter you learned how to lock a user account with the **passwd** command. Now we will see all the commands you can use to lock and unlock user accounts.

Using the **usermod** command along with the **-L** option will lock the user's account by placing an exclamation mark in front of the encrypted password in the /etc/shadow file; **usermod -U <name>** will unlock the account.

The command **passwd -l <name>** will also lock the account by placing two exclamation marks in front of the encrypted password in the /etc/shadow file. To unlock the account using the **passwd** command, use the **-u** option.

The last way, which is not used as often as the others, is by changing the user's default shell to an invalid directory using the **chsh** command. You will still use the **lock** command but with the option: to lock the user account, give it a bad directory name; to unlock it, give it the correct directory. Without a valid shell, the users can't log into a host.

---

### Key Facts

### Lock / Unlock user accounts

- Lock - **usermod –L <name>**.
- ! is put in front of the encrypted password in /etc/shadow.
- Unlock – **usermod –U <name>**.

OR

- Lock - **passwd –l <name>**.
- Two !s (!!) are put in front of the encrypted password.
- Unlock – **passwd –u <name>**.

OR

- Change the shell to an invalid shell – i.e., /bin/false.
- Lock – **chsh –s /bin/false <name>**.
- Unlock – **chsh –s /bin/bash <name>**.

---

# Deleting a User Account

The command **userdel <options> <name>** will remove that user's records from the /etc/passwd and /etc/shadow files. Again, using this command is safer than deleting the lines manually.

Normally, you will not use an option with this command, because you don't want to delete all the user's files. They will need to be transferred to the person taking over that job or to archive. Only the user's records in /etc/passwd, /etc/shadow, /etc/group, and /etc/gshadow will be removed.

If you know that user had nothing that needs to be saved, you can use the **-r** option which will remove that user's home directory and all the files it contains. It also removes the user's mail spool.

The **-f** option can be used, but it is not recommended. This option forces the same actions as above, but it works even if the user is logged in or if someone else is using that home directory or the user's primary group.

It was just mentioned that you may need to transfer that user's file to a new or existing user. Here's how you do that.

If the account has not been created yet, you can use the **-u** option along with the old user's user ID. This assigns that number to the new user rather than getting the next available number from the /etc/login.defs file. If an existing user needs access to the files, you can make them a member of the user's primary group.

After all the files have been transferred, the home directory and mail spool will have to be removed manually.

---

### Key Facts

Command – **userdel <options> <name>**

- Removes user account from /etc/passwd and /etc/shadow files
- Options
    - **-f** = forces the deletion of the account, its home directories, and mail spool – even if they are being used by other users

- **-r** = removes the account and its home directories and files

- no option = leaves home directory in tack so files can be transferred to their new owner

*** Additional options can be found by using the **man chage** command.

---

Command – **useradd –u <old user's UID> <new user name>**

- To assign deleted account's files to a new user, create the new user and assign the old account's UID.

# Group Accounts

Management of group accounts is similar to managing user accounts. You can add, remove, and modify membership of groups. You can add and remove a password from groups.

## Add Groups

The syntax used to add a group is **groupadd <options> <group>**. The most commonly used options are listed in Table 7-2.

***Table 7-2.*** *Options Used with the groupadd Command*

| Options | Description |
| --- | --- |
| -f | Exit if group exists/Cancel –g if GID is used |
| -g <GID> | Assign GID to group |
| -p <password> | Assign encrypted password to group |
| -r | Create a system account |

## Modify Groups

To modify a group, use the syntax **groupmod <options> <group>**. Table 7-3 lists two options used with the **groupmod** command. More options can be found in the manual pages – **man groupmod**.

**Table 7-3.**  *Options Used with the groupmod Command*

| Options | Description |
|---|---|
| -g <GID> | Changes the GID of the group |
| -n <newname> | Changes the group name |

# Deleting Groups

Before deleting a group, you should ensure that no files remain owned by this group.

The command to delete a group is: **groupdel <group name>**. If you find you can't delete the group, it is likely because the group is the primary group of an existing user. You will see the following message: *groupdel: cannot remove the primary group of user 'Sam.'* You must change the primary group to another group or delete the user account before continuing.

# Managing Group

A group can have administrators, members, and a password. Changes to a group can be made with the **gpasswd** and **newgrp** commands (Table 7-4).

Syntax: **gpasswd [options] group**.

Using this command, you can add or remove a password for the group; you can also change the membership of the group.

A caveat is that you must execute this command on the server that holds the group since the group is only located on that server. Changes made using this command only effect the local /etc/group and /etc/gshadow files.

**Table 7-4.**  *Options Used with the gpasswd Command*

| Options | Description |
|---|---|
| | Add or change a password |
| -a | Add a user |
| -d | Remove a user |
| -r | Remove group password |

The **newgrp <-> <group>** command allows a user to log into the group account if they have the group's password. Using the dash with this command gives the user extra permissions that belong to that group. The main use of this command is to temporarily change a user's primary group. This command has some definite disadvantages:

- It is never wise to share any password, especially to an entity that can modify access to a resource.

- There is no accountability for the use of the group password.

## Helpful Group Commands

Two additional commands that will come in handy are **groups** and **id**.

- The **groups** command allows you to list all the groups of which the logged in user is a member.

- The **id** command gives you more flexibility than **groups**. It not only gives you the group names but the UID and the GID for each group listed.

# Best Practices

The sysadmin should control the naming convention used for user and group names. If they are all the same format, it is much easier to troubleshoot issues.

Set all the options available on passwords. Require users to change their passwords – typically every 45 to 60 days. Set the *min* field so a user can't change their password to something new and then change it back to the old one the same day. There may be some initial resistance to these practices, but users will learn to work within the security best practices.

Make sure users are aware of strong password requirements – uppercase, lowercase, special characters – length, at least 8 characters.

The best password is totally random. One good way to create a secure password, other than using a password generator, is to pick a long phrase you can remember. Use the first character of each word then scatter a few numbers or symbols around in those characters.

Periodically run the **pwck** command to verify the user account and group account files are in sync. This can help to eliminate calls from frustrated users.

The most important practice you can perform is creating a group for a job or function – such as Sales. Make user accounts members of that group if they all perform the same type function. The vmware group allows any member (user account) to use the vmware software. If you are a member of the log group, you can access all log files in the /var/log directory. This eliminates the individual management of each user; you only have to manage the group and its membership. Using groups increases accuracy and efficiency for the sysadmin.

### Key Facts

### Best Practices

- Create a naming standard for users and groups.

- Set all options available to require passwords.

- Make sure users are aware of the password requirements and consequences for non-compliance.

- Periodically run the **pwck** command.

- Create a group for a job and put user accounts in it.

# Summary

- User accounts can be stored in several locations: NIS database, a directory such as Microsoft's Active Directory and Novell's eDirectory. It can be in a single, global location or can be stored locally on each host.

- There are two types of user accounts; standard user accounts which are normally used by people to log into a host and system user accounts which are used to perform a specific task. System user accounts cannot be used to log into a host.

- Information about each standard user account is stored in the /etc/passwd and /etc/shadow files. These two files must remain in sync in order for a user to log into a host.

- Group accounts are stored in the same location as the user accounts.

- Group accounts group users into a container that has a specific purpose such as location, function, or role.

- There are also two types of group accounts, primary and secondary. A primary group is created for each user when the user account is created. The secondary groups are used mainly to provide the proper access to files and directories.

- Two files hold information on group accounts also: /etc/group and /etc/gshadow. As with the user account files, they must stay in sync.

- Several commands are used to create, delete, and manage user accounts; **useradd**, **passwd**, **usermod**, **chge**, and **userdel** are the most commonly used ones. Password settings can be established by corporate policies and applied to all users, or specific settings can be applied to a single user account.

- Managing group accounts can also be done using one of several commands such as **groupadd**, **groupmod**, **groupdel**, **gpasswd**, **newgrp groups,** and **id**.

- As with any procedure, a list of "Best Practices" should be established and followed when managing both user and group accounts.

# CHAPTER 8

# Administrative Tasks

This chapter introduces you to several management tasks which will make your job as a systems administrator much easier. You will first learn to use the **at** and **cron** commands to schedule jobs that can perform tasks automatically. Then you will learn how to control the locale time settings on servers and desktops.

By the end of this chapter, you will be able to

1. Create and manage tasks
2. Customize localization and internationalization
3. Modify time zone settings

## Task Management

Have you ever had a report you needed to print in the middle of the night or a task that should NOT be run during the day because of the bandwidth it would take? Sure you have! There are two commands that are available to do both of those which are **at** and **cron**. The **at** command allows you flexibility about when you can schedule a job or task. Its only drawback is it will only run once.

The **cron** command allows you to schedule a job to run multiple times on some kind of a schedule. Aside from the frequency, the functionality and syntax of the commands are similar.

## ATD Daemon

Before using the **at** command, you should verify the atd daemon is installed and running.

147

© Ahmed F. Sheikh 2024
A. F. Sheikh, *CompTIA Linux+ Certification Companion*, Certification Study Companion Series,
https://doi.org/10.1007/979-8-8688-0128-0_8

To verify the at daemon (atd) is running, type the following:

- **cd /etc/rc.d/init.d**   #changes directory

- **ls at***               #lists all files starting with at

- **./atd status**         #verifies the atd daemon is installed and running

- **./atd**                #starts atd daemon if it is not running

# at Command

The "at" command integrates with the Linux scheduling system, serving as a tool to schedule tasks for execution at a predetermined time. It operates as a one-time scheduler, intended for tasks scheduled to run only once. From a terminal session, you can use the **at** command with a variety of options. The basic syntax is **at**, the time and possibly a date as you see below. That establishes when the commands you are about to schedule will be executed. The next line you see will be an "at>" prompt. Enter a single command there. You will continue to get the "at>" prompt for additional commands until you press <ctrl>+D to save the schedule. Only one command can be entered on each line. That command may be a long, complex command with piping and redirection.

After you have saved the file, the system will assign a job number. That number becomes the name of the job.

Syntax: **at <time> <date>**

- at> **<command>**

- at> **<command>**

- **<ctrl> + D** - saves schedule

- Returns job #

# Shell Script

Shell scripting is predominantly used for automating recurrent system tasks, including file backups, system resource monitoring, and user account management. Transforming a sequence of commands into a script enables system administrators to save time, enhance accuracy, and streamline complex tasks. If you have a long list of commands or ones that are very complicated to type, save them in a shell script which is something you can edit. There does not appear to be any way to edit a job scheduled with the **at** command. This example is a simple one, and the concept is applicable to more complex jobs. Create a shell script (remember to make it executable so it can run) and use that file along with the **–f** option to create a job. Note you didn't get any at> prompts using this syntax, but you did get a job number.

Be sure you have the proper permissions to execute a command. This is a common issue to troubleshoot when a scheduled job is not working properly.

Syntax: **at <time> <date> -f <shell script>**

- Returns job #

# at Optional Additions

Table 8-1 lists the optional additions for the **at** command. With **at <time>**, you use a.m., p.m., or military time. Next you see the various formats in which you can enter a date. You can also use times like midnight and noon or teatime (4:00 p.m.). If you do not add a date, the current day is assumed.

*Table 8-1.* *Use of the at Command*

| Command | Example |
| --- | --- |
| at <time> | at 10:00 pm |
|  | at 22:00 |
| at <time> <date> | at 11:00 am June 1 |
|  | at 11:00 am 06/01/2013 |
|  | at 11:00 am 06012013 |
|  | at 11:00 am 06.01.2013 |
| at midnight I noon I teatime [date] | at noon July 1 |
| at <time> tomorrow | at 9:00 pm tomorrow |
|  | at 21:00 tomorrow + 2 days |
| at now [ + <time> } I batch | at now |
|  | at now + 5 minutes |
|  | at now + 5 hours |
|  | at now + 5 days |
|  | at now + 5 weeks |

There are two options you can use along with adding time: tomorrow and now. Table 8-1 shows both options with the plus sign and number of days, weeks, and hours. The most important options are **–l,–d,–f,** and **–c**.

- The **at –l** command displays all the scheduled jobs. You can also use the **atq** command for this purpose. Did you see the difference in the two screen shots? The user who is logged in as root shows all scheduled jobs, whereas the one logged in as a regular user can only see theirs.

- To remove a scheduled job, you need to know the job number. Then you can use the **at –d <job #>** or **atrm <job #>** command.

- You have already seen the **–f** option which is used to execute a shell script.

- The last one is the **at –c <job#>** which shows the current environment variables followed by the contents of the scheduled job.

- The at -b command runs the scheduled job in the background.

- The at -m command send an email to the user once the job is done.

You can view all available options that can be used with the **at** command using **man at**.

---

### Key Facts

### Options

- **at –l** or **atq** – displays scheduled jobs

- **at –d <job #>** or **atrm <job #>** – removes numbered job

- **at –f** – specifies script to execute

- **at –c <job #>** – shows current environment variables and the contents of the job

---

# Results

There are two ways to see the results of running a job: printing it to paper and sending the results to a file. If you printed something, that one is easy. The most logical way is to redirect the output to a file. Then you can view the contents of the output file.

If you forget to include an output file, it will be sent to your mail. Use the **mail** command to see what mail you have received.

All **at** jobs are stored in the /var/spool/at directory.

---

### Key Facts
### Results

- Output to file

    - **at midnight –f <script> > <output>**

- Output to Mail

    - **at midnight –f <script>**

---

# Control Use of at Command

If you want to control who can or can't use the **at** command, use the at.allow and at.deny files in the /etc directory. In Fedora, the default is to create an empty at.deny file and to not create an at.allow file. Be careful when working with the at.allow file. If you create that file and leave it empty, no one can create **at** jobs. If you add a single user, only that user can create an **at** job.

# Cron Command

**Cron** jobs and jobs scheduled with the **at** command are very similar in their purpose, but their configuration files and their locations are very different. An **at** job only runs once; **cron** jobs can be scheduled to run multiple times. Also, the cron daemon is always installed and starts automatically at boot up. If it is not running, your system will have major issues and will not work properly.

The **cron** daemon can be in one of several places according to different Linux distributions. For example, the **cron** daemon for Suse and Fedora are in different directories.

### Key Facts

- Use the **cron** command to schedule tasks or jobs that execute more than once.

- **Location of** the **cron** daemon is not always the same across distributions.

  - Suse - /etc/init.d

  - Fedora - /etc/rc.d/init.d

# Cron Jobs

In addition there are two types of **cron** jobs: user defined and system defined.

- User defined **cron** jobs can be created by an individual user and are found in a different place than system **cron** jobs. These are only available to the user who created them.

- The system **cron** jobs can only be run by someone with root access. Normally, **cron** jobs perform system-wide tasks such as log rotation or system database updates.

# Configuration Files

The configuration files and their locations are very important to a sysadmin since much of their routine jobs can be scheduled and run by the cron daemon.

### Key Facts

- User Defined configuration file

  - /var/spool/cron/<username>

# System cron Jobs

The system **cron** jobs are located in the /etc directory or one of its subdirectories. The **cron** daemon checks the /etc/crontab file every minute to see if there is a job that should be run. In addition it checks files in the /etc/crontab.d and the /etc/cron.<time> directories and runs any scheduled jobs. **Cron** also has the cron.allow and cron.deny files which add a layer of security to who can schedule a job. The only difference is the cron.deny job includes the guest user whereas the at.deny is empty by default.

Having the different directories for hourly, daily, weekly, and monthly jobs makes it easier to keep track of what is running when. There are jobs that need to run at each of these time frames that a sysadmin doesn't want to have to do manually such as doing an incremental backup daily and a full backup weekly. What if you have to change all the passwords for root on each of your supported servers each month? Using a monthly **cron** job, you never forget to do it at a certain time.

If you have a job that needs to run at a time not covered by these directories, it is considered a custom job and is added as a file to the /etc/crontab.d directory. What if you need to back up the /var/log/messages log file every Monday, Wednesday, and Friday nights? Using the **logrotate** utility, you could create a custom job that would compress the file and then back it up on just those days.

Every **cron** job scheduled by a user is in /var/spool/cron directory in a file that is the same as the currently logged in user's name. Root does have the ability to specify a username and work with a user defined cron schedule file.

---

## Key Facts

### Files

- /etc/crontab
- /etc/cron.allow
- /etc/cron.deny

### Directories

- /etc/cron.d
- /etc/cron.hourly
- /etc/cron.daily

- /etc/cron.weekly

- /etc/cron.monthly

# Content for cron Files

The crontab file shows you the format that the file must be in for the job to run.

There are six spaces (or tab-delimited fields) that must contain information. Each field is well defined for minute, second, and the hour, down to the actual command that you want executed. This command must include the absolute path name, and it cannot be relative to any directory. In other words, if you want to run a shell script that is located in your home directory, you would have to use /home/<username>/<script>.

# Working with cron Jobs

If you have root access, you can use **vi** to edit any of the system configuration files or use the **crontab –u** command for a specific user's file.

As a user, you would create and edit your own configuration file with **crontab –e** (opens **vi** editor), display or list its contents with the **–l** (that is lower case L not the number one), or delete it with **–r**.

Each time a cron job is added or modified, the cron daemon restarts so it can re-read the appropriate files.

---

### Key Facts

- **crontab –e** = creates or edits the configuration file for the current user

- **crontab –l** = displays the contents to of the <username> file

- **crontab –r** = removes the <username> file

- **crontab –u** = works with other options and specifies the user's configuration file – requires root access

---

# Localization

## Locale

Locale is a set of parameters that defines a variety of settings depending on where a user lives. It is what determines the language you speak and the format of options like date and time, currency, and numbers. If you support Linux boxes globally, you may connect remotely to one in Japan that has a different date format and is in Japanese! A Canadian user will have the date format set with day, month, year, which can be confusing if you are reading 02/05. Is this February 5 or May 2? Understanding the locale command and its options is important for a system administrator. The following information covers codes that are used to change these settings.

The most common parameters include

- Language
- Character sets
- Currency
- Date/time display
- Number format
- Sort order

## Locale Code

The locale code is the language, then the territory, and then the code set. The language uses the ISO 639 language code, and it must be in lower case. The territory must be in upper case. It uses the ISO 3166 standard country codes. The code set is almost always now Unicode or UTF-8. The code set or character map is what contains all the different characters you will use like tilde (ñ) if writing in Spanish or umlaut (ä or ë) in German.

A few examples are listed below. The language spoken in the USA, English, uses en_US.UTF-8. So why does Canada have two – en_CA and fr_CA? English and French are both used in Canada. There are many areas of the world that are just like Canada where more than one language is commonly used.

## Key Facts

### Locale code

- language_territory.codeset <modifier>

    - Language is always lower case.

    - List of language codes in ISO 639.

    - Territory is always upper case.

    - List of territory codes in ISO 3166.

    - Code set – usually UTF-8 or ASCII.

- Example

    - en_US.UTF-8

    - en_CA.UTF-8

    - fr_CA.UTF-8

Table 8-2 lists two commands that are commonly used when working with locale, along with their options. The **locale** command shows you information about the current locale, and **iconv** allows you to change character encodings. A common character set conversion is US-ASCII to UTF-8.

***Table 8-2.*** *Commands Used When Working with Locale Settings*

| Commands | Description |
| --- | --- |
| locale -a | Displays all installed locales |
| locale -m | Displays all installed character set options |
| locale charmap | Display the character encoding |
| iconv -t | Convert to new encoding type |
| iconv -f | Convert from old encoding type |
| iconv -l (lower L) | Lists of supported encodings (lower L) |
| iconv -o | Indicates input and output file to use with conversion |

# Environmental Variables

There are many environment variables that can be set to change locale information in Linux. A few of the most common ones are shown in Table 8-3. There is an order of precedence used by the system when it reads the environment variables.

1. If there is a value in the LC_ALL variable, it is used, and all individual locale variables are skipped. If it is blank, the system moves to the individual variables.

2. If there is a value in the individual variable, it is used; otherwise, the system moves on to the LANG variable.

3. The value of the LANG variable is used when the two previous variables are blank.

Most distributions place the following variables (Table 8-3) in the /etc/ environment file.

*Table 8-3.* *Sample of Environment Variables for Locale Settings*

| Variable | Description |
| --- | --- |
| LC_ALL | Overrides all other all locale variables – set all to the same thing |
| LANG | Sets all local variables but allows individual LC_* settings |
| LC_PAPER | Defines paper size |
| LC_TIME | Defines time format |
| LC_NUMERIC | Defines numeric value except money |
| LC_MONETARY | Defines monetary settings |
| LC_MESSAGES | Prints out messages in a specific language. |

# Time Management

## Linux Clocks

The two clocks used by every Linux system are the hardware clock and the system clock. The hardware clock is the one the CMOS battery maintains when your computer is turned off. The system clock is used by the kernel and is the time stamp used by the system and applications. At boot up each Linux system sync's its system (internal) clock with the hardware clock. Linux uses its internal clock to run all applications and systems.

---

### Key Facts

### Clocks used by Linux

- Hardware clock – in BIOS
  - Continues running when system is off
  - Time is kept in /proc/driver/rtc file
- System clock – time used by Kernel
  - Sync's to hardware clock at boot up
  - Clock used by system and applications

---

# Local Time and Universal Time

Linux differentiates between local time and UTC Time. Local time is just that, the time you see on your local clock. UTC is the abbreviation for Universal Time Coordinated or Coordinated Universal time. You will see it written both ways. This was previously known as Greenwich Mean Time or GMT. All time zones are based off the time in Greenwich, England, which is located near London at a longitude of zero degrees.

Linux can use either local or UTC for its hardware clock and its system clock, but it prefers UTC. By default, hardware is usually set to local time so you will need to change that for Linux systems. You will see UTC time written in several different ways.

The UTC offset is the number of hours before or after UTC time. For example, US Central time is six hours behind UTC and Germany is one hour ahead of UTC.

Local time is the time you would set on your watch or clocks at home. This is the default time on most computers, but as covered earlier, Linux does better using UTC for the hardware and system time.

---

### Key Facts

### Local time vs. UTC time

- UTC time – Universal Time Coordinated (or Coordinated Universal Time)
    - Also called Zulu time
    - Previously called Greenwich Mean Time (GMT)
    - 08:00 UTC = 08:00Z = 0800Z
- UTC offset – hours that local time is ahead or behind UTC time
    - Central time is UTC -06
    - Germany is UTC +01
- Local time
    - Time where you are located
    - Default setting for most computers
    - Not recommended for Linux systems

---

If you live in Central Standard Time (CST) and you want to call someone in Germany before their bed time of 10:00 p.m., you have to call them by 3:00 p.m. local time (10 - 1 - 6 = 3).

# Time Zone

At time of installation, you are asked which time zone your system will use. That is written to the /etc/timezone file in Ubuntu and /etc/sysconfig/clock file in Red Hat and Suse. In the clock file there is a parameter called ZONE where the time zone is written.

To see your time zone setting from a terminal session, you can use the **date** command. This will give you not only the day, date, and time but the time zone. Displaying the contents of the appropriate file, /etc/sysconfig/clock for Fedora, you see the ZONE parameter.

# Changing the Time Zone

There are several ways to change the time zone in Linux. The easiest is through the GUI, but you have to have root access. Select System ➤ Administration ➤ Date and Time and the Time Zone tab. The system clock uses UTC and is checked by default. Pick your time zone and OK to make the change. Changing the time zone this way is persistent; changes are saved after the system is rebooted.

The **tzselect** command can be used to change the time zone from a terminal session. You will be provided with several menus where you pick what applies to your area. It starts with continents and oceans, moves to countries, then states, and then to zones. The environment variable TZ stores this time zone information. This change is not permanent after reboot.

You can also find files for all the time zones in the /usr/share/zoneinfo directory. List all the files there to see the abbreviation for all the time zones.

You can make a temporary change as a regular user; permanent changes must be made by root. Remember, to make the changes permanent, you must edit the ~/.bash_ profile file by adding **TZ=<timezone>; export TZ**.

# Summary

- Task management is an important function of any sysadmin's job. Creating tasks that can be scheduled to run at a future time or on a regular basis helps to lessen the workload. These task, commonly referred to as jobs, are usually created with the **at** or **cron** commands. The **at** command can only run once, whereas the **cron** command can be scheduled to run multiple times.

- Different countries or regions often speak different languages that use different characters such as tilde (ñ) in Spanish and umlaut (ä or ë) in German. They also use different formatting for date/time display, number format, sort order, paper size, and money. All these options are controlled through locale settings. Commands such as **locale** and **iconv** can be used to change these settings.

- Time management in Linux is very important. Linux has two clocks: hardware and system clocks. The internal clock, which is the one used by the kernel, sync's with the hardware clock at bootup. The hardware clock is maintained by a CMOS battery. All time stamps on files, folders, and in logs are based off the internal clock's time.

- In addition to the clocks, a time zone is selected for each host. Each time zone is based off the distance the host is away from Greenwich, England, which is currently call UTC or Zulu time. The time zone can be changed either in the GUI or with the command **tzselect**.

# CHAPTER 9

# Working with Linux: Part 1

In this chapter, you will gain an understanding of foundational concepts related to customizing environment variables and managing Linux using shell commands and help resources.

By the end of this chapter, you will be able to

1.  Discuss kernels, terminals, and shells

2.  Customize environment variables

3.  Use shell commands to manage Linux

4.  Use help resources to manage Linux

## Kernels, Terminals, and Shells

Before the chapter begins, it is important to understand a few basics about the Linux system.

## Kernel

The core of the Linux operating system is the kernel. It locates and loads various components for the current installation. It also controls the activities performed on the host. Without this program, all you would have is a bunch of hardware sitting and waiting for someone or something to tell it what to do. The kernel is what makes the hardware go into action. Once the kernel is talking to the hardware, it is the user's turn to make something happen.

© Ahmed F. Sheikh 2024
A. F. Sheikh, *CompTIA Linux+ Certification Companion*, Certification Study Companion Series,
https://doi.org/10.1007/979-8-8688-0128-0_9

# Shell

When the user interacts with the host, there is a middle man that takes the user's instructions and sends them to the kernel called the shell. It is a text-based command line interface (CLI). You might remember the days when there was no GUI. The host booted into DOS, and you were ready to enter commands to make the host do something. Administrators still prefer using shell commands to work with Windows and Linux. A big part of the Linux+ exam will cover shell commands so it is important to learn to use them.

When a host first boots, you are put into a GUI interface and are asked to log on or you are put directly into a shell without a GUI. Each shell has built-in commands that perform various functions as does the GUI interface.

# Terminal

If the GUI is not loaded, the user inputs a command in a terminal session, and the shell passes this command to the kernel. The kernel processes the command and returns the output.

If you are a Windows user, you may be familiar with this process. A host is turned on, it boots into a Windows operating system, and a GUI is presented with a login request. You can then start using your mouse and keyboard to open applications and do other tasks. If you want to perform tasks without using the GUI, you would open the command or DOS window and start working with DOS commands.

There is one big difference between Windows and Linux though. Linux has a variety of shells it can boot into. Windows only has one, the DOS shell.

# Shells Available in Linux

Now that you better understand what a shell is, it is time to learn a little about the most commonly known ones. Review Table 9-1 which includes descriptions of common shells.

*Table 9-1.* *Common Shells*

| Shells | Description |
| --- | --- |
| bash | Bourne Again Shell - default |
| sh | Bourne Shell – bash predecessor |
| ksh | Korn Shell |
| csh | C Shell (programming language C) |
| tcsh | Enhanced C Shell |

The bash shell is the most commonly used because of its advanced features. Bash (Bourne Again SHell) is an improved version of the Bourne shell (sh), which was created by Steve Bourne. It includes some special features that make using this shell much easier than its predecessor, like the tab complete and command history.

Next, there is the ksh (Korn shell) created by David Korn in the early 1980s, which is still used by people writing a lot of scripts. It is the default shell for AIX, which is a version of UNIX. Scripts can be created in bash; however, bash does not contain some of the scripting features included in the Korn shell. It is considerably easier to use, so inexperienced users prefer it. The next two shells use the C programming language syntax rather than what is used with the bash, sh, or ksh shells. The csh uses C shell and tcsh uses an enhanced version of the C shell.

The needs of the user determine the shell choice. We will use the bash shell throughout this book since it is the most commonly used one.

# Kernel Architecture

The kernel architecture is divided into two parts: (1) the user space where the user's processes and library routines run, and (2) the kernel space where the system calls, kernel services run, and the device drivers are located (Figure 9-1).

Data flows between the user and kernel spaces. However, the only way the kernel is accessed is by a system call.

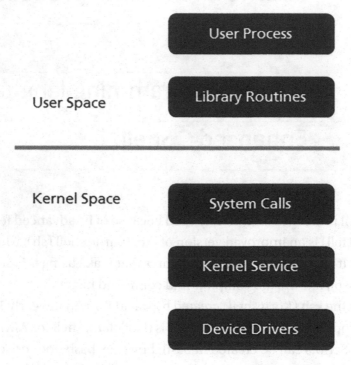

***Figure 9-1.*** *Kernel architecture has two parts: the user space and the kernel space*

# Terminal Session

A terminal session looks like a DOS or command window in Windows (Figure 9-2). They are command-driven interfaces that work directly with the kernel.

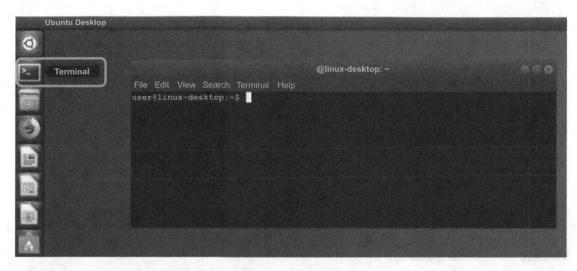

*Figure 9-2.* *View of a terminal session in Ubuntu*

# Environment Variables

When a shell starts in the Linux system, there are variables that are critical to making the system work properly. These are known as environment variables. What is a variable? You can think of a variable like a glass. You have a container, and you can put whatever you want to in it.

## Two Types of Variables

There are two types of variables. The first type is the environment variable which is used by the system and some applications. The second type of variable can be modified to meet a user's needs. User-defined variables also are used in scripting and have no effect on the environment of the system. They can be used to pass information into another script and to gather information. For instance, if you want to capture a user's name when you are running a certain script, it can store this user name to use in the rest of the script. User-defined variables come in handy when you are doing shell scripting.

Environment variables modify the way the shell functions at boot up. There are a couple of things you need to remember when working with environment variables: they always start with a dollar mark, and they are always written in capital letters. To display the value of a variable, use the echo command. At your prompt, type echo, dollar mark, and, in all caps, the environment variable you want to see. If you want to see a list of all the environment variables used by your system, use the set command. It will tell you the variable names and their values.

## Variables Used in Linux

Table 9-2 gives you an example of the several environment variables that are used in Linux.

***Table 9-2.*** *Environment Variables*

| Variable | Description |
| --- | --- |
| $SHELL | Name of the shell you are using |
| $PATH | Search path for commands; list of directories, separated by : , in which the shell looks for a command |
| $HOME | Home directory of current user |
| $HOSTNAME | Name of your computer |
| $HISTFILE | Name of the file in which command history is saved |
| $HISTFILESIZE | Maximum number of lines contained in the history file |
| $HISTSIZE | Number of commands to remember in the history command – default=500 |
| $PS1 | Your prompt settings |
| $PWD | Provides the path of the current working directory |

Review the Environment Variable page on Wikipedia's website for more information. View the following video: *Environment Variables* (3:40).

## Path Variable

The PATH environment variable serves as a critical security measure by specifying the directories searched to locate a command. This variable tells the system where to look for the command you are trying to execute. Make sure that you do not overwrite your existing settings. The way to do that is to use the PATH=$PATH:<new path>. That causes the new path to be appended to the end of the existing one. If you use different sessions, export the path command so it will be the same in all sessions.

**PATH = $PATH:<newpath>**
**export PATH**

An important thing to remember is that everything you just changed is not permanent. When you reboot your system, it will all go away. The way you save these settings is to modify your bash configuration files. If you want to save the changes just for the particular user, you would put the two commands shown in the .bash/rc, or .bash/login, or .bash/profile file. Modifying any of those files will save the changes for that user. If you are going to save the changes for **all** users, add those two commands to the /etc/profile file.

**Files to update**

- User only – ~/.bash/rc, ~/.bash/login, ~/.bash/profile

- All users – /etc/profile

# Working with Shell Commands

There are three characters that have a very special meaning in Linux, which are the dollar mark, pound sign or hash, and tilde. Table 9-3 and video in this section will help you understand exactly how they are used and what they mean.

*Table 9-3.* *Characters with Special Meaning*

| Character | Use | Description |
|---|---|---|
| $ | <prompt>$ | Indicates the user does not have root access |
| # | <prompt># | Indicates the user has root access |
| ~ | [Julie @ ~]$ | Indicates the present working directory is the user's home directory |
| ~ | cd ~ | Changes to the user's home directory |

View the following: *Characters with Special Meaning* (1:14).

# Shell Commands: Case Sensitive

Before you learn more about the Linux shell commands, you need to understand one of the major differences between DOS/Windows and Linux. Commands are case sensitive.

The name of a file or directory is not case sensitive in DOS and Windows. If you have a file named MyFile, one can refer to it in any of the following ways and still be talking about the exact same file:

- MyFile
- myfile
- Myfile
- myFILE

This rule does not hold true in UNIX/Linux. If you review the following list of five variations on MyFile, there would be five different and distinct files:

- MyFile
- myfile
- Myfile
- myFILE

Do not forget that Linux is case sensitive! This is one of the first things that will get you in trouble when working in Linux.

# Shell Commands: Path

Another problematic area is how you address the location of an executable file.

In DOS and Windows, when a command is issued, the shell looks for the file first in the current directory. If it is found, it is executed. If it is not found, the directories in the PATH environment variable are searched. If it is not found in one of those directories, an error message is returned to the user.

Linux only looks in the PATH for the command, even if the file is in the current directory. If that current directory is not in the PATH statement, it will not be executed. You can work around this issue by adding "./" in front of the command. The period tells the system the command is located in the current directory.

| DOS/Windows | UNIX/Linux |
|---|---|
| • Current directory<br>• Directories included in the PATH environment variable | • Directories included in the PATH environment variable |

View the following video: *Case Sensitivity and Location of Files (2:25)*.

# Good to Know

The period is one of those characters that have more meanings than just a period.

If you find a period in front of a file name, the file is hidden from sight. Only people that know it is there can access it. Windows has this same type function. To see hidden files in Linux, use the ls -a command. Also, you can use "./" to indicate you are starting in the current folder, which will be demonstrated in an upcoming video.

- Hidden files begin with a period.

- .<filename> - i.e., ~/.bash_profile.

- To view hidden files – ls –a.

- " ." also indicates the current directory.

- "./" indicates that what follows is in the current directory; for example, cat ./.bash_profile from user's home directory.

# History File

Learning to use the history file will save you a huge amount of time when working in a terminal session. By default, this file stores up to the last 1000 commands you have entered. The most common way to access these commands is to use the <up arrow> to scroll through the history file. Another way is to use an exclamation mark and the first few letters of a command. You can also use the history command to show a list of the commands and then use an exclamation mark and the number of the command shown in your list.

Be aware that each user has their own history file in their home directory – ~/.bash_ history. If you use this function by hitting the up-arrow key after switching to another user, you will get the last command issued by the root user, which may not be what you were looking for.

Why not just retype the command? If it is ls -l, or ping, or a similarly short command, retyping it is not a problem. If a command consists of 40 or 50 characters with various options and values, it is better to use the history option. This method does not require you to remember everything to type it correctly.

Another function that can be very helpful, especially if you are not good at typing, is tab complete. You can start typing the command and hit the <tab> key. If you have enough characters to identify a single command, the system will complete the command and execute it. Try it with the history command, type hi <tab>. It will complete the word history and execute the command. If there had been more than one command starting with hi, you would get an error "ding," and if you press <tab> again you get a list of everything that starts with hi. Try it with just the letter h. This function is helpful if you forget how to spell a command. You can get it started, but do not need to finish it correctly.

## Purpose of Configuration Files

Before going into detail about the shell configuration files, you need to understand the purpose of a configuration file. These files are actually scripts, or a list of commands, that execute when the configuration file is executed during boot up. Have you ever written a Windows batch file? That is a list of commands that are executed one after the other to perform a task. Batch files are the same as shell scripts and are called that by some.

When a shell loads, scripts found in shell configuration files are executed. Which files are executed depends on the type of shell used.

There are two shell types:

- Login shells run only when the system starts in the Text User Interface, in other words no-GUI.

- Non-login shells run when the GUI is started at boot up, and a terminal session is subsequently started by the user.

Couple of reminders:

- Tilde is the shortcut for the user's home directory – in Fedora, /home/<user?

- Period at the beginning of a filename indicates it is a hidden file.

Review Table 9-4 which includes the configuration files that are executed in the following order:

*Table 9-4.* *Configuration Files*

| Configuration Files | Shell Type | Description |
|---|---|---|
| ~/.bashrc | non-login (login on some distros) | Stores shell preferences for individuals |
| /etc/profile | login | Stores system-wide configuration preferences and is used mainly to set environment variables |
| ~/.bash_profile | login | Stores shell preferences for individuals |
| ~/.bash_login | login | Stores commands that execute at login |
| ~/.profile | login | Stores configuration preferences for individual users |
| ~/.bash_logout | login | Stores commands that execute at log-out |

# Basic Shell Commands

You have learned a lot about how the backend of Linux works. Now, you will learn more about the command line.

The following provides a few basic commands you can use in a terminal session.

- exit – closed the terminal session

- clear – clears the screen

- date – displays date and time

- cal – displays the current month's calendar

- w – displays all logged-in users and their tasks

- who – displays all currently logged-in users

- whoami – displays current user's login name

- finger – displays details on system users

- uname – displays system information

- id – displays user IDs (UIDs) and group IDs (GIDs)

- cd – changes the working directory

- rm – deletes a file

- kill – terminates a running command

- file – check file's type

These commands and more can be found at Simple Commands.

# Metacharacters

The following list includes several special characters that the shell uses to perform functions. The redirection, pipe, and comment characters are probably the most used.

**Special Characters That Shells Use to Perform Functions**

> – redirects output to screen or file

>> – redirects output to end of a file

< – redirects input

<< – redirects output to end of previous command

; – separates a series of commands

# – used to start a comment

& – runs command in background

| – pipe – takes output of 1 command and sends it to another as input

? or * – used as wildcard characters

If any of these symbols are needed as the actual character, it has to be enclosed by "" quotes. Otherwise the shell will interpret them as a symbol with a special task.

These and more special characters can be found at Special Characters.

View the following video: *Metacharacters* (4:49).

This video shows how to use special characters and how they can help you.

# How to Get Help

After learning how to shut down a Linux system, the next most important thing to know is how to get help in Linux. There are two local help documents that come with the operating system: man (manual) pages and info (information) pages.

## Man and Info Pages

The main use for the man and info pages is to learn the syntax of a command and what options are available. To find this information, type man <command> or info <command>. Some commands, like ping, will give you the usage by typing the command. Others will give you a help screen by using the -h option.

Apropos with a keyword will search the whatis database for the keyword and display the results.

Man pages – Manual Reference pages in OS

- Includes Library and system calls

- Details syntax used by the command

- man <command>

Info pages – Documentation similar to man pages in OS

- Easier to use

- Contains more up-to-date information

- info <command>

Apropos "<keyword>" – Searches the whatis database for strings
The following are some common websites with information about Linux:

- linux.org

- linux.com

You can also search the Internet to find more resources.

# Summary

In this chapter, you learned about important concepts that relate to customizing environment variables and understanding how to use shell commands and help resources. Keep the following in mind:

- The kernel is the core of the Linux OS.

- A shell is a user interface that accepts input from the user and passes the input to the kernel for processing.

- A terminal session is a channel that allows a user to log in and communicate with the kernel via a user interface.

- Basic shell commands help manage Linux.

- Metacharacters are special characters used by the system.

- Help is available through the man and info commands in a terminal session – additional help is readily available on the Internet.

# Resources

- **Environment Variables**: http://en.wikipedia.org/wiki/ Environment_variable

- **Simple Commands**: www.digitalocean.com/community/tutorials/ linux-commands

- **Special Characters**: https://devdojo.com/bobbyiliev/17- special-characters-in-the-shell-that-you-should-know

# CHAPTER 10

# Essential System Services

This chapter will introduce you to four of the essential system services any Linux sysadmin needs to understand – system time, system logging, mail, and printing.

By the end of this chapter, you will be able to

1. Configure Network Time Protocol to maintain system time

2. Describe system logging

3. Understand the Mail Transfer Agent

4. Install and manage a printing environment

## System Time Management

Previously, you learned about localizing your system which included the format of your time. You also learned about how time zones and their offsets work. Now you will learn about how to keep your system at the current date and time using **hwclock**, **date**, and **NTP**.

## Hardware Clock

When a Linux system boots, the system clock synchronizes with the hardware clock; therefore, it is important to keep it very close to the correct time. As your CMOS battery gets older, you may notice your hardware clock is losing very small amounts of time. You will eventually need to reset it. This can be done with the BIOS utility or with the **hwclock** command.

© Ahmed F. Sheikh 2024

A. F. Sheikh, *CompTIA Linux+ Certification Companion*, Certification Study Companion Series, https://doi.org/10.1007/979-8-8688-0128-0_10

## Key Facts

### Change hardware clock's time

- BIOS utility to change time

- **hwclock** command

  - **hwclock --set --date="05/01/13" 16:00:00" to 5/1/13 at 4:00 p.m.** – sets the hardware clock

  - **hwclock --show** – displays syntax for command

# System Clock

If you need to change the system clock, it can also be done with a command or with the GUI. By selecting System ➤ Administration ➤ Date and Time, you will get the screen which allows you to set the date and time.

The **date** command also allows changes to the system clock as well as displaying the current date and time. Be aware that changing the date and time in this manner can cause issues with system services and with timestamps. This is more of a brute force way to make your change. It is much better to use the process discussed below – using **NTP**.

## Key Facts

### Change system clock's time

- GUI – System ➤ Administration ➤ Date and Time

- **date** command

  - **date –d "05/01/23 16:00:00"** – changes the date to 5/1/23 at 4:00 p.m.

  - **date** – displays the current date and time

# Network Time Protocol (NTP)

The best way to synchronize your time is with a time provider located on the Internet using the Network Time Protocol. This protocol is used by most, if not all, operating systems to keep their time in sync with the rest of the world's clocks. Linux automatically installs and starts the NTP daemon, **ntpd**, when the system boots up. Each system starts synchronizing with the designated servers unless the time difference is greater than 17 minutes.

Time providers are set up in a hierarchy that is similar to the Internet. There is one main time provider that maintains an atomic clock – stratum 0. Several time servers get their time from that one server in stratum 0 and make up stratum 1. Each of the stratum 1 time servers has servers that get their time from them making stratum 2. This continues until the end user's system is reached. You can think of this like a family tree.

Internet time providers are usually in stratum 1 and are provided by sources such as Apple, Microsoft, and NTP Pool Project which provides a pool of time servers.

---

### Key Facts

### Network Time Protocol (NTP)

- Aids in synchronization of time with a time provider on the Internet.

- Uses Time Zone settings.

- UDP protocol using port 123.

- NTP daemon is installed and runs by default.

- Updates occur every 60 seconds until system is synchronized, then checks every 17 minutes.

- Stratum – hierarchy of time providers – max of 256.

---

The easiest way to set up NTP is through the GUI system – select *Administration* ➤ *Date and Time*. Click on the *Synchronize date and time over the network* box, and you will see the screen change to allow you to enter two or three Internet time servers. One problem with doing it this way is if you are over 17 minutes out of synch, your system will never synchronize with a time server. Therefore, it is better to use the command line method.

The /etc/ntp.conf file contains at least two entries. The entries begin with the work "server" followed by a few spaces or a tab, then the DNS name or IP address. The first entry is "server 127.127.1.0" which causes the ntp daemon to check your hardware clock as a starting point. Then it tries to synch with the first Internet server in your list. It will continue through the list until it finds a time server with which it can synchronize.

- Sample /etc/ntp.conf

    - server 127.127.1.0

    - server <name or IP address of time server>

    - server <name or IP address of time server>

    - server <name or IP address of time server>

At this point, stop the ntp daemon and run the command **ntpdate**. You will probably need to run it two or three times before it gets in sync. Restart the ntpd service and verify your offset is no more than 5 minutes. You can find the current time at WORLDTIMESERVER.COM.

The ntp daemon will automatically keep your host in sync with one of the time servers you provided.

You can also learn what your ntp daemon is doing by reviewing the log files. Start with the log files when troubleshooting problems with your NTP setup.

A Linux system is configured by default to not be a time server. The /etc/ntp.conf file contains a line "restrict 127.0.0.1" which means that only the loop back address has access. By adding lines to this configuration file, you allow the local host to become a time server for the machines you indicate. For example, any host on the subnet 192.168.1.0 with a 24-bit mask can get time from this local host, but no changes can be made to it and, for security reasons, information cannot be obtained by anyone on that subnet.

The ntp daemon must be restarted for it to recognize any changes.

# System Logging

The **syslog** utility is responsible for tracking and logging all system messages. These messages are placed in log files and provide from general to emergency type information that is helpful for troubleshooting problems. Each message is made up of two labels: the daemon that created the message, and its severity. They are called the facility and the priority. These labels determine the log file in which the message will be recorded and are placed in the /dev/log and then in the log file specified in the /etc/syslog.conf file. Some distributions use the /etc/rsyslog.conf file. The /dev/log file collects a message and then looks in the /etc/syslog.conf configuration file to determine where the message should be placed. This configuration file is discussed in more detail as the chapter progresses.

Logs are usually text files although there are a few files that are in a binary format, requiring a special application to read them. An example of a binary file is the lastlog log file; it can only be read by the **lastlog** command.

One more thing to consider is remote logging. Often a sysadmin will configure the supported Linux systems so all their messages go to a central server whose only function is to hold all log files. This not only adds convenience when troubleshooting a supported system, but it adds a layer of security. When a hacker is able to access your system, tracks are normally left in log files. The first thing a hacker does is remove those messages. If the logs are not on the hacked system, the hacker would then have to know where the logs are being stored and break into that system too. Details on configuring remote logging are not covered in this book. If you want to learn more about this feature, review How to Setup Rsyslog Remote Logging on Linux (Central Log Server).

The facility is what service or process is being tracked. The priority is categorized, based on the type of result or error. Note that facility and priority are separated by a period and followed by one or more spaces. Next is the name of the file where the message should be written. Review the tables at Wikipedia's page on syslog to see some of the more common facilities and what daemon generates the message and the priority with their descriptions.

- /etc/syslog.conf (/etc/rsyslog.conf)

    - facility.priority <destination file>

    - Example – kern.warning /var/log/logfile

You can put these messages in any file with any combination of facilities and priorities you wish. For example, if you are the printer admin, you could break up the printer message into three files:

- lpr.alert /var/log/printer_alert – All "alert" printer messages would go to this file.

- lpr.crit /var/log/printer_crit – All "critical" printer messages would go to this file.

- lpr.*; lpr.!=alert; lpr.!=crit /var/log/printer – All printer messages would go to this file except alerts and critical ones.

This eliminates all the messages except the ones the printer admin needs to see right away.

Run the **ls** command from the /var/log directory to see them all. Some log files are written to directories in the /var/log directory such as /var/log/cups. If you will be working with log files, you should become familiar with what is available.

You can read about many of the log files and what type messages they hold in the Wikipedia article on /var. Scroll down a few screens until you see the /var/log directory. You will then see several log files.

# Logrotate

Log files can quickly exceed capacity. Then the oldest messages are deleted. This can happen to several log files within a day depending on the size of the company and the amount of activity on the system. Because of this, you will want to back up your log files periodically. This can be done by using the **logrorate** utility. Global settings are put in the /etc/logrotate.conf file. If some log files need special configurations, a file is added to the /etc/logrotate.d directory.

---

### Key Facts

### Logrotate – Utility used to manage log files

- /etc/logrotate.conf – global settings

- /etc/logrotate.d directory – add file that  overrides global setting for single log file or include options in /etc/logrotate.conf

---

The following list discusses many of the options that are available to configure your logrotate.conf file.

- The *compress* or *nocompress* options say whether the file you are backing up should be compressed or not.

- The *delaycompress* or *nodelaycompress* indicates if the file should be compressed when it is rotated or the next time the file is rotated. If you have to look at the backup often, you may not want to have to uncompress the file before viewing it.

- *Ifempty* or *notifempty* determines if an empty file should be backed up.

- *Maxage* sets the number of days before the file can be deleted.

- *Dateext* is a great option; it adds the date to the end of the file so you can keep track of the backups more easily.

- The *rotate* option kind of goes with the maxage option; it sets how many rotations should be made before a backup can be deleted.

- *Size* can help to control the number of backups you have by setting the maximum size of a log file before it is rotated. If a file grows larger than the indicated size during the day and the default option is daily, the log could not only get backed up each day, but it could be two or more times.

- You can schedule the backup to occur daily, weekly, or monthly.

- The create option says to create a new log file; you can set permissions and ownership with this option.

- The *prerotate* and *postrotate* allow you to run a process before or after the rotation.

These are only some of the options available to use when doing log rotation.

Figures 10-1 and 10-2 provide an overview of how the options should be used to schedule the rotations or backups. Comments make the file longer, but they document the commands and are good practice. By using the # sign, you can explain the upcoming options and why it is being used. Did you notice the include statement? That is another way to create the override for special backups. Messages created by **lastlog** will be backed up monthly rather than weekly, and 12 months of backups will be retained.

```
cat /etc/logrotate.conf
weekly        #rotate log files weekly
rotate 4      #keep 4 weeks of backlogs
create        #create new (empty) log files after rotating old ones
Include /etc/logrotate.d  #change options in /etc/logrotate.d file
/var/log/lastlog {
     monthly
     rotate 12
}
```

***Figure 10-1.*** *Sample logrotate.conf** 

For more detail on the logrotate.conf file, read the article Manage Linux log files with Logrotate.

```
cat /etc/logrotate.d/yum  #displays content of /ect/logrotate.d/yum file

/var/log/yum.log  {
   missingok
   notifempty
   size 30k
   yearly
   create 0600 root root
 }
```

***Figure 10-2.*** *Sample of a logrotate.d file*

## Managing Log Files

There are two types of log files: text-based and binary.

When working with text files, there are several of the commands you learned in earlier chapters such as **cat**, **head**, **tail**, **more**, **less** that can be used with log files. **Gedit** or **vi** can be used to edit these log files. Because of the massive size of many of these files, you may want to use **grep** to filter only what you want to see from the **cat** command.

Commands used to view and edit text-based log files:

- **cat** displays the content of <logfile> and **grep** searches for lines that match the pattern given – only matching lines are displayed

  - **cat <logfile> | grep <pattern>**

- Display first 10 lines of a file
  - **head**
- Display last 10 lines of a file
  - **tail**
- Displays a file page at the time
  - **more**
- Similar to **more** command but allows backward as well as forward movement
  - **less**
- Text editor often used by programmers and seasoned Unix/Linux sysadmins
  - **vi**
- GUI based text editor
  - **gedit**

Binary files are a little different; you have to use a specific file to open and review a binary log file. The /var/log/faillog log file has to be viewed with the **faillog** command. That log file lists all users and when they last logged in. The /var/log/wtmp file lists that same information and more – list of users, their last login/logout time, and where they were logged in. That log file gives you much better information for security verification.

---

## Key Facts

- **Binary log files**
  - **Lastlog  /var/log/lastlog**
  - **Faillog /var/log/faillog**
  - **Last /var/log/wtmp**
  - **Dmesg /var/log/boot.msg**

---

For better troubleshooting, study the log files and know what information each captures. Know where messages are coming from. That way you will know which files you should review when you have an issue.

The **logger** command allows you to change where messages are sent and their severity. It can also write a message to a log file.

The Kernel Log Daemon, **klogd**, is a system daemon that intercepts and logs kernel messages. It is used if the /proc file system is not mounted.

# Mail Transfer Agent (MTA)

A Mail Transfer Agent (MTA) is important to any Linux system. Many services depend on an MTA to deliver messages to local users. **Cron** is one of those services. System errors can also be set to go to the root user. By default, all distributions of Linux start an MTA when the system boots.

The three parts of any e-mail system are the

- Mail Transfer Agent (MTA) – the MTA is the server that distributes e-mail across a network.

- Mail Distribution Agent (MDA) – the MDA, which can be on an MTA, accepts inbound e-mail from an MTA and delivers it to the appropriate user's directory on the local server.

- Mail User Agent (MUA) – the Mail User Agent (MUA) is what allows the end user to review their mail.

The MUA can pull mail from their local MTA with the **mail** command, or POP3/IMAP4 can be installed on the MTA so the end user can use a more friendly application like Thunderbird.

Figure 10-3 shows you two ways a host can get their mail – internally and over the Internet.

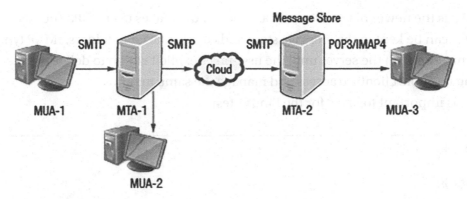

***Figure 10-3.*** *MUA mail process*

### E-Mail from MUA-1 to MUA-2 using the mail command

- Simple Mail Transfer Protocol (SMTP) takes mail from MUA-1 to MTA-1.

- MTA-1 becomes an MDA and puts mail in user's mail directory.

- MUA-2 gets mail with mail command.

### E-Mail from MUA-1 to MUA-3 using a GUI or Browser-Based Application

- SMTP takes mail from MUA-1 to MTA-1.

- SMTP takes mail from MTA-1 to MTA-2.

- MTA-2 puts mail in Message Store.

- POP3/IMAP4 takes mail from MTA-2 to MUA-3.

## Mail Protocols

Linux mail uses several mail protocols, Simple Mail Transfer Protocol (SMTP) uses TCP port 25, Enhanced Simple Mail Transfer Protocol (ESMTP) which uses TCP port 27, Post Office Protocol (POP3) uses TCP port 110, and Internet Message Access Protocol (IMAP4) uses TCP port 143.

IMAP is the newer of the two and has several advantages over POP3 such as messages can be kept in the message store and can be placed in folders. IMAP typically retains messages on the server until the user takes explicit action to delete them, enabling multiple clients to access and manage the same mailbox.

This is important to know for the Linux+ test.

---

### Key Facts

### Protocols

- SMTP – TCP port 25
- ESMTP – TCP port 27
- POP3 – TCP port 110
- IMAP4 – TCP port 143

---

# MTAs

There are five widely used MTAs which are

- *Sendmail* has been around for a long time, and some say it is very hard to work with. It is still the default for Fedora.

- *Postfix* is commonly used on Fedora and it is the default for Suse.

- *Exim*, Postfix Qmail are much easier to use than Sendmail.

- *Qmail* has the best security of the four.

- *Alpine*, built on the Pine messaging system, is a fast and user-friendly terminal-based email client designed for Linux.

### MDAs and MUAs

Common MDAs and MUAs are listed below. For the Linux+ test, you need to know the names of the different common agents. If you will be setting up e-mail for use on a Linux system, you will need to have more knowledge.

**MDA – Mail Distribution Agent**

- Procmail
- Fetchmail

**MUA – Mail User Agent**

- mail
- Thunderbird
- Evolution
- Eudora
- mutt

# Redirecting Mail

There are circumstances where e-mail should always go to someone other than to whom it is addressed. Any e-mail that would normally go to root, such as a system-generated e-mail, really should be redirected to a sysadmin for immediate attention. This can be done by adding an entry to the /etc/aliases file. Add a line that starts with the userid of the e-mail that should be redirected (called an alias in this situation), followed by a colon then by an e-mail address or addresses that should receive the e-mail. Several entries are added during installation, but modify that last line so that all e-mail addressed to root is redirected to the appropriate person or persons.

**Way to redirect e-mail**

- /etc/aliases file
- Syntax – <alias name>: <email_address>, <email_address>, ...
- Example – jsmith: julie
- Example – sspade: julie, susie, joe

After changes have been made, rebuild the aliases database using the **newaliases** command (/etc/aliases.db).

If you need to redirect e-mail for a short period of time, such as for a vacation, you can use the .forward file in your home directory. Type **vi ~/.forward** because that will create a new file or open the current one for editing. If you want to see if the file already exists, you can use the **ls –a** command. (Remember hidden files are not visible with just the **ls**.) The MTA looks in this file to see if anything should be forwarded elsewhere.

Add an entry to this file, and include the recipients. You can use the complete e-mail address or just the userid if you and the recipient are in the same domain. You can also forward to more than one user using a comma as a separator.

---

**Caution**   No mail that is forwarded will be saved in your local user's directory.

---

When you want to cancel the forwarding, rename (**mv <oldfile> <newfile>**) or delete (**rm <file>**) the file.

---

**Key Facts**

- Use ~/.forward file for temporary redirection.

- The MTA looks in ~/.forward.

- Syntax – <ksanders, lmorgan | ksanders@domain.xxx>.

- Note:  Forwarded mail will not be saved in your directory.

- Rename or delete /etc/.forward when it is not needed.

---

# Print Management

## Linux Printing Systems

The original printing system used by Linux was inherited from UNIX and is still in use today on some older Linux computers. It is called the Line Printer Daemon or LPD Printing System. Since it is not widely used today, only an overview of LPD will be included in this chapter.

The most commonly used printing system is Common UNIX Printing System (CUPS). This printing system is usually installed by default in almost all Linux distributions.

# LPD Printing System

There are four basic command line tools used to manage printing in Linux. Use the **man** command to get options that go with each of these commands. These four commands allow you to send a job to a printer, check the status of a printer, show all the jobs that are in a print queue, and remove jobs from a queue. LPD's configuration file is /etc/lpd.perms.

---

**Key Facts**

**Four LPD Commands**

- **lpr -P <printer> <file>** – sends jobs to printer
- **lpc status** – used to view the status of printers
- **lpq** – displays jobs in the print queue
- **lprm <job #>** – used to remove jobs from the queue

---

# Common Unix Printing System (CUPS)

CUPS is a modular printing system designed for Unix-like computer operating systems, enabling a computer to function as a print server. With CUPS, a computer serves as a host capable of receiving print jobs from client computers, processing them, and routing them to the correct printer. The important concepts related to Common Unix Printing System (CUPS) are client, job, scheduler, queue, backend, and printer language.

The client is the device that creates the print job. That job is sent to the print server which can be on the same machine as the client, where the CUPS daemon passes it to the scheduler. The scheduler is actually a website that manages all the printers. You can get to this site from the local host using http://localhost:631 and a remote host using the URL http://<ip_address>:631.

The job is then placed in the queue which is a temporary location to hold the jobs until they are ready to be printed. That location is normally the /var/spool/cups directory. The filter processes each print job by converting it to the proper Page Description Language (PDL). PDL is the language that is used to describe the look of a printed page of information. Most Linux jobs are created using Abode's PostScript. Other

191

common PDLs are Hewlett Packard's (HP) Printer Control Language (PCL) and Epson's ESC/P (Epson Standard Code for Printers), respectively. Without this conversion, only garbage would be printed. These filters are located in the /usr/lib/cups/filter directory.

The backend stores all the different interfaces that are being used by installed printers such as LPT, serial or USB. This backend information is stored in the /usr/lib/cups/backend directory. The job converted by the filter is sent to the appropriate backend and then to the actual print device. The backend lets the scheduler know the job has been processed and the print job is deleted from the queue.

The last item on this list is the PostScript Printer Description (PPD). These files tell the CUPS daemon what each printer is capable of doing. They are located in the /etc/cups/ppd directory.

---

### Key Facts

### Components of Linux Common Unix Print System (CUPS)

- Client – creates the print job
- Server – processes the print job
  - Scheduler – web interface – http://<ip_address>:631
  - Queue – /var/spool/cups
  - Filter – / var/lib/cups/filter
  - Backend – /usr/lib/cups/backend
  - Postscript Printer Descriptions (PPD) – /etc/cups/ppd file
- Printer

---

# Print Job Flow

Figure 10-4 shows the flow of a print job. When the CUPS service is started, it queries the printers and records their capabilities such as paper size, single or double-sided, and other functions.

When the client creates a print job, the CUPS daemon writes the job to the print queue. The filter then converts the job to the PDL used by the destination printer and sends it to the backend which then sends it to the printer.

The backend notifies the scheduler that the job has successfully printed, and the job is deleted from the queue.

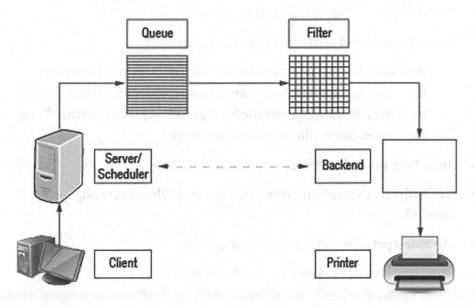

***Figure 10-4.***  *Flow of a print job from the client to the printer*

# CUPS Configuration

CUPS is a little different than printing as we know it in Windows; a printer is shared and is there waiting for someone to print to it. CUPS broadcasts the fact that a printer is there. The first option in these tables is the name of the server that will be broadcast to all users. This configuration file holds all the information needed for the CUPS service to run properly. The **cupsctl** utility or a text editor can be used to modify the cupsd. conf file.

Review some of the options that can be used in the /etc/cups/cupsd.conf file in the article CUPS Troubleshooting.

# CUPS Print Job Management

Most of the commands used to manage LPD printing can also be used with CUPS. Additional commands shown below can be used to manage CUPS.

- **lpstat -t** – displays information about all print jobs

- **cancel <job #>** – removes a print job

- **lp or lpoptions -d <printer>** – sets default printer

  - Be aware that this command will set the default for all users on that system. If a single user wants to use a different printer as their default, they can add the line "default=<printer_name>" to a file in their home directory – ~/.lpoptions.

- **lp** or **lpoptions -l** – shows printer settings

- **accept|reject <print_queue>** – enables or disables receiving new jobs

- **disable <printer>** – disables printing

- /usr/bin/**enable <printer>** – enables printing

# Printer Set-Up

After CUPS is installed and configured, the printers have to be set up. All printer configuration information is stored in the /etc/cups/printers.conf file. The web-based tool is used to set up printers and to manage queues and print jobs. Using this tool is the safest way of setting up and managing printers. To set up a printer, follow these steps:

1. Open a browser to http://localhost:631/.

2. Select the Administration tab.

3. Select Add Printer.

4. Enter a User Name and Password that has access to manage Printers.

5. After all local printers are loaded, the Add Printer screen appears.

6. Select the appropriate type of printer and select Continue.

7. Enter the Connection type and select Continue.

8. Type the name of the printer in the Name box.

9. Select the box for Sharing and select Continue.

10. Select the Make of the printer and select Continue.

11. Select the Model of the printer and select Add Printer.

12. On the Set Default Options for <printer name> screen, make any changes needed for your specific printer, and select Set Default Options.

13. Your printer has now been added.

Any future maintenance on this printer can be done from this same web-based tool. You can also use the Printer Configuration tool found in the System menu ➤ Administration ➤ Printing GUI. You have to be working on the system to use the GUI tool, whereas you can manage printing on any system both locally and remotely using the system's IP address and a web browser.

# Summary

- System Time Management is very important to any Linux host. You learned how to change the date and time and how to manually sync a local host to an Internet time server. In this chapter, you learned how to keep that host's time using the NTP daemon. By adding the names of up to three Internet time providers, the host's date and time will always be accurate.

- The easiest way to configure NTP on a host is to use the GUI: System ➤ Administration ➤ Date and Time. The **ntpdate** command is used to synchronize the host's time with an Internet time server. A system reboot is required after any changes to NTP.

- System logging is used to troubleshoot problems and to gather usage information on a host. The syslog utility is responsible for tracking and logging informative to critical system messages. Some log files are saved in a binary format which cannot be read by a text editor; a special command such as **lastlog**, **last**, **dmesg**, and **faillog** are used to read these logs. As an added security measure, log files can be written to a central location.

- Each entry in a system log file is made up of two labels and a location: facility=daemon running process and the priority=severity of the message. The location is the name and location of the log file to which the message should be written.

- Other log files are saved in a text-based format which can be edited by **vi** or a GUI application such as **gedit**. Additional commands that can be used with text-based files are **cat**, **head**, **tail**, **more**, and **less**.

- By default, a mail transfer agent (MTA) is started on boot up and is used by several services. This MTA works with a mail distribution agent (MDA) and a mail user agent (MUA) to enable the use of e-mail. System error logging and **cron** jobs are two of the services that can use the MTA.

- Linux's mail service uses one of the following protocols: SMTP (TCP port 25), ESMTP (TCP port 27), POP3 (TCP port 110), or IMAP4 (TCP port 143).

- Commonly used MTAs are Sendmail, Postfix, Exim, and Qmail; MDAs, Procmail and Fetchmail; MUAs – mail, Thunderbird, Evolution, Eudora, and mutt.

- The **logrotate** command is used to manage the size and location of log files.

- As with most e-mail systems, you can redirect mail when necessary, by adding recipients to the /etc/.forward file.

- Common UNIX Printing System (CUPS) is the printing system most used by Linux distributions. The components of this system are client, job, scheduler, queue, backend, and printer language. A print job is created by the client and is passed through the other components in the order listed above. Commands commonly used with CUPS are **lpr**, **lpc**, **lpq**, **lprm**, **lpstat**, **lp**, and **lpoptions**.

- CUPS can be managed through the System ➤ Administration ➤ Printing GUI or through a browser using the URL http://<ip address of print server>:631.

# Resources

- **NTP Pool Project**: www.ntppool.org/en/use.html

- **World Time Server:** www.worldtimeserver.com/current_time_in_ UTC.aspx

- **How to Set Up Centralized Logging on Linux with Rsyslog:** https://betterstack.com/community/guides/logging/how-to- configure-centralised-rsyslog-server/

- **Log Files**: https://tldp.org/LDP/Linux-Filesystem-Hierarchy/ html/var.html

- **Syslog**: https://en.wikipedia.org/wiki/Syslog

- **Managing log files using logrotate**: www.datadoghq.com/blog/log- file-control-with-logrotate/

- **CUPS Troubleshooting:** https://wiki.archlinux.org/title/ CUPS/Troubleshooting

# CHAPTER 11

# Working with Linux: Part 2

In this chapter, you will gain an understanding of the Linux directory structure, file types and extensions, and additional shell commands. You also will learn how to perform compression and backups when working with Linux.

By the end of this chapter, you will be able to

1. Describe the Linux directory structure

2. Identify the Filesystem Hierarchy Standard (FHS)

3. Describe file types and extensions

4. Use additional shell commands to manage Linux

5. Perform compression and backups

## Directory Structure

### What Is a Directory Structure?

A directory structure refers to how an operating system organizes files for user access, usually displayed in a hierarchical tree structure. Most computer users are used to the Windows directory structure. The Windows structure has a C: drive, a D: drive, and an E: drive, and each drive has its own root and a breakdown of directories, as seen in Figure 11-1. With Linux, there is one single root for all drives and partitions, and everything branches out from it, as seen in Figure 11-2. Linux has a single root as compared to Windows having multiple drives each with a root.

© Ahmed F. Sheikh 2024
A. F. Sheikh, *CompTIA Linux+ Certification Companion*, Certification Study Companion Series,
https://doi.org/10.1007/979-8-8688-0128-0_11

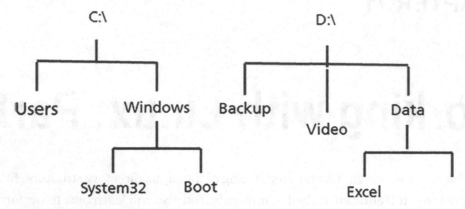

***Figure 11-1.*** *The directory structure of Windows*

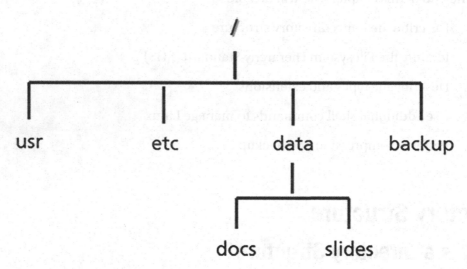

***Figure 11-2.*** *The directory structure of Linux*

# Filesystem Hierarchy

Linux has the Filesystem Hierarchy Standard (FHS) that defines what folders should be created at installation and what their function will be. Its purpose was to standardize the directory structure, making it easier to move from distro to distro. You need to know where important files are located, such as the configuration files used when the system boots.

As a sysadmin, it is important to know about the standard directories and their purpose (Table 11-1). It will save you time while troubleshooting and working with Linux.

***Table 11-1.*** *Standard Directories*

| Command | Description |
| --- | --- |
| /lib | Libraries essential for the binaries in /bin/ and /sbin/ |
| /media | Mount points for removable media such as CD-ROMs |
| /mnt | Temporarily mounted filesystems |
| /opt | Optional application software packages |
| /proc | Virtual filesystem providing information about processes and kernel information as files |
| /root | Home directory for the user |
| /bin | Essential command binaries that need to be available in single user mode |
| /sbin | Essential system binaries |
| /tmp | Temporary files (see also /var/tmp). Often not preserved between system reboots |
| /usr | *Secondary hierarchy* for read-only user data; contains the majority of (multi-)user utilities and applications |
| /usr/local | *Tertiary hierarchy* for local data, specific to this host. Typically has further subdirectories |
| /var | Variable files – files whose content is expected to continually change during normal operation of the system – such as logs, spool files, and temporary e-mail files |
| /etc | System configuration files |
| /home | Home directory |
| / | Root directory. It marks the starting point of the file system hierarchy |

These and other standards directories are found at Filesystem Hierarchy Standard on the Wikipedia website. You can also review the table in Unix Filesystem on the Wikipedia website.

Remember the /usr directory is not where users' home folders are located; that is /home.

Be very careful with the /tmp directory. This is not an area that you want to intentionally store files. It is used more by the system as a temporary holding area – like for files during the installation of an application. It is periodically cleaned out automatically, so anything you put there will be cleaned out also. If you want to share files, even for a day or two, it is much safer to create a directory just for that.

# File Types

Table 11-2 lists some file types with which you should be familiar and understand. If you do not understand the purpose of any of the file types, you can Google them to learn more. You will find articles that explain them in more detail and that show how they are used or problems encountered when working with them.

***Table 11-2.***  *File Types*

| Type | Description |
|---|---|
| Text files | Contains configuration information |
| Binary data files | Stores information such as graphics and functions |
| Executable program files | Contains files that can become a process |
| Directory files | Acts as a place holder in the file system |
| Linked files | Contains files that are associated with each other or point to the other (i.e., shortcut) |
| Special device files | Represents different devices on the system – usually found in /dev directory |
| Named pipes files | Identifies a channel to pass information from one process to another while in memory |
| Sockets files | Allows a process from another host to write to a file on a local host while another process reads from that file |

# Common Filename Extensions

Linux extensions usually range from one to four characters and can be a combination of uppercase and lowercase letters. Two extensions are sometimes combined as with the file ghex.tar.gz.

Familiarity with these can help you to work better in Linux. For example, you know a file is a Word file if it has a .doc or .docx extension. You can also tell a .docx file was created in Word 2007 or later. The same holds true for Linux. When you see an extension of .tar.gz, you know the file has been compressed and archived. The .sh extension tells you the file is probably a shell script. For additional file extensions, review List of File Formats on the Wikipedia website.

# More Linux Commands

You will use most of the commands in Table 11-3 almost every time you open a terminal session.

***Table 11-3.*** *Linux Commands*

| Command | Description |
| --- | --- |
| pwd | Print working directory |
| cd <new directory> | Changes to a another directory |
| cd .. | Moves you up a level in the directory |
| cd ~ | Moves to user's home directory |
| history | Displays the last xxx issued commands |
| ↑ | Displays the last command issued |
| file <command> | Displays the file type of the command |
| <cmd>\| <cmd> | Pipe symbol used in conjunction with two commands (i.e., ls –a \| more – displays a list of files one page at the time) |
| ls | Displays a columnar list of files in a directory |

**Table 11-4.**  *Symbols Used with the ls -F Command*

| Symbol | Description |
|--------|-------------|
| * | Executable file |
| \| | Named pipe |
| / | Subdirectory |
| @ | Linked file |
| = | Socket |

The ls command used with the –F option (Table 11-4) appends a special symbol at the end of the filename that indicates the file type (Table 11-5).

**Table 11-5.**  *Display File Contents*

| Command | Description |
|---------|-------------|
| cat <file> | Displays the entire file; short for *concatenate* |
| tac <file> | Displays the entire file backward |
| head <file> | Displays the first 10 lines of the file |
| tail <file> | Displays the last 10 lines of the file |
| more <file> | Displays the file one page at the time |
| less <file> | Displays the file one page at the time using <space> or one line at the time using the <enter> |
| strings <file> | Searches for and displays text characters in a binary file |
| od <file> | Displays the content of a file in octal format |

# Wildcard Characters

Periodically, you need to find, rename, copy, or move a group of files that have similar character groupings.

You may have worked with the asterisk and question mark in Windows to look for files. For example, if you want to list all the files starting with Chapter 2, you would simply add an asterisk at the end, and you would see them all – ls -l Chapter 2*.

The asterisk will match anything that follows the number two. The question mark only matches one character. For example, ls –l Chapter? would display all files that begin with Chapter followed by a single character.

To display only files that begin with Chapter and 1, 2, 3, or 4, you would use ls –l Chapter[1234]. You could also use ls –l Chapter[1-4] to see that same list of files.

What if you wanted to see all files except the ones containing 1, 2, 3, 4? You can use the ls –l [!1-4]. The exclamation mark works as "not."

# Regular Expressions

Have you ever wanted to use some information that you do not want to have to recreate, but you do not remember what file it is in? The following characters can help you find it when combined with some commands.

In addition to the wildcard metacharacters, there are additional special characters called *regular expressions* that you can use to look inside files. There are two types: common and extended.

- Common – available in most text tools

- Extended – not always available in text tools

## Common Regular Expressions

Common regular expressions work in most files. For example, if you are looking for text that you know contained an x, then you could use the [x].

Another option is the caret. If you know you had a paper with section headers – one of which started with Quote – you can use ^Q to find it.

For additional regular expressions, see Regular Expressions: A Brief Tutorial.

## Extended Regular Expressions

In addition to common Regular Expressions, there are Extended Regular Expressions which do not work with all tools.

You can find more on regular expressions as well as Table 11-6 at Regular Expressions from the Wikipedia website.

**Table 11-6.** *Extended Regular Expressions*

| Expression | Description |
| --- | --- |
| ? | Matches the preceding element zero or one time. For example, ab?c matches only "ac" or "abc" |
| + | Matches the preceding element one or more times. For example, ab+c matches "abc," "abbc," "abbbc," and so on, but not "ac" |
| (…l…) | The choice (also known as alternation or set union) operator matches either the expression before or the expression after the operator. For example, abcldef matches "abc" or "def." |

One of the most common commands used to search for text inside a file or files is grep (Table 11-7).

**Table 11-7.** *Tools Used to Search for Text Within Files*

| Command | Description |
| --- | --- |
| grep <pattern> <file> Global Regular Expression | Displays lines of text that match requested common regular expressions |
| grep –e <pattern>  <file> | Displays lines of text that match requested extended regular expressions |

Using grep with the regular expressions will help you find what you need in a group of files much faster than looking in each file.

The upcoming video will show you more on how to use grep and expressions.

View the following: *How to Use the grep Command* (2:06).

# Compression

Compression serves as a fundamental utility across various platforms, aiding in the reduction of file sizes for efficient sharing. Additionally, compressed files facilitate easier copying to remote servers. You likely have worked with compression already and did not know it. Rather than using the term *compress* when discussing it, you likely said you *zipped* a file to reduce its size. There are several different applications that

Windows uses to compress a file including: WinZip, 7Zip, PKzip, and RAR (WinRAR). The most commonly used Linux compression applications are compress, gzip, and bzip2 (Table 11-8).

There are multiple applications, and there are just as many compression algorithms. Each application uses an algorithm (or a process) that is used in a calculation operation.

An advantage that gzip has over the other applications is that you can control if you want faster compression with a lower ratio or a slower compression with a higher ratio.

Terms you should know:

- Compression – process of reducing the size of a file by removing characters

- Compression Algorithm – instructions used to make the file smaller

- Compression Utilities – the application used to reduce the size of a file

***Table 11-8.*** *Compression Utilities*

| Compress Command | Uncompress Command | Extension | Algorithm | % Compressed (Compression Ratio) |
|---|---|---|---|---|
| compress | uncompress | .Z | Adaptive Lempel-Ziv (LZW) | 40-50 |
| gzip | gunzip or gzip | .gz | Kempel-Ziv (LZ77) | 60-70 |
| bzip2 | bunzip2 | .bz2 | Burrows-Wheeler Block Sorting Huffman Coding | 50-75 |

# Compress Utility

The compress utility is the oldest of the currently used compression utilities. Because newer ones were developed, it is not installed by default. Consider using the yum package installer to add this application to your system.

| Key Facts | |
| --- | --- |
| Compress Utility | • Oldest compression utility |
| | • Compression algorithm – Adaptive Lempel-Ziv (LZW) |
| | • Average 40–50% compression ratio |
| | • Compressed file extension – .Z |
| | • Not installed by default; can use yum install compress |
| | • Maintains original ownership, modification, and access time information |
| | • Works with standard input and output |

The options shown in the following table includes common options you can use with the compress utility. Note that there is –f with compress and uncompress, but they mean different things.

Use the man and info pages for details on options that are used with the compress and uncompress utilities (Table 11-9).

*Table 11-9.*  *Commands Used with Compress*

| Commands | Description |
| --- | --- |
| zcat | Displays content of compressed file |
| zmore/zless | Displays content of compressed file one page at the time |

# GNU Utility

The following information is about the GNU zip (gzip) utility. The advantage of using gzip over compress and bzip2 is that you can control the level of compression. You can set it to have the best compression ratio available with the cost of it taking longer to complete, or you can speed up the compression time at the cost of the compression ratio.

The following items are key facts about the GNU Utility:

- Compression algorithm – Lempel-Ziv (LZ77)

- Average 60–70% compression ratio

- Compressed file extension – .gz

- Maintains original ownership, modification, and access time information

- Works with standard input and output

- Advantage of gzip is ability to control level of compression

Notice in the gzip options that you have a way to uncompress files using –d. You can also use the gunzip command.

The other difference is the level of compression. Minus one gives you the fastest compression with the lowest compression ratio. You can move that number up to a maximum of -9, which allows you to find the level that works best for you.

Use the man and info pages for details on options (Table 11-10) that are used with the gzip and gunzip utilities.

***Table 11-10.*** *Commands Used with gzip*

| Commands | Description |
| --- | --- |
| zcat | Displays content of compressed file |
| zmore/zless | Displays content of compressed file one page at the time |

# Bzip2 Utility

The following are key facts on the bzip2 utility:

- Compression algorithm; Burrows-Wheeler Block Sorting Huffman Coding

- Average 50–75% compression ratio

- Compressed file extension – .bz2

- Maintains original ownership, modification, and access time information

The main difference between this utility and the other two utilities are the options.

Per the following tables, you can see that bzip2 cannot compress symbolic links or compress directories. It also does not use the zcat and zmore utilities. To work with bzip2 files, use the bzcat and bzmore commands.

Use the man and info pages for details on options (Table 11-11) that are used with the bzip2 and bunzip2 utilities.

**Table 11-11.**  *Commands Used with bzip2*

| Commands | Description |
| --- | --- |
| zcat (Not available) | Displays content of compressed file |
| zmore/zless (Not available) | Displays content of compressed file one page at the time |
| bzcat | Displays content of compressed file |
| bzmore/bzless | Displays content of compressed file one page at the time |

Table 11-12 provides a comparison between the options and commands that are used with the main three compression utilities.

**Table 11-12.**  *Options and Commands*

| Command | -v | -f | -r | (-f) | -d | | | |
| --- | --- | --- | --- | --- | --- | --- | --- | --- |
| compress | Yes | Yes | Yes | | | zcat | zmore | Maintains ownership and times |
| uncompress | | | | Yes | | | | |
| gzip * | Yes | Yes | Yes | | Yes | zcat | zmore | Maintains ownership and times |
| gunzip | | | | Yes | | | | |
| bzip2 | Yes | No | No | | | bzcat | bzmore | Maintains ownership and times |
| bunzip2 | | | | Yes | | | | |

The –f option has two different functions depending on which command uses it, compress or decompress.

As you can see, most of the options mean the same in each except the –r which compresses a directory with its contents. Bzip2 can't compress an entire directory just the files inside the directory.

One other thing to note, the zmore and zless commands do basically the same thing. This seems to be a holdout by "older" Unix Linux users.

# Archiving

Archives are copies of backups. A backup is simply a copy of data. Everyone, not just companies, should back up at least some of their data.

Linux has two commonly used backup or archiving utilities – tar and cpio. As with most Windows backup applications, these utilities allow you to compress the files while you are backing them up.

Before learning about each of these utilities, it is important to be aware of backup strategies. You can create a backup of everything you want each day (full) or combine a full with either an incremental or differential backup. An incremental backup only backs up what changed in the previous time period, such as a day. A differential backup backs up everything that changed from the last full backup. Both options work well, but you have to pick the one that fits your needs the best. Copies of backups are called archives.

### Common Backup Utilities

- tar
- cpio (copy in/out)

### Tarballs

- Compressed tar archives – .tar.gz or .tgz

### Backup Strategy

- Full – backs up everything each day
- Incremental – backs up only what changed from previous day; faster to backup, but slower to recover
- Differential – backs up what changed from previous full backup; slower to backup, but faster to recover

# Tar

Tar is the oldest and probably the most common backup utility for Linux. It has a couple of drawbacks, which are that it cannot back up device files or files with names longer than 255 characters. It is also used to group several files into one large file for ease of distribution.

The options listed in the following chart are used most often. The –c, -f <filename>, -r, and -t either create a backup or work with one. The –x extracts the files from an archive. The –j, -z, and -Z are used to compress the backup.

Use the man and info pages for details on options that are used with the tar command.

- The tar –cvf /accounting/acct.tar /accounting/* command will create a backup called acct.tar of all files in the accounting directory and lets you see results as the process is happening. You do not have to add .tar to the end of the backup file, but it is a good idea because it helps identify that it is a backup file.

- The tar –tvf /accounting/acct.tar command allows you to view a list of files in the acct.tar file located in the /accounting directory.

- The tar –zcvf /accounting/acct.tar.gz /accounting/* command creates a backup file called acct.tar.gz of all files in the accounting directory and compresses it by using gzip compression.

- The tar –rvf /accounting/acct.tar /accounting/f1 command allows you to add files to a previous backup. It adds the f1 file to the previously created acct.tar file.

You will often see a group of files archived into a .tar file and then compressed with one of the utilities just detailed. Figure 11-3 is a great visual to understand this concept.

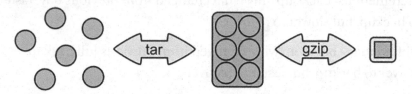

**Figure 11-3.** *Demonstration of a group of files archived into a .tar file and then compressed with a utility*

# Cpio

The cpio utility has additional features (when compared to tar) that include backing up device files and filenames that are longer than 255 characters. It also has more options available than tar. To view all the options, type man cpio.

The syntax for cpio is similar to the tar command, but it has an added piece – the file command. You first have to find the files you wish to back up. Then using standard input (SI) or the pipe command, you send what was found to the cpio command.

Review the following for examples:

- find <files> | cpio <options> <destination>

- find /acct/* | cpio -vocB –O /dev/st0

- find /acct/* | cpio -vocB –O /acct/acct.cpio

- cpio -vicduB –I /dev/st0

- cpio –vitB –I /dev/st0

The find /acct/* | cpio -vocB –O /dev/st0 option allows you to back up all the files in the acct directory to tape. The –O tells it where to send the backup. In this case, it is to the first tape device. In verbose mode, you do the following: create a new archive, use the SVR4 storage format that is known by a different version of cpio, and change the block size to 5KB from 512KB so it will speed up the transfer of data.

The find /acct/* | cpio -vocB –O /acct/acct.cpio option is the same as the first example, except that the backup goes to the file called /acct/acct.cpio. Notice that the extension cpio was added for identification.

The cpio -vicduB –I /dev/st0 option extracts files in verbose mode from the archive on the tape using the known format in 5KB blocks. It also creates directories when needed and overwrites without asking for an OK.

The cpio –vitB –I /dev/st0 option allows you to view a list of files in the archive on the tape. Again, it uses verbose mode and 5KB blocks.

# Summary

In this chapter, you learned about Linux's directory structure, regular expressions, compression, and archiving. Keep the following in mind:

- Linux's directory structure has a single root.

- Filesystem Hierarchy Standard (FHS) created a standard for the location of required files and directories.

- There are several standard file types.

- More file system commands were reviewed.
- How backups (archives) are created was reviewed.

## Resources

- **File System Hierarchy System:** http://en.wikipedia.org/wiki/Filesystem_Hierarchy_Standard
- **Unix File System:** http://en.wikipedia.org/wiki/Unix_filesystem
- **List of File Formats:** http://en.wikipedia.org/wiki/List_of_file_formats_(alphabetical)
- **Regular Expressions:** www.guru99.com/linux-regular-expressions.html

# CHAPTER 12

# Networking Fundamentals

As a Linux system administrator, you will be managing systems that use Internet protocols and networking, so it is essential to have a basic understanding of the underlying concepts. The OSI and TCP/IP are the two main models used in networking. Networks have physical and logical addresses, and addresses can be assigned manually or dynamically. IPv4 was the protocol used to address hosts, until the Internet became so large that all the numbers were used. IPv6 was developed to add more addressing capability. Decimal (base 10), Binary (base 2), and Hexadecimal (base 16) are the three numeric methods used to represent addresses to a computer. Port numbers map to different services, such as FTP and HTTP. Linux commands allow detection of the NIC and provide powerful troubleshooting functions.

By the end of this chapter, you will be able to

1. Identify the fundamentals of Internet protocols

2. Describe and set up basic network configuration

3. Configure DNS on a host

4. Identify and use basic network tools for troubleshooting

## Internet Protocol

When you first start learning about networking, the term protocol can be a mystery. Governments have protocols (procedures or conventions) they follow when working together, but what does it mean in networking?

A network protocol is a set of rules by which two devices communicate. Think of making a long distance phone call to your sister who lives in Germany. She speaks German as her main language and English as a second one. You live in the USA and speak only English. You call her, and she answers in German. You, while speaking

215

A. F. Sheikh, *CompTIA Linux+ Certification Companion*, Certification Study Companion Series, https://doi.org/10.1007/979-8-8688-0128-0_12

English, say hi and identify yourself. She knows you do not speak German so she agrees to talk to you in English. The English language is a protocol for communicating that has been agreed upon by both parties.

The main protocol that is used on the Internet today is Internet Protocol (IP). Devices have to be configured to use this protocol along with others when using the Transmission Control Protocol/Internet Protocol suite (TCP/IP).

## Networking Models

Figure 12-1 outlines the two main models used in networking today, the OSI model (7 layers) and the TCP/IP model (4 layers). The OSI model was developed by the International Standard Organization (ISO), whereas the TCP Model was developed by the Advanced Research Project Agency Network (ARPANET). The chapter will review the protocols on two of the layers of the TCP/IP model that are used by Linux.

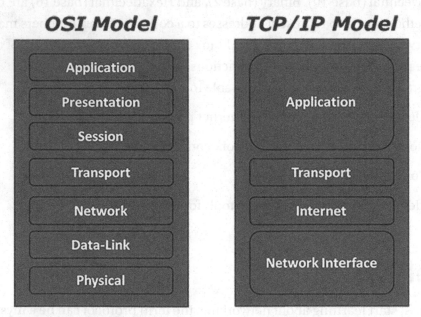

*Figure 12-1.* *Mapping of layers in the OSI model to the TCP/IP model*

# OSI Model

As you can see from Figure 12-1, the OSI model is broken into more modules than is the TCP/IP model. For this book, your main concern is the Transport layer and Network layer. Those two layers map directly to the Transport and Internet layers of the TCP/IP model and perform the same functions using the same protocols.

# TCP/IP Model

Starting at the bottom of the TCP/IP model, you will remember the Network Interface layer covers the physical part of the configuration and the creation of packets which carries data to its destination. What happens on the Internet and Transport layer is what will be discussed here.

- Internet Protocol (IP) is responsible for addressing and routing. Addressing and Routing will be covered later in this chapter. Internet Control Message Protocol (ICMP) works with IP to return error messages but does not carry any actual data.

- Transmission Control Protocol (TCP) and User Datagram Protocol (UDP) are responsible for getting the packets from one computer to another.

---

### Key Facts

### Layers of TCP/IP model

- Application
- Transport
  - TCP – Transmission Control Protocol
  - UDP – User Datagram Protocol
- Internet
  - IP – Internet Protocol
  - ICMP – Internet Control Message Protocol
- Network Interface

---

# TCP and UDP

TCP takes the packets which are created at the Network Interface layer and divided into smaller packets at the IP layer, keeping track of them as they move across the network. It is responsible for sequencing of data packets which is putting each of the packets in the correct order once they all get to the destination. TCP also manages flow control and performs error checking. Because of these tasks, TCP is known as a very reliable method of transporting data.

TCP is known as a connection-oriented protocol, because it acknowledges each packet as it is received. For example, when host 1 sends packet A to host 2, host 1 sends a notice to host 2 that packet A is on its way. When host 2 receives packet A, host 2 notifies host 1 that packet A was received. This process continues until all packets have been received. Packets are then put in the correct order. But what if a packet didn't get to host 2? Host 1 keeps track of the packets so if it doesn't get an acknowledgment for one, it resends it. You can see why TCP is considered slow. This protocol is used by network services that need reliability such as FTP, Web, or mail.

UDP is a fast protocol, because it doesn't use acknowledgments like TCP. That is why it is referred to as a connectionless protocol (Table 12-1). It is more interested in getting the next packet to the destination as quickly as possible. Services such as streaming audio or video use UDP because losing a packet is not as critical as with one like mail.

***Table 12-1.***  *Differences Between TCP and UDP*

| UDP | TCP |
| --- | --- |
| Unreliable | Reliable |
| Connectionless | Connection-oriented |
| Unordered packet delivery | Ordered packet delivery |
| Fast | Slow |

# Internet Control Message Protocol (ICMP)

The Internet Control Message Protocol (ICMP) serves as a supporting protocol utilized by diverse network devices such as routers to send error messages, indicating issues like the unavailability of a requested service. ICMP does not carry data – just messages.

It sends either an echo request or an echo response. This protocol (Table 12-2) is usually not used by end-user applications; however, the **ping** and **traceroute** utilities which are widely used by sysadmins do use ICMP.

The **ping** command can determine if a host is up and reachable. When host A pings host B, host A sends an ICMP echo request to host B. Host B either replies with an ICMP echo response, or host A gets an error stating host B is not responding. The **traceroute** command acts much in the same way except it reports on each host it passes on the network until host B is reached.

***Table 12-2.*** *Other Protocols Used in the TCP/IP Suite*

| Protocol | Description |
| --- | --- |
| HTTP – HyperText Transfer Protocol | Used with Web servers and browsers to handle requests and responses |
| DHCP – Dynamic Host Configuration Protocol | Assigns addressing information automatically |
| SMTP – Simple Mail Transfer Protocol | Routes electronic mail through the Internet or intranet |
| NTP – Network Time Protocol | Synchronizes time between systems |
| SSH – Secure Shell | Allows for secure connection – uses public key encryption – substitute for telnet |
| Telnet – Remote Terminal Emulation | Used to connect systems – not secure |
| DNS – Domain Name System | Provides address to name resolution |
| ICMP | Detects and reports network error conditions |
| FTP | Used for file transfer from one host to another host |

# Addressing

## Physical and Logical Addresses

There are two types of addresses used in networking: the physical address and a logical address. The physical address is the burned-in address on your network interface card (NIC). This is called the Media Access Control (MAC) address and is unique to each NIC. This address can be changed on some NICs but is usually left as it is.

The logical address is an address that is either assigned manually by a sysadmin or automatically assigned by a Dynamic Host Configuration Protocol (DHCP) server on the network. This must be unique but can be changed as needed.

There are two versions of the IP protocol that are in use today which are IPv4 and IPv6. Both of these will be discussed in more detail as the chapter progresses.

Before a system can function on any public network, it must have a globally unique IP address. Most of us get our IP address from our service provider; however, in the past, you could go to Internet Assigned Number Authority (IANA) and request an IP address. Since all IPv4 addresses have now been issued, requesting an IP address from IANA is not possible.

---

### Key Facts

### Addressing

- Logical address – Unique IP address assigned manually or by a DHCP server
- Physical address – burned-in Media Access Control (MAC) address on a Network Interface Card (NIC)

### IP protocol versions

- IPv4
- IPv6

---

# IPv4

Each address is made up of four numbers – four octets (Table 12-3) separated by a period. These octets represent an 8-bit binary number or a number between 0 and 255. You will also hear an IPv4 address called a 32-bit address – 4 octets times 8 bits equal 32 bits.

Each computer has what is called a Loop Back or Local address which is 127.0.0.1. Sysadmins use this address to verify the TCP/IP stack of protocols is functioning properly. Some software uses this address in their services/applications. No actual hardware is associated with this address.

You will also hear another term used with an IPv4 address which is valid or invalid. A valid IP address cannot have an octet with a value of more than 255. If it does, it is considered invalid and cannot be used. For example, 222.1.2.45 is a valid IP address; none of the octets have a value of more than 255. On the other hand, 400.290.1.3 is not valid because two of the octets are greater than 255.

Have you ever been watching TV and noticed the IP address of a computer being examined by a tech? TV and movies always use invalid IP addresses, as well as fake phone numbers.

There is a little math to review (or learn) before getting started with addressing. Humans, with 10 fingers, chose base 10 for counting, using 10 digits from 0 to 9. Computers use binary (base 2), utilizing only the digits 0 and 1. These digits correspond to current off (0) or current on (1) in a chip. It is very simple to convert between binary, octal (base 8), and hexadecimal (base 16), and these bases are used extensively to represent the contents of computer memory. Conversion between base 10 and other bases can be done, but it is not as easy.

As was explained earlier, an IP address can have four octets or 4 8-bit values separated by a period. Each bit in the octet has a value. This value is based on binary numbering.

**Table 12-3.**  *Value of Each Bit in an IPv4 Octet*

| | |
|---|---|
| $2^0$ | 1 |
| $2^1$ | 2 |
| $2^2$ | 4 |
| $2^3$ | 8 |
| $2^4$ | 16 |
| $2^5$ | 32 |
| $2^6$ | 64 |
| $2^7$ | 128 |

The computer starts numbering with 0; therefore, the highest number represented in eight bits is 1111 1111, or 256 − 1, or 255.

Table 12-4 shows another view of bit values. With one in each location, the sum is 255. Starting with the right most bit, its value is 1. To find the value of the second bit, you would double the value of the first bit. Continue doubling the value as you move to the left to get that bit's value until you reach the eighth bit. Understanding these concepts is critical to understanding addressing.

***Table 12-4.*** *Binary Bit Value*

| Bit | 8 | 7 | 6 | 5 | 4 | 3 | 2 | 1 | |
|-----|-----|-----|-----|-----|-----|-----|-----|-----|------|
| | $2^7$ | $2^6$ | $2^5$ | $2^4$ | $2^3$ | $2^2$ | $2^1$ | $2^0$ | |
| Value | 128 | 64 | 32 | 16 | 8 | 4 | 2 | 1 | =255 |

# Binary Values

Figure 12-2 demonstrates how to determine the binary value for each octet when the IP address is 192.168.1.1. The easier way to convert from a decimal value to a binary value is to use the scientific calculator on your PC. To best understand addressing though, you should learn how it is done. To do the conversion manually, follow this process.

1. Start with the number 192. Compare 192 to the value of the 8th bit (128); it is greater. Result: "1" is in the 8th bit.

2. Subtract 128 from 192 to find what's remaining; result is 64.

3. Look at the 7th bit; its value is 64. Is 64 greater than or equal to 64? Yes. Result: "1" is in the 7th bit.

4. Subtract the number 64 (from step 2) from 64 (value of the 7th bit.) The answer is 0.

   That means all remaining bits are zero.

   Final Answer: 11000000 (128 + 64 = 192.)

The example uses the same process with 168. You can see some of the values could not be used, such as 64 and 16 so that bit became a 0. The last two octets are very easy to convert.

Remember that (theoretically) each octet could be from 0 to 255? Well, that is not totally true. The host portion of an IP address can never be a 0 or 255. Those are reserved for special purposes. The 0 is reserved for the network segment's address and the 255 for a broadcast address.

Figure 12-2 demonstrates the four steps outlined above when converting decimal to binary.

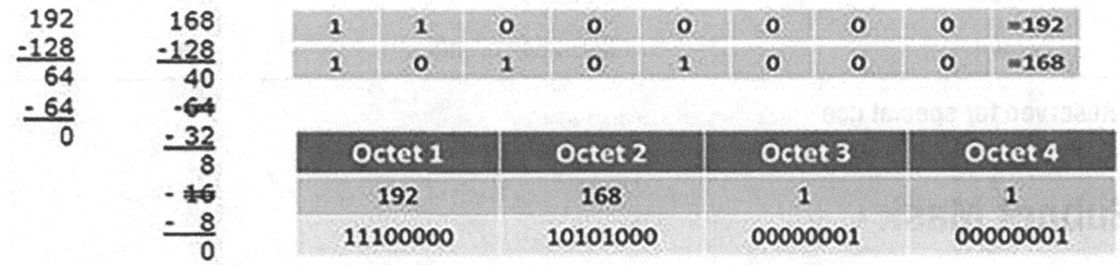

| | | | | | | | |
|---|---|---|---|---|---|---|---|
| 1 | 1 | 0 | 0 | 0 | 0 | 0 | 0 | =192 |
| 1 | 0 | 1 | 0 | 1 | 0 | 0 | 0 | =168 |

| Octet 1 | Octet 2 | Octet 3 | Octet 4 |
|---|---|---|---|
| 192 | 168 | 1 | 1 |
| 11100000 | 10101000 | 00000001 | 00000001 |

```
192      168
-128     -128
 64       40
- 64     -64
  0      - 32
           8
         - 16
           8
         - 8
           0
```

***Figure 12-2.*** *Decimal to binary conversion*

# IPv4 Address Classes

To make managing IPv4 addresses easier, they were divided into classes (Table 12-5). Classes A, B, and C are for public use, D is for multicasting, and E is for experimental use. Each has a default subnet mask and a range of numbers.

You may have noticed the large number for "Maximum # of Hosts" for a Class A address. Because no one network would ever have that many IP addresses in its collision domain, class A, and class B, addresses are almost always subnetted. Subnetting is the process of breaking up a single network into smaller, more manageable ones. Class C addresses can also be subnetted. The /## is called Classless InterDomain Routing (CIDR) notation and is simply a shorter and faster way of noting a subnet mask.

**Table 12-5.** *IPv4 Address Classes*

| Class | Subnet Mask /CIDR Notation | Range | Max # Networks | Max # Hosts |
|-------|----------------------------|-------|----------------|-------------|
| A | 255.0.0.0 OR /8 | 1-127 | 127 | 16,777,214 |
| B | 255.255.0.0 OR /16 | 128-191 | 16,384 | 65,534 |
| C | 255.255.255.0 OR /24 | 192-223 | 2,097,152 | 254 |
| D* | n/a | 224-239 | n/a | n/a |
| E* | n/a | 240-254 | n/a | n/a |

*Reserved for special use

# Subnet Mask

The purpose of a subnet mask is to determine which portion of an IP address is the address of the network and which portion is the address of the host. A subnet mask is also made up of four octets separated by a period. Each bit in an octet has a value just like an IP address does. Classful subnet masks are 255.0.0.0, 255.255.0.0, 255.255.255.0, or /8, /16, /24. They can be defined with /## such as /24 which is a CIDR notation.

This information below explains how a computer takes an IP address and its subnet mask in binary format and determines what the network portion of an IP address is versus the host portion. A process called ANDing (Figure 12-3) is used by the computer to determine the network address. ANDing works as a logical AND. Are both bits 1? If yes, then the network bit is 1. Specifically, the computer compares the 8th bit of the IP address with the 8th bit of the subnet mask; in this case, they are both 1s; therefore, the network address's 8th bit is also a 1. The 7th bits are both 1s again so the network address is also a 1. The 7th to the 1st bits are all 0s which means those bits in the network address will be 0. The only time ANDing the bits will give you a 1 is if the bits for both the IP address and subnet mask are both a 1.

# ANDing Process

- If both #s are 1, then 1

- If both are 0, then 0

- If one is 1 and the other is 0, then 0

| Network Address | | | | Host Address |
|---|---|---|---|---|
| IP Address-decimal | 192 | 168 | 1 | 1 |
| IP Address-binary | 11000000 | 10101000 | 00000001 | 00000001 |
| Subnet Mask-decimal | 255 | 255 | 255 | 0 |
| Subnet Mask-binary | 11111111 | 11111111 | 11111111 | 00000000 |
| After ANDing | 11000000 | 10101000 | 00000001 | 00000000 |

*Figure 12-3.* *Example of ANDing*

# Default Gateway

Why does the computer need to know this information? It has to plan where a packet will be sent on the local network segment or to another segment. If it is destined for another network segment, the computer must have a default gateway. The default gateway is the address of a local router that will take the packets destined for another network and help deliver them to their destination.

# Broadcast Address

The last special IPv4 address is the broadcast address (Table 12-6). It is used to broadcast packets to all hosts on a network segment. The last IP address on each network segment is considered the broadcast address. The last address cannot be used by a host just like the first network address can't, because the first address is used to indicate the address of the network.

*Table 12-6.* *Sample Range of IP Addresses*

| Network Address | Subnet Mask | First Address | Broadcast Address |
|---|---|---|---|
| 10.0.0.0 | 255.0.0.0 | 10.0.0.1 | 10.255.255.255 |
| 172.16.0.0 | 255.255.0.0 | 172.16.0.1 | 172.16.255.255 |
| 192.168.10.0 | 255.255.255.0 | 192.168.10.1 | 192.168.10.255 |

# Lack of IPv4 Addresses

Earlier you learned that there are no more IPv4 addresses available to the public. The explosion of devices that use IP addresses caused this to happen very quickly by using all available routable addresses. In preparation for this happening, development of a new version of IP was started about 1994. It is known as IPv6 and uses a 128-bit ($2^{128}$) address size, compared to the 32-bit ($2^{32}$) length used by IPv4. Implementation of this new protocol is still underway in enough places that IPv4 continues to be widely used. Because of this, other temporary solutions had to be developed.

- NAT (Network Address Translation) and private addressing has helped to keep everyone going until IPv6 can be implemented. NAT is a protocol that allows a single IPv4 address to be used on the public side of a personal Internet router and multiple addresses be used on the private side. This process is being used by small businesses and home users alike. NAT keeps track of the internal IP address of each request that goes out to the Internet on the network's public address. When a response comes back to the public address, NAT determines to which internal network address it should be sent. This also adds a layer of security to that network, because the outside world does not know your internal network's IP addressing scheme.

- In addition to using NAT, three address ranges, one from each class, were designated as "private" addresses. They are considered non-routable addresses, because they are blocked by all Internet routers. If for some reason one of your internal computers gets to the Internet, it cannot be routed anywhere else. These non-routable addresses are:

  - The entire Class A – 10.0.0.0/8

  - A portion of the Class B – 172.16.0.0-172.31.0.0/16

  - The entire Class C – 192.168.0.0/24

# Comparing IPv4 and IPv6

Table 12-7 compares IPv4 to IPv6. This by no means a complete list; however, it does cover the most common points.

*Table 12-7.* *Comparing Ipv4 to IPv6*

| IPv4 | IPv6 |
|---|---|
| decimal | hexadecimal |
| 32-bit address | 128-bit address |
| 4 period-delimited octets / 8- bit numbers | 8 colon-delimited  quartets / 4 hex characters |
| 192.168.1.1 | 2010:***0000***:3c4d:abcd:1111:***0000:0000***:0012 or |
| | 2010:***0000***:3c4d:abcd:1111:**:**:0012 |
| 127.0.0.1 - loopback | 0000:0000:0000:0000:0000:0000:0000:0001or ::1 |
| Uses subnetting | Does not use subnetting |
| +16,777 million addresses | + 340 trillion trillion trillion addresses |
| none | Built-in authentication and privacy support |

The two main advantages IPv6 has over IPv4 are the built-in security and the massive number of available IP addresses.

The main difference between IPv6 and IPv4 is the layout of the addresses.

- There are eight parts (quartets) when there had been four (octets).

- The delimiter is a colon rather than period.

- Hexadecimal characters are used so you will need to learn to "think" in hex, not decimal.

- Addresses can be shortened by dropping leading zeros in a quartet and eliminating two quartets of all zeros (only two).

  - Let's look at dropping the leading zeros:

    2010:***00***20:3c4d:abcd:1111:***0***145:1000:***00***12

    2010:20:3c4d:abcd:1111:145:1000:12

    If there are less than four characters in a quartet, you know the missing characters are zeros.

- Eliminating two consecutive quartets of all zeros is a little more complicated. Let's take this one in two steps:

  2010:***0000***:3c4d:abcd:1111:***0000:0000***:0012

  2010:***0***:3c4d:abcd:1111:***0:0***:0012

  2010:0:3c4d:abcd:1111**::**0012

  The first step removed the leading zeros. The last step removed the 0:0 which left two colons next to each other. When you look the last address, you will see six quartets when there should be eight. However, you know the two missing quartets were all zeros and are located between the double colon.

- What about the IPv6 loop-back address shown in Table 12-7?

  ***0000:0000:0000:0000:0000:0000:0000:000***1

  Can more than one set of zeros be omitted by replacing them with double colons?

  The answer is yes. ::1 (again as shown in Table 12-7)

- Let's look at a different variation of all zeros:

  2010:***0000:0000***:abcd:1111:***0000:0000***:0012

  2010:***0:0***:abcd:1111:***0:0***:12

  2010::abcd:1111::12

Will that work? How would you know where the missing zero quartets are located when there are two colons next to each other? Therefore, only one set of consecutive zero quartets can be removed. The proper conversion would be

2010:***0:0***:abcd:1111:***0:0***:12

2010:***0:0***:abcd:1111::12 **or** 2010::abcd:1111:***0:0***:12

# IPv6 Addressing

The conversion to IPv6 has been coming for years; however, it has been a slow process. Hardware has to be able to use IPv6. Support personnel also need to be able to work with it. IPv6 is very different from IPv4 in several ways. The biggest difference you will see is it has eight quartets instead of four octets. It is also represented in hexadecimal rather than binary, and it doesn't use a subnet mask. The Key Facts listed below list more of the most common differences.

# Converting Hex to Decimal or Binary

This is a quick refresher on converting hex to binary or decimal.

First, please review the conversions in Table 12-8 below for Hexadecimal to Binary and to Decimal. Hex (base 16) uses 16 different digits: 0 through 9, and A through F. Table 12-8 shows how hex values are represented in base 2 (binary) and base 10 (decimal).

***Table 12-8.*** *Number Conversions – Hexadecimal, Decimal, and Binary*

| Hex | Binary | Dec |
| --- | --- | --- |
| 1 | 0001 | 1 |
| 2 | 0010 | 2 |
| 3 | 0011 | 3 |
| 4 | 0100 | 4 |
| 5 | 0101 | 5 |
| 6 | 0110 | 6 |
| 7 | 0111 | 7 |
| 8 | 1000 | 8 |
| 9 | 1001 | 9 |
| A | 1010 | 10 |
| B | 1011 | 11 |
| C | 1100 | 12 |
| D | 1101 | 13 |
| E | 1110 | 14 |
| F | 1111 | 15 |

In Table 12-9, each IPv6 hexadecimal address has to be broken into 4 parts (quartets) to determine the binary value of each. Then, review the values of the 4-bits. Just like in IPv4 addresses, the values from right to left are 1, 2, 4, and 8. FFFF is easy. F = 15 which is all 1's (8 + 4 + 2 + 1).

***Table 12-9.*** *Converting Hexadecimal to Binary – Examples*

| Hex | Binary 8 4 2 1 | Binary 8 4 2 1 | Binary 8 4 2 1 | Binary 8 4 2 1 |
|-----|----------------|----------------|----------------|----------------|
| FFFF | 1 1 1 1 <br> 8 + 4 + 2 + 1 = 15 | 1 1 1 1 | 1 1 1 1 | 1 1 1 1 |
| C30D | 1 1 0 0 <br> 8 + 4 = 12 | 0 0 1 1 <br> 2 + 1 = 3 | 0 0 0 0 <br> 0 | 1 1 0 1 <br> 8 + 4 + 1 = 13 |
| 1A2B | 0 0 0 1 <br> 1 | 1 0 1 0 <br> 8 + 2 = 10 | 0 0 0 1 0 <br> 2 | 1 0 1 1 <br> 8 + 2 + 1 = 11 |

# Parts of an IPv6 Addresses

An IPv6 address is divided into two parts, the Prefix and the Interface ID. The Prefix is the first 64 bits of the address and is referred to as a global routing prefix since it knows the geography of the address. The Interface ID is made up of the last 64 bits and is assigned to the interface rather than the host. This is like the host portion of an IPv4 address that must be unique. Because of automatic host identification, an interface can get an address assigned automatically even if there is no DHCP server enabled.

---

**Key Facts**

**Prefix**

- First 64-bits

- Referred to as a global routing prefix

- Can be divided into parts – region, ISP, network, subnet

### Interface ID

- Second 64-bits

- Assigned to interface – not host

- Unique within a subnet

- Can use automatic host ID to get address

# Ports
## Port Numbers

When information arrives at a host that has a single IP address, how does the system know what service or protocol will use that data? Each network service is assigned a port number by the TCP or UDP protocol. Having a port number assigned allows a single host to provide multiple services such as FTP, Telnet, SSH, or HTTP.

The /etc/services file stores a mapping of port numbers to named services.

There is a pool of over 65,000 port numbers that are managed by the Internet Corporation for Assigned Names and Numbers (ICANN). This pool is divided into three categories (Table 12-10) which are well-known ports, registered ports, and dynamic ports.

- Well-known ports, 0 through 1023, are assigned to common protocols and services such as DNS, FTP, HTTP, etc.

- Registered ports, 1024 through 49152, are assigned to companies who write their own software and want to use a specific port for their service.

- Dynamic Ports, 49151 through 65535, are available for services that need to make a temporary connection for a single session.

**Table 12-10.** *Categories of Port*

| Categories | Range of Port #s | Purpose |
| --- | --- | --- |
| Well-known ports | 0 – 1023 | Common protocols and services |
| Registered ports | 1024 – 49151 | Specific service |
| Dynamic ports | 49151 – 65535 | Temporary service used only for single session |

Table 12-11 lists well-known ports used by all operating systems including Linux and Windows. If you want to see a list of all network services available on your Linux system, look at the contents of the /etc/services file.

For security purposes, you should always close any port that is not being used.

**Table 12-11.** *Commonly Used Well-Known Ports*

| Service | Port |
| --- | --- |
| FTP – File Transfer Protocol | TCP 20 |
|  | TCP 21 |
| SSH – Secure Shell | TCP 22 |
|  | UDP 22 |
| Telnet | TCP 23 |
| SMTP – Simple Mail Transfer Protocol | TCP 25 |
| DNS – Domain Name System | TCP 53 |
|  | UDP 53 |
| DHCP – Dynamic Host Configuration Protocol | UDP 67 |
|  | UDP 68 |
| TFTP – Trivial File Transfer Protocol | UDP 68 |
| HTTP – HyperText Transfer Protocol | TCP 80 |
| POP3 – Post Office Protocol | TCP 110 |
| NNTP - Network News Transport Protocol | TCP 119 |
| NTP – Network Time Protocol | UDP 123 |

(*continued*)

***Table 12-11.*** (*continued*)

| Service | Port |
|---|---|
| NetBIOS | UDP 137 |
| | UDP 138 |
| | TCP 139 |
| IMAP4 – Internet Message Access Protocol | TCP 143 |
| | UDP 143 |
| SNMP – Simple Network Management Protocol | TCP 161 |
| | UDP 161 |
| | TCP 162 |
| | UDP 162 |
| LDAP – Lightweight Directory Access Protocol | TCP 389 |
| | UDP 389 |
| SSL – HTTP with Secure Sockets Layer | TCP 443 |
| | UDP 443 |

# Configuring an Interface
## Network Interface Card (NIC)

A network interface card (NIC) is a hardware component responsible for establishing the connection between a computer and a computer network. Normally, all network interface cards (NICs) are detected during the Linux installation so no manual work is required. If they are not found, you will have to manually add them to the Linux kernel using the **insmod** or **modprobe** commands. To remove a module, you should use the **rmmod** command. If you only want to view the currently loaded modules, use the **lsmod** command.

Now that you know how interfaces are set up, you need to know how to identify them and how to configure them. Linux interfaces are labeled either eth# for wired connections or wlan# for wireless connections. Depending on your infrastructure, you will configure your NIC as static or dynamic.

Dynamic configuration can happen one of two ways, from a DHCP server or using a Linux version of Automatic Private Internet Protocol Addressing (APIPA). APIPA gives out an address starting with 169.254. IPv6 does not use APIPA. The same type address can be obtained from an IPv6-configured router. If that type router is not available, your system will convert the IPv4 address to the hexadecimal equivalent and add the NIC's MAC address to the end.

---

### Key Facts

### NIC – Network Interface Card

- Usually detected during Linux installation

- Add with **insmod** or **modprobe** commands

- Deleted with **rmmod** command

- List loaded modules, **lsmod**

- Naming convention

  - First wired interface is eth0, second is eth1, etc.

  - First wireless is wlan0, second is wlan1, etc.

### Configure each NIC

- Static settings – manual

- Dynamic settings – DHCP

- APIPA – Automatic Private IP Addressing – (169.254.x.x)

---

# Static Settings

To manually configure an interface, modify the /etc/sysconfig/network-scripts/ifcfg-<eth#> file. Each of the options found in this file is needed to properly configure an interface. In order for these changes to take effect, you must restart the interface using the **ifdown eth#** then **ifup eth#**. These changes are persistent; that means they will be available after a reboot.

## Key Facts

### Static settings

- /etc/sysconfig/network-scripts/ifcfg-eth0
- Options
    - DEVICE=eth0
    - ONBOOT=YES
    - BOOTPROTO=static
    - IPADDR=<IP address>
    - NETMASK=<xxx.xxx.xxx.xxx>
    - NETWORK=<network address>
    - BROADCAST=<broadcast address>
- Restart interface

# DHCP Settings

Options that are available when configuring DHCP settings are very similar to the manual configuration options. They even use the same file. You will still have to restart the interface by using **ifdown and ifup** commands or by rebooting your system.

Both the static and DHCP are usually set using the Network Configuration Utility under System ➤ Administration ➤ Network.

## Key Facts

### DHCP settings

- /etc/sysconfig/network-scripts/ifcfg-eth0
- Options
    - DEVICE=eth0
    - ONBOOT=YES
    - BOOTPROTO=dhcp
- Restart interface

# ifconfig Command

The **ifconfig** command is used often especially in troubleshooting. It gives you a wealth of knowledge about the NICs on your system such as the MAC address, IP address, subnet mask, broadcast address, collisions, receive and transmit packets and bytes. It does not give you the default gateway.

# Configuring Routes

## Routers

A router is a device that carries traffic from a sending host to a receiving host across a network. One of the functions of a router is to determine the best path to the destination host. If you want to send traffic to a host on another network, you have to have a router; otherwise, the traffic will only travel on your local network segment.

Normally, your network will have a physical device whose main purpose is to act as a router. If your Linux host has more than one network interface card, it too can act as a router. No matter the type of router you use, it will contain a routing table that provides information about all its known routes.

## Gateway Router

The router that takes you out of your local network segment is known as a gateway router or default router. You must configure your host so it knows the IP address of this router. Add the line **default <IP of router>** to the /etc/sysconfig/routes file if it is not there already. Before this change can take effect, you must restart the interface with the **ifdown** or **ifup** commands.

---

### Key Facts

Gateway Router

- IP address of the device that takes packets out of local network
- /etc/sysconfig/routes file
    - default <IP address of router>

- Restart interface
  - **ifdown** <interface>
  - **ifup** <interface>

## Local Routing Table

The **route** command can display the contents of a routing table or add or remove routes from this table. It can also set the default or gateway router.

---

**Key Facts**

Local Routing Table

- Route displays routing information
- Add or remove a route
  - **route add –net <remote network IP address> netmask <xxx.xxx. xxx.xxx> gw <router's IP address>**
  - **route del –net <remote network IP address> netmask <xxx.xxx. xxx.xxx> gw <router's IP address>**
  - **route add default gw <router's IP address>**

---

# Configuring DNS
## Name Resolution

You may know that using a URL like www.google.com or www.linux.org does not mean anything to a computer. A computer has to have an address to which to send a packet. In Linux, as in Windows, there are two ways to accomplish this resolution: hosts file and Domain Name Service (DNS).

Using the /etc/hosts file was the original way to do this conversion. By including an IP address, host name, and an alias in this file, the computer could determine the IP address of a host. When there were only a few hosts on a network, this was a good solution; however, with the size of the Internet, it is impossible to include information on every host. The hosts file still exists on all Linux systems and must include at least the local host's information. There are system processes that use this information.

An example would be a trouble ticket about a PC that cannot reach a server. The first step is to do the regular troubleshooting, checking connectivity to other servers, and checking DNS among other processes. The final step was to look at the hosts file. Even though it is rarely used any more, it may have an entry for that server that is wrong.

You can see at least two disadvantages for using the hosts file for name resolution. IP addresses can change, even on a local network. Server addresses can seamlessly change without end users being notified. The other obvious issue is the number of entries that would be required because of the Internet. Can you imagine trying to add every name and IP address for each and every host you want to communicate with on the Internet?

Even though the hosts file is still used at least for local name resolution, DNS is now the tool used for name to IP address resolution. Each host can have up to three DNS servers in its resolv.conf file. When a host wants to go to google.com, it checks the first server for the IP address. If it does not respond, it checks the second one. This continues through all DNS server IP addresses in the resolv.conf file. Note the spelling of resolv, with no "e" at the end.

There is one more file that works with the hosts and resolv.conf files – nsswitch.conf. This file sets the order the system should use for resolution – host or DNS first.

# /etc/hosts

The /etc/hosts file is tab-delimited with three columns: the IP address, hostname, and alias (optional). Why set an alias? Many times a host is assigned a name created by a predetermined naming convention. This name may not make sense to the average user. A more user-friendly name can be created as an alias.

**The syntax used in the /etc/hosts file:**

- <IP address> <hostname> <alias>

# /etc/resolv.conf

The resolv.conf file has two sections: search and address. The address is self-explanatory; the DNS name servers are listed there. The search is not so intuitive. The domain name is placed there. In order to use just the hostname of a machine the system has to know the rest of the name or the domain name. If you worked at Google, you might want to reach a server on the internal network named "hammer." You could use "hammer.google.com" or add "google.com" to the search section of the resolv.conf file and then only use "hammer." The system automatically adds the domain information. More than one domain listed there also. In the same way the system progresses through the list of DNS name servers, it will move through the list of domain names.

**The syntax use in the /etc/resolv.conf file:**

- Search

  - <domain name>.<com>

- IP addresses of nameserver

  - <192.168.0.1>

  - <192.168.0.2>

## /etc/nsswitch.conf

The /etc/nsswitch.conf file contains a section labeled #hosts. The line "hosts: files dns" can be included so the system will first use local files and then DNS for name resolution.

**The syntax for /etc/resolv.conf:**

- hosts: files dns

# Configuring with GUI
## Network Configuration Tool

Using the Network Configuration tool, you can configure static IP address or DHCP information. This tool is located in System ➤ Administration ➤ Network. Just as with the command line, you must be a root user to change the interface settings. You can also configure the DNS and search path in this tool.

## Troubleshooting

This section will cover the most common utilities used for troubleshooting.

# ping

The Linux ping command, short for packet internet groper, is a utility used to troubleshoot network problems within a server or network infrastructure. Its functionality involves sending a data packet to the target device and awaiting its response. If a response is returned, the interface is up; if not, there is a problem somewhere along the way. It could be in your NIC's configuration, your default gateway, a router along the way to the destination or at the destination. It could also just mean that ICMP is being blocked by a firewall at the destination. In past years, what has been referred to as a "ping of death" could take a host down, because it could not handle the large number of pings it was receiving; therefore, many hosts now block the ICMP requests.

It is a good idea to first **ping** the IP address of the destination host rather than their DNS name. If you cannot reach the host by the DNS name, you do not know if there is a connectivity issue or the problem is with DNS. Work out any connectivity issue first, and then move to correcting any DNS problems. Be aware that you have to stop the **ping** command with a <ctrl>C; otherwise, you will continue to receive responses.

The responses give you some very helpful information in addition to the fact the destination is reachable. The source and round-trip time are the most helpful to the troubleshooter. Take a look at the man page for **ping** for available options.

# traceroute

The **traceroute** command is another command that works with the ICMP protocol. Where this one really differs from **ping** is that you see how many hops are between the source and the destination. A client worked from home for a large corporation that was about 15 minutes away. The response time was getting worse and worse; the client ran a **traceroute** and learned traffic was going from the PC in Dallas through Los Angeles and back to the corporate offices in Dallas. No wonder it was slow! After a call to their ISP, the issue was resolved.

You can verify the settings for your NIC are correct using the **ifconfig** command.

# netstat

The **netstat** command is another very useful tool. It displays all ports on your system (listening and non-listening), sockets that are in the listening state, stats on each protocol, routing information, and more. Using the -i option shows a list of all network interfaces.

## telnet

The **telnet** command is a good tool to test port status on a destination host by using a command prompt, type **telnet <IP address of destination> <port #>.** If you are connected, you know the port is open, and you can type **quit** to break the connection. Some software needs to talk to a specific port, and if that port is not open, the connection cannot be made.

## nslookup

The **nslookup** command queries a DNS server for the IP address or hostname as well as the DNS server being used. It is not as extensive as the next command, **dig**, but it is still very helpful.

## dig

Another good command for troubleshooting DNS is **dig**. It requests a name to IP address resolution, and depending on the option used, you get more than just the requested resolution. Again, review dig's man page for options.

## host

The **host** command aids in DNS name resolution. By adding a hostname or an IP address at the end of the host command, you can test the DNS resolution for that host.

## hostname

The **hostname** command allows you to set the host's name or to display the current setting.

## sar

The **sar** command is used to collect, report, or save system activity information. The default version of **sar** (CPU utilization) monitors major system resources which makes this a good starting point for looking for problem areas.

# Summary

- The main protocol used on the Internet now is the IP. It and many others are found in the TCP/IP Model. This model is made up of four layers with each having a different function in moving data.

- Starting at the top of the TCP/IP model, its four layers are the Application layer, the Transport layer, which uses the TCP and UDP protocols; the Internet layer which uses the IP and ICMP protocols, and the Network Interface protocols.

- The Transport layer protocols are responsible for dividing packets into smaller packets and keeping track of them as they go from one host to another.

- The Internet layer is best known for routing and route decisions. IP and ICMP are the most commonly used protocols on this layer.

- Other protocols, which are found on the Application layer, are HTTP, DHCP, SMTP, NTP, DNS, Telnet, and SSH.

- There are two types of addressing used with the TCP/IP model: physical and logical. The physical address is the burned-in MAC address on a NIC. The logical address is assigned by DHCP or manually by the system's administrator. Currently, there are two versions of the local address: IPv4 and IPv6.

- IPv4 addresses use four octets of binary numbers separated by a period and are associated with a subnet mask. Together the address and mask are used to route packets to their destination. Because of the explosion of the number of devices using an IP address now, almost all these addresses are in use.

- IPv6 was developed to solve the lack of addresses issue. In addition to the extremely large number of IP addresses it makes available, it includes added advantages, including built-in authentication and privacy support. IPv6 uses hexadecimal (hex) numbers separated by colons. IPv4 uses binary number separated by periods.

- Using port numbers, packets are able to travel to the appropriate service on a single host with a single IP address. Well-known ports are TCP port 80 for HTTP, TCP port 23 for Telnet, TCP 25 for SMTP, and UDP 123 for NTP.

- Each network card in a host must be configured and managed. In addition to the burned-in MAC address, it must have an IP address and a subnet mask before it can talk to another host. If traffic is to leave the local network, such as going to the Internet, it must also have a gateway address (IP address of the router connected to that host's network). That IP address can be assigned manually by the host's administrator or automatically by DHCP or APIPA. Commands used to manage NICs are **ifconfig**, **insmod**, **modprobe**, **rmmod**, **lsmod**, **ifdown**, and **ifup**.

- A routing table is stored on each host that is on a network, and it contains information about where a packet should go after leaving the host and going to a specific IP address. The **route** command is used to add or remove a route from the host's local routing table.

- DNS is used to resolve a host name to an IP address so a packet can be routed to the proper host. The /etc/hosts file was the way first used to do this conversion. As networks started to grow and grow, this was no longer a good solution. The DNS service was developed to dynamically maintain information on each host's name and IP address.

- The Network Configuration Tool GUI application can be used to configure and maintain most of the functions from the command line. This application can be found in System ➤ Administration ➤ Network.

- There are many troubleshooting tools available for use with the TCP/IP model; only the most commonly used ones were covered: **ping**, **traceroute**, **netstat**, **telnet**, **nslookup**, **dig**, **host**, **hostname**, and **sar**.

# CHAPTER 13

# Software Installation

In this chapter, you will gain an understanding of the software-installation process, including using package managers, libraries for scripting, and tools for troubleshooting.

By the end of this chapter, you will be able to

1. Use package managers to install software

2. Describe libraries used in scripting

3. Discuss tools for troubleshooting software installations

## Package Managers

A package is a group of files that work together to make an application function properly. A package manager is an application that maintains a database with information about all installed software; it provides a standard format for installing packages.

This is similar to what Microsoft does with its .msi files. Microsoft's packages are called *installation packages*, which also include a database that maintains information on all installed applications.

Package managers, like Windows installers, are prebuilt for a specific architecture, such as 32-bit and 64-bit systems. Some are even built for a specific distribution of Linux. They can be used to install and update packages, to manage installed packages, or to remove packages. They also verify that the package is the same as it was when it left the developer and that no one has tampered with the code.

245

© Ahmed F. Sheikh 2024
A. F. Sheikh, *CompTIA Linux+ Certification Companion*, Certification Study Companion Series,
https://doi.org/10.1007/979-8-8688-0128-0_13

# Source or Binary

A package is either source or binary. The code in a source package can be read by real people, not just computers. Binary code is written for a specific computer, such as an Intel PC or PowerPC. It is in machine code, which cannot be read by most humans.

You may have seen applications that need other applications to be installed before installing properly. For example, iTunes will install QuickTime before it starts the actual iTunes application – this is called a dependency. In Linux, dependencies refer to the libraries, packages, or modules required for smooth execution of a program. Occasionally, when installing a package, its dependencies may not be automatically installed or might be absent. Therefore, it is crucial for Linux administrators to understand how to install these dependencies. Most vendor applications will bundle all the required applications into one installation; however, others, such as with open-source software, will just tell you to install several applications in a particular order.

**Common Package Managers**

- Red Hat Package Manager (RPM)

- Yellowdog Updater, Modified (YUM)

- Debian Advanced Packaging Tool (APT)

- Debian Package Manager (DPM)

- KPackageKit

- Zypper (Zypp)

When you start installing packages on Linux, you might ask yourself "How do I know the name of the installer I need?" If you want to install a time server, it is commonly referred to as *ntp*. At this point, you can use the rpm –q --whatprovides ntp to get the package installer's name. If that does not work, an Internet search is your next best choice.

Once you know the name of the package installer, you need to know where you can find it.

The most common location is on the installation CD/DVD. That is one of the safest places to find it. You can download it from the Internet and install the package from your local host. You also can install it directly from the Internet if you know the complete URL for the location of the package. Use the command rpm -1 <complete URL>.

You learned about dependencies earlier in the chapter. As a review, some packages require other packages be installed before you can install the one you want. If you are trying to install such a package, you will get an error message that tells you what dependencies are required before the installation can complete successfully. This can be frustrating, but not as frustrating as when your software does not work, and you have no idea why.

# Red Hat Package Manager (RPM)

Redhat Package Manager, or RPM, is used on Suse, Redhat, Fedora, and many other Linux distributions. Debian uses a package manager that is very similar to RPM, Debian Package Manager, or DPM.

Remember that the previous package manager can be built for a specific architecture or distribution. That means you could have multiple versions of a package for the same software. The naming convention (Table 13-1) used for a package will tell you when it should be used.

***Table 13-1.*** *Naming Convention for ntp Installer*

| Name | Version # | Release | Distribution | Architecture |
|------|-----------|---------|--------------|--------------|
| ntp | 4.2.8p17 | 1 | Fc38 | i686 |

**RPM**

- Database stored in /var/lib/rpm directory

- Database repair – rpm -rebuilddbBefore installing – rpm –k or --checksig <pkg>

- Convert RPM package to cpio archive – rpm2cpio <installer> > name.cpio

As you can see in the "Naming Convention for ntp Installer" table, ntp is the name of the package, 4.2.8p17 is the version number, 1 is the release number, fc38 is for Fedora Core 38, and i686 is for an Intel Pentium II processor or later.

Information about all installed packages is stored in a database in the /var/lib/rpm directory. The database is updated any time you update or remove a package. As with any database, it can be corrupted and might need to be rebuilt. You will know if it must be fixed, because installed packages will start to misbehave.

247

In an effort to make sure packages are not tampered with along the way, you should use the rpm –checksig command. It verifies that the package has not been changed in any way.

There may be a time that you need a single file from an RPM package. You can use the rmp2cpio command to convert the package to individual files, much like you can expand an .iso file.

# RPM Commands

The commands in Table 13-2 are only a few of the options that can be used with the rpm command. Each of these is fairly self-explanatory so this chapter will review a few commands.

You can display all options that were used with rpm by using the rpm command, or you can use the man and info commands for more detailed information.

Also, you will be able to see that something is actually happening during installation. If you use the rpm –ihv <installer> command, it displays a progress bar with hash marks on your screen. The –v means verbose and shows something on the screen. If you use only the –i, all you will see is a blank screen waiting for the install to complete. You will not know if the installation is hung, if there are errors, or what is going on. Rather than starting the installation, you can use the --test option with rpm command. That will tell you what, if anything, is missing. Then you can install those first.

You will notice that the name changes from installer to package after installation. After the software is installed, the rpm database knows the name of the package, so the full name of the installer package is no longer needed. The only other time the installer name will be used is with the update option. The old package is actually removed and the new, updated package is then installed.

Lastly, if you try to uninstall a package that is a dependency of another installed package, it will not install but will tell you about the dependency.

**Table 13-2.** *RPM Commands*

| Command | Description |
| --- | --- |
| rpm | Displays options |
| rpm -i <installer> | Installs software; no display |
| rpm –ihv <installer> | Installs and shows hash marks for a progress update |
| rpm -U <installer> | Upgrades software |
| rpm –e <package> | Uninstalls software |
| rpm -q <package> | Basic query |
| rpm –qa | Basic query against all packages |
| rpm -qi <package> | Basic query with information |
| rpm –ql <package> | Displays files in a package |
| rpm –V <package> | Identifies missing package(s) |
| rpm -h <package> | Displays hash marks (#) indicating progress during installation or removal. |

For a more extensive list of options, use the man rpm command.

# Yellowdog Updater Modified (YUM)

Yellowdog Updater Modified (YUM) is even better than using only RPM for installing packages. YUM looks first for dependencies and installs them; then YUM handles the installation using RPM. This Package Manager is used on Redhat, Fedora, and other distributions; however, you may need to install it after the default installation.

YUM works with repositories rather than with a database (like RPM). A repository, in Linux terms, is a location where installer packages are located on the Internet. These repositories also are referred to as software mirrors.

**YUM**

- Automatically downloads and installs a package and its dependencies

- May not be included with the default installation of Linux

- Works with repositories (a collection of packages)

# YUM Commands

YUM has command options (Table 13-3) very similar to RPM's options, except it uses words rather than options. You can install, update, and remove using YUM. You can also list all your installed software, search for software, or get information about a particular piece of software. You can even download the installer package without installing it. This comes in handy when you have several hosts on which you want to install the software.

***Table 13-3.***  *YUM Commands*

| Command | Description |
| --- | --- |
| Yum | Displays options |
| yum install <package> | Installs software |
| yum remove <package> | Removes software |
| yum update <package> | Updates software |
| yum list installed | Displays  list of all software |
| yum info <package> | Displays information about the software |
| yum search <package> | Searches for the software |
| yumdownloader <installer> | Downloads installer file without installing it |

# YUM Configuration Files

YUM uses a configuration file – /etc/yum.conf – that contains the directory that includes the following: the YUM log files storage location, the location of downloaded packages, and a list of the URLs of RPM repositories. The log file is usually located in /var/log and is named yum.log. This file is not often modified, because it has everything it needs.

The /etc/yum.repos.d directory contains a .repo file for repositories and is where the YUM command normally starts when looking for repositories. For example, the main .repo file for Fedora is fedora.repo. This directory is where YUM normally looks first for repositories.

If you have a medium to large number of Linux installations on your network, you may want to set up your own repository. You can create a .repo file that points to a repository located on a local server. Your repository server can get everything it needs from the Internet. Then, your group of Linux hosts can look there for installers for new and updated software rather than going out on the Internet. This will speed up the install or updates and save on bandwidth that goes to the Internet.

# Debian Package Manager

Debian Package Manager (DPM) is used with Debian or its derivatives. As with RPM and YUM, it is used to manage software.

Like RPM having the .rpm extension, DPM uses .deb extension. The /etc/apt/sources.list tells the installer where to get its packages (Table 13-4).

***Table 13-4.*** *Debian Package Manager*

| Command | Description |
| --- | --- |
| dpkg <option> <package> | Installs, updates, and so on |
| dpkg-reconfigure | Reconfigures install package |

# Debian APT

Debian's Advanced Packaging Tool (APT) is another package manager like YUM. It was originally written to work with DPM and was later updated to work with RPM, too. It finds the packages and all the dependencies and installs everything.

Table 13-5 shows some of the apt commands. You can type apt-get or apt-cache for more details.

***Table 13-5.*** *Debian APT*

| Command | Description |
| --- | --- |
| apt-get | Displays options |
| apt-get install <package> | Installs software |
| apt-get update | Updates package index |
| apt-get upgrade <package> | Upgrades software |
| apt-get remove <package> | Removes software |
| apt-cache <options> <cmd> | Cache manipulator |

# KPackageKit Package Manager

KPackageKit is more user-friendly than other package managers and is more Windows-like than others. It is located in a slightly different place depending on the distribution, but can usually be found under the application section.

Choosing a package manager to work with depends on your installed distribution and which one you are most comfortable using.

# Libraries

A shared library is a file containing code that performs a specific task, such as opening or closing a file. This code can be used by any developer free of charge. Plus, the developer does not have to waste their time creating something that is already readily available. This saves time and reduces the size of the application.

Applications look for dynamic shared libraries in the default locations (/lib or /usr/lib) or the configuration file (/etc/ld.so.conf) that lists non-default locations. These files end with .so.

Static shared libraries contain code that becomes part of the actual application when it is compiled. Static libraries are made part of the software when it is compiled; therefore, it makes the application larger.

With dynamic libraries, an application makes a call to a library and uses it as it is needed, saving space in memory and in storage.

You might ask, then why would anyone use static libraries? What if the dynamic library becomes unavailable? It could be deleted, moved, or updated so it is incompatible with the calling application. The area where it is stored could become unavailable. If you have a mission-critical application that cannot fail, it must run. Static files end in .a and can be found in the /usr/lib or /usr/local/lib directories.

Shared Library – a single file (holding other files) that contains common routines that any program can use.

- Dynamic

    - Software references library

    - /etc/ld.so.conf file tells application where libraries are located

    - Default location – /lib or /usr/lib

    - File names end in .so

- Static

  - Collection of code that becomes part of an application when compiled

  - File names end in .a

  - Default location – /usr/lib or /usr/local/lib

# Troubleshooting

Another important aspect of software installation is troubleshooting. You will learn many of the common reasons a program fails to start.

Use the following questions to start the troubleshooting process:

- Is the software actually installed? If so, did someone delete a file needed for this program to function?

- Has the software ever worked properly? Did a dependent package not get installed originally, or did it get removed later in error?

The database that RPM uses might be corrupted and may need to be rebuilt.

When a program fails to execute, the most common reasons are the following:

- The program was not installed.

- Some of the program files were deleted.

- Sometimes, all dependencies were not installed when the program was installed.

- Dependent programs were uninstalled in error.

- The database was corrupted if RPM was used.

*Table 13-6.* *Troubleshooting Commands*

| Command | Description |
|---|---|
| rpm –V <package> | Displays missing files |
| rpm -rebuilddb | Rebuilds the RPM database |
| ldd <software> | Displays required libraries |
| ldconfig  <options> | Creates, updates, and removes required links and cache in libraries |
| Ping | Helps identify the availability of a network and host |

Consider the following question and the subsequent answers: What does a piece of software require to function properly?

- It requires that you install all files with the package manager. The rpm –V <package> can tell you if any files are missing (Table 13-6).

- If a database is involved to help the package manager do its job, it could have become corrupt. Try the rpm –rebuilddb command, which often fixes a corrupt database.

- If the software is linked to a shared library, is that library still in the correct place and still compatible with the software? Use the ldd command to display all libraries that are required by that application. It will also tell you if any of them are not installed.

- In connection with shared libraries, you also can use the ldconfig –p command to display a list of all shared libraries that are available. If you know there is a library file that does not show up in this list and it is not in the /etc/ld.so.conf file, you can set the LD_LIBRARY_PATH environment variable to the path where that library is located. Another option is to add the location of that library to the /etc/ld.so. conf file.

  - Be sure to run the ldconfig command again so your library cache is updated. This creates or recreates all the links required for the shared library directories listed in the /etc/ld.so.conf file and in the default locations.

# Summary

In this chapter, you learned about how to install software on Linux, which included an overview of package managers, libraries, and troubleshooting tools. Keep the following in mind:

- Package managers are used to install, remove, and update software in Linux.

- Repositories hold packages and the dependent packages.

- Libraries are where code is stored for use by multiple applications to avoid duplication in storage and in RAM.

- The ldd and ldconfig commands help find missing libraries or broken links that cause applications to not execute properly.

## CHAPTER 14

# Security

Securing our data is one of today's biggest challenges. In this chapter, you will learn some of the ways you can secure a Linux system. You will also learn how to audit some of the activity that has occurred on a host.

By the end of this chapter, you will be able to

1. Perform security administration tasks

2. Configure security on a host

3. Identify tools and technologies used to encrypt data to ensure network security

## Root User Security

Working with admin access is something that is very difficult to get users to understand. Every user, even administrators, should always have a regular user account they use to log onto a machine or network. This account should give them access to ONLY what they HAVE TO have to do their job. The su or sudo commands can give a standard user temporary admin access for a single command or group of commands.

## su Command

The "su" command enables a user to switch to another user account and access all of its privileges. If the user is a sysadmin, the person probably knows the root user's password. In this case, they could use the **su** (switch user) command. Using just **su** implies you are switching to the root user account so adding root to **su** is not required. Like most commands, **su** has several options that can be used. The most commonly used one is

© Ahmed F. Sheikh 2024
A. F. Sheikh, *CompTIA Linux+ Certification Companion*, Certification Study Companion Series,
https://doi.org/10.1007/979-8-8688-0128-0_14

the "-" which not only changes the user to root but also changes the environment to that of the root user. Another good option is the **-c** option; it changes to root, executes the command, and then put you back in your standard user's environment.

## sudo Command

A second way a user can execute a command is with the **sudo** command. You type **sudo** plus the command, and the command is executed with root access. The "sudo" command permits a user to run a particular command with the privileges of another user.

In most distributions, the user doesn't have to know the root password. In order for the **sudo** command to work, the /etc/sudoers configuration file must give you the proper access.

Always use the **visudo** command to edit the /etc/sudoers file. It opens the file in **vi**, but it also checks for errors as it saves the changes.

## Sudoers File

The /etc/sudoers file is a list of which users or computers can do what without having the root password. It uses two types of entries: aliases and specifications.

- Think of the term *alias* more as a variable than the normal meaning of the word alias. It is more like a group to which permissions can be assigned.

- The *specification* is like permissions. It is used to say what an alias can do and to what resource.

The alias has to be defined before it can be used. Aliases are defined in one of the four basic sections of the sudoers file:

- User_Alias
- Cmnd_Alias
- Host_Alias
- Runas_Alias

The *User_Alias* assigns a name to a list of one or more users and is used later in the sudoers file to say what those users can do and to what resources.

- User_Alias PRINTERS = sspade, knguyen

- User_Alias INSTALLERS = dvanburen, squeue

The *Cmnd_Alias* sets an alias for specific commands. A common example is the install command. Normally, you would need root access to install something like the package yum.

- Cmnd_Alias INSTALL = /user/bin/yum

- Cmnd_Alias PRINT_CMDS = /usr/sbin/lpc, /usr/sbin/lprm

The *Host_Alias* lists hosts on which commands can be executed.

- Host_Alias SERVERS = serv1, serv2, serv3

The *Runas_Alias* lists user names that are tasked to run specific commands that require root access and a password (the %administrators is a group that exists on a system).

- Runas_Alias ADMINS = root, %administrators

After the aliases (or variables) are defined, you can then use them to assign an action. The format or syntax that makes these assignments in the /etc/sudoers file is: User + Host = Runas + Authentication + Command

- PRINTERS SERVERS = (ADMINS)PRINT_CMDS

- INSTALLERS ALL = (ADMINS) NOPASSWD: PRINT_CMDS

The Authentication option is either **PASSWD** where the user must use the password tied to their user account or **NOPASSWD** where a password is not required.

# User Security Administration

User password security was covered in a Chapter 6, but a quick review might be helpful.

## Passwd and Shadow File

User passwords and aging requirements are stored in the shadow file which has to stay synchronized with the passwd file. Having two files make it that much harder for a hacker to retrieve the list of passwords.

## passwd Command

The **passwd** command is used to create or change a password. Remember that a password can't be changed by anyone other than the root account.

## usermod Command

The command **usermod** is used to modify account information. More can be found on its man page.

## chage Command

The **chage** command is used to change password expiry information in / shadow file.

# Best Practices

Best practices were discussed when working with passwords in Chapter 6, but more have been added here. The chapter covered using upper and lower case letters, numbers and special characters when creating your password, and to make it at least eight characters long. It also mentions that you should NEVER use a word that can be found in the dictionary. They can be "cracked" too easily using most password cracking tools that can easily be found on the Internet.

One thing not covered was social engineering. That is where someone either asks for your password outright or obtains enough information from you to guess what it is. You should not use the name of friends, family, or pets. Most of that information can be obtained from the Internet. Never give your password to anyone including a tech working on your PC, close friend, or family member. Also NEVER write your password down and put it in a convenient place you can reach.

One last item pertaining to password security is the password should be changed periodically. Unfortunately, we humans will put this off if we are not forced to make the change. You can set the number of days after which you should change your password. This will range from 30 to 120 days depending on who is setting the policy. Even at home, you should periodically change your password.

### Key Facts

### Best Practices when working with passwords

- Do NOT use a word that can be found in the dictionary.

- Include uppercase, lowercase, numbers, and a special symbol.

- Make the password at least eight characters but more is preferable.

- Never write the password down and save it.

- NEVER give it to anyone – even someone you trust.

- Select a phrase you can remember and use the first letter of each work – then add a few numbers and special characters.

- Always set to expire and lock the account if password is not changed.

# User Limits

The amount of resources used by applications in a terminal session should always be set using the **ulimit** command.

Without these limits, the machine could be shut down by running the system out of resources. If a hacker gets into your system, limits will prevent the machine from shutting down. Even a user could accidentally do the same thing.

The main thing to remember about setting limits with **ulimit** is that they only apply to terminal sessions or shells. They do not work in the GUI.

The description of most of the options shown in Table 14-1 is easy to understand; the Hard (-H) and Soft (-S) option need more detail.

- A hard setting is the maximum that can be used. A process cannot run if it exceeds this limit.

- A soft setting is a little more flexible in that a process can temporarily exceed the soft limit. Soft settings can be set by users as well as root. Hard settings can only be set by root.

**Table 14-1.**  *ulimit Command Options*

| Option | Description |
|--------|-------------|
| -a | Displays existing limits |
| -S | Sets a soft resource limit |
| -H | Sets a hard resource limit |
| -u | Limits number of concurrent processes that can be run |
| -t | Limits the amount of time in seconds a process can use the CPU |
| -n | Limits the number of files open |
| -d | Limits the number of kb of RAM a process can use |
| -f | Limits file size in blocks of files created in a terminal session |
| -m | Physical memory size in kilobytes (kB) |
| -R | Maximum process running time in microseconds |
| -v | Maximum virtual memory available for processes |

# Changing Limits

To change these limits, you need to modify the /etc/security/limits.conf file
(Figure 14-1). There are four parts of each limit you set:

- entity

- type

- limit

- value

The *entity* can be asterisk for all, a user's name, or a group name preceded by an
ampersand. The *type* is either hard or soft. The *limits* shown in Figure 14-1 are the most
used of the options. The *value* is a number to indicate the number of times, seconds, or
kilobyte used by the limit.

| Entity | Limit | Description |
|--------|-------|-------------|
| User_name | core | Limits size of core dump file in kb |
| @group_name | data | Limits amount of RAM an application can use in kb |
|  | rss | Limits amount of RAM that can be used by user in kb |
| * | cpu | Limits amount of time a process can use the CPU in minutes |
|  | fsize | Limits the size of a file in kb |
| **Type** | nofile | Limits the number of open files |
| Hard | nproc | Limits the number of processes that can run at the same time |
| Soft | maxlogins | Limits the maximum number of concurrent logins |
|  | priority | Sets process priority limits |

*Figure 14-1.* *Syntax used in limits.conf file*

### Key Facts

- The /etc/security/limits.conf file is used to limit resources that can be used by applications.

- Syntax – <Entity>   <Type>   <Limit>   <Value>

- Example – Julie       hard     maxlogins     3

# Auditing Files

A big security risk involves files that give too much access to too many people. Audit for this type file is on a regular basis. Create a cron job that will review the permissions on all files on a system and report any risks to the root user in a file. That file can then be used to "close" this security hole.

The SUID bit can help or hurt you. Rather than say it should never be used on a file, a regular review should be done to verify the file really should have this bit set. The SUID bit allows any user to execute the file in the same way as the owner of the file. Since many applications require root access to execute a command, that does give a standard user lots of access on that file.

The **ping** command is an example. Any user can execute the **ping** commands since the SUID bit is set. Using the find command, you can start at the root directory and look at the permissions on all files. The files with the u=s permission should be recorded and reviewed.

Files that are both writeable and executable are risks that should be audited. If a file is writeable, it can be modified to perform harmful tasks. If it is also executable, then the tasks can be performed (Table 14-2). Using the find command, you can start at the root directory and look for all files with the permissions –o=w,-o=x. If any files are located, the permissions should be modified right away.

***Table 14-2.*** *Permissions That Can Create a Security Risk*

| Permission | Description |
|---|---|
| X | Execute |
| W | Write |
| S | SUID |

In addition to auditing permissions on files, monitor what files are open. Again, by creating a cron job, you can periodically produce a report of what files are open at a time when the machine is usually dormant. You could catch some inappropriate activity that way.

The following are examples of where an entity has a permission that could be exploited:

- Groups have execute permissions on a file: -g=x

- Owner of file has execute permissions: -u=x

- Others have write permissions on a file: -o=w

- SUID bit: -u=s

# Host Security

You have looked at ways to secure your system with password protection, removing unneeded permissions to files, and setting limits on resources. Now consider a few other areas where we can help better secure our machines and network.

During the normal Linux installation many more services are installed and started than are actually needed or used. These should be removed. Your distribution's init.d directory (/etc/init.d or /etc/rc.d/init.d) is where those services or scripts are located. Review them all to see what can be removed. You will probably find many with which you are not familiar; use the **man** command to learn what they do or google them. Before removing what you think are unneeded services, it is a good idea to disable it and see if anyone yells. The **chkconfig**, **init**, and **insserv** commands can all help with this process. Using the command **chkconfig <service> off** will disable the service at all run levels which means it will never start at boot up. Stop the services using the command **<service> STOP**. After you are comfortable that the services or application is really not being used, you should remove it with the appropriate **rpm** command.

### Key Facts

- Disable before uninstalling – **chkconfig <service> off**

- Uninstall service or application – **rpm –e <package>**

## Open Network Connections (Sockets)

One of the areas where hackers can crawl into a system is through an open port or an open socket. The **netstat** command (Figure 14-2) shows information such as open network connections (open sockets), your routing table, and your interfaces. The options in Table 14-3 are only a few of what is available for use with **netstat**, but these are the ones used to see what network connections are open. Again, if you determine the socket should not be listening, close it and remove the services/application.

### Key Facts

### Open network connections (sockets)

- **Netstat** – network statistics – displays TCP/IP network connections and protocol statistics.

- Syntax – **netstat <option>**.

***Table 14-3.***  *netstat Command Options*

| Option | Description |
|--------|-------------|
| -a | Displays all listening ports and connections |
| -at | Displays TCP connections only |
| -al | Displays listening sockets only |
| -i | Displays a table of every network interface |
| -s | Displays per protocol stats |
| -p | Displays only specified protocol |

```
[root tecmint-centos8:~]█ netstat -ant
Active Internet connections (servers and established)
Proto Recv-Q Send-Q Local Address           Foreign Address         State
tcp        0      0 192.168.122.1:53        0.0.0.0:*               LISTEN
tcp        0      0 0.0.0.0:22              0.0.0.0:*               LISTEN
tcp        0      0 127.0.0.1:631           0.0.0.0:*               LISTEN
tcp        0      0 0.0.0.0:25              0.0.0.0:*               LISTEN
tcp        0      0 0.0.0.0:111             0.0.0.0:*               LISTEN
tcp        0      0 192.168.43.13:44926     216.58.223.106:443      ESTABLISHED
tcp        0      0 192.168.43.13:45048     3.227.150.182:443       ESTABLISHED
tcp        0      0 192.168.43.13:51392     52.45.212.92:443        TIME_WAIT
tcp        0      0 192.168.43.13:36176     99.84.13.50:80          ESTABLISHED
tcp        0      0 192.168.43.13:36736     93.184.220.29:80        TIME_WAIT
tcp        0      0 192.168.43.13:45046     3.227.150.182:443       ESTABLISHED
tcp        0      0 192.168.43.13:51390     52.45.212.92:443        TIME_WAIT
```

***Figure 14-2.***  *Sample of **netstat** command*

# Open Ports

A great application that scans for open ports is Network Mapper (**nmap**). This is a free
application that all sysadmins should have in their tool kit. Using this tool allows you
to see what ports are open and ready to accept communications from other systems.
By default, many distributions install Apache, the web server most used by Linux.
Unless the machine on which it is installed is going to be a web service, this service is
not needed and should at the least be disabled. Using the –**sT** for TCP and –**sU** for UTP
options will give you a listing of open ports that use those protocols. You can either
search for information on each port on the Internet or in the /etc/services file.

## Key Facts

### Open Ports

- **nmap** – application that scans for open ports

- Syntax for TCP scan – **nmap –sT <ip_address>**

- Syntax for UDP scan – **nmap –sU <ip_address>**

# Firewalls

Firewalls are good for blocking unwanted traffic coming into your system or leaving your system. Most firewalls are in routers or special appliances, but they can and are often now included in a single host. If your system is dual-homed (two NICS), it can act as a router. The /netfilter/iptables file stores the rules created by using the **iptables** command. You can set rules based on a source IP address, a destination IP address, a protocol, or a packet status.

## Key Facts

### Firewalls

- Stores rules in /netfilter/iptables.

- Modify iptables with the **iptables** command.

- Chain of rules – no rules are set by default.

  - INPUT – packets coming into your computer

  - FORWARD – packets passing through your computer

  - OUTPUT – packets leaving your computer

- Rules can be set on source or destination IP address, protocol, or packet status.

# User Running a Service

The chapter has explained how to get rid of unneeded services and applications but did not discuss when a user is running the services that are required. Many of these required services must run as the root user, but if they do not, change the user. It is best to create and use a "service" account. You should also change the shell field in the /etc/passwd file to /sbin/nologin which will prevent those services accounts from actually logging into the system. If someone tries to login with a service account, they will get a message from the /sbin/nologin.txt file stating that the account can't log in. If that file does not exist, a generic message will be displayed.

Just like the operating system gets patches periodically, services are fixed or patched to close holes hackers have found. Because of this, you should always monitor for updates to your applications and services.

---

### Key Facts

### User Running a Service

- Change user running a service to a "service account" if possible.

- Set the shell field in the /etc/passwd file to /sbin/nologin.

- /sbin/nologin displays message in the /sbin/nologin.txt file if it exists.

---

# TCP Wrappers

To understand TCP wrappers, you first need to understand what a super daemon is. The xinetd daemon, which acts as a super daemon, is normally installed by default, and it acts as an interface between the user and the actual daemon. When a user asks for a service such as FTP or telnet, the super daemon gets the request, starts the service, and delivers it to the user. When the user is finished using the service, the super daemon stops the service. As a matter of fact, it can manage multiple requests at basically the same time.

This can be a good or a bad thing. It is good that it saves resources, but it is bad because it slows down the response to the user. Evaluate which is best for you, load the service as needed, or set it to load permanently.

A small change in the /etc/xinetd.conf file may be needed but that is rare. Usually it is the individual service configuration files that need to be updated. These are the files located in the /etc/xinetd.d directory. Be careful not to confuse these configuration files with the ones that set up how the service will run. Those only direct how the service will be stopped and started by the xinetd super daemon. If you need a service to NOT be started by xinetd, make sure the value of the disable parameter is set to "yes." This means the service will not be controlled by xinetd. Remember, any time you make a change, you need to restart the service.

If you want to use a TCP wrapper to add more security, add more parameters to the service's configuration file in the /etc/xinetd.d directory. Tell xinetd to use the tcpd daemon rather than the service's daemon and the location of the actual service's daemon. Next, you have to configure the /etc/hosts.allow and /etc/hosts.deny files. Those two files act as a type of access control list; hosts.deny is read first-then host.allow. Again, don't forget to restart the service that was updated.

Xinetd super daemon's predecessor, inetd, is also considered a super daemon, because it also controlled how services were started. The biggest difference in the two is that inetd had a line for each service that outlined how it would start while xinted has a single file for each service in the xinetd.d directory. Also, TCP wrappers can't be used with inetd.

# Encryption

To gain an understanding about encryption, you must understand why it is needed. Transmitting information across the wire has been done for a long time, but security was not an issue in the distant past. Telnet was used to make connections to remote machines. All information including a password was sent in clear text for anyone to see. A savvy hacker would put a sniffer, such as Wireshark, on the wire, and grab your data. Today, **telnet** is very seldom used except maybe for troubleshooting. Encryption is required on anything that leaves a secure environment; it is not always safe on your own network. The following material provides a beginning foundation of knowledge needed to properly secure a Linux network or any network.

Encryption is a method used to encode data so that only the users with the proper key can decode it. There are two types of encryption used today: Asymmetric and Symmetric.

# Asymmetric Key Encryption

Asymmetric key encryption uses a key pair which includes a public key that is known to everyone and a private key that is only known to the owner of the key. Data is encrypted by the sender with the recipient's public key and decrypted by the recipient with their private key. The secrecy of this key pair is imperative. If you even think it has been compromised, a new key pair should be generated.

# Symmetric Key Encryption

Symmetric key encryption uses a single key to encrypt and decrypt data. This type of encryption is also known as secret key, private key, or pre-shared key. The key has to be exchanged before encrypted data should be sent. Can you see a problem with this? Yes, if a hacker is capturing traffic to a user's computer, how does the sender get that key to the recipient? Other than hand delivering it, the only secure way is to use some form of asymmetric encryption to send it.

Both asymmetric and symmetric key encryptions are still widely used, and each has its place. Table 14-4 summarizes the features of each.

***Table 14-4.*** *Asymmetric and Symmetric Keys*

| Asymmetric | Symmetric |
| --- | --- |
| Key pair (public/private) | Single key |
| More CPU intensive than symmetric | Less CPU intensive than asymmetric |
| Most secure | Less secure |
| Only one key pair required | Different key needed for each user pair (sender/receiver) |
| Provides confidentiality, authenticity, and non-repudiation | Only provides confidentiality |
| The length of key is 2048 bits or higher | The length of key is 128 or 256 bits |
| Slow encryption process | Very fast encryption process |
| Used to transmit small data | Used to transmit big data |

Table 14-5 lists the most common encryption standards used today and shows which type of key it uses.

*Table 14-5.* *Commonly Used Encryption Standards*

| Standard | Asymmetric | Symmetric |
|---|---|---|
| RSA – Rivest, Shamir Adleman | X | |
| DSA – Digital Signature Algorithm | X | |
| Diffie-Hellman Key Exchange | X | |
| ECC – Elliptic-curve cryptography | X | |
| DES – Data Encryption Standard | | X |
| 3DES – Triple DES | | X |
| AES – Advanced Encryption Standard | | X |
| Blowfish | | X |
| Twofish | | X |

# Secure Shell

Secure Shell (**SSH**) is the tool that is used to encrypt data as it crosses a network. Linux uses an open source version of SSH called OpenSSH. **SSH** version 1 is seldom used any more since it is less secure than version 2. Version 2 uses both RSA for encryption and DSA for digital signatures; version 1 only used RSA.

The first time a system boots, it loads the sshd daemon and creates a system-wide key pair which is stored in the /etc/ssh directory.

---

**Key Facts**

**Secure Shell v2 (SSH) Daemon - sshd**

- **OpenSSH** – open source version of SSH

- Installed by default – uses port 22

- Loads automatically with runlevel 5

- Uses RSA for encryption and DSA for digital signature

- System-wide key pairs

  - Created first time **ssh** daemon starts

  - Stored in /etc/ssh directory

# Connection with SSH

There are two ways you can connect to a server using SSH. Note the first one that does not list a user name will attempt to connect using the current user's login and password. If that account doesn't exist on the server, the connection will be denied. You can add a user name that does exist on the server, such as root, using the –l option.

Upon your first connection, information is then stored in the ~/.ssh/known_hosts file on the server and can be used for future connections. If the user ever has to regenerate their keys, the known_hosts file has to be removed so the new information can be added.

---

### Key Facts

### Remote connection with SSH

- Connects using current user name / password

  - Syntax – **ssh <host_name or IP address>**

- Connects using remote host's <user_name> / password

  - Syntax – **ssh –l <user_name> <host_name or IP address>** OR
    **ssh <user_name>@<domain>**

- Connection information is stored in the ~/.ssh/known_hosts file or the /etc/ssh/ssh_known_hosts file

- Regenerate keys with **ssh-keygen**

---

# Key Pair

To make an SSH connection even more secure, you can generate a key pair (Figure 14-3), which creates the files shown below. Rather than logging in with a user account's password, you can then use your new key pair. Your public key will be stored on the remote host in the user's /.ssh/authorized_key file. In fact, this key can be added to any remote host to which you want to connect – in this same file. You will still be asked to provide a passphrase which is required by the local ssh process – not the remote host.

```
[root@tecmint ~]# ssh-keygen
Generating public/private rsa key pair.
Enter file in which to save the key (/root/.ssh/id_rsa): /root/.ssh/prod_rsa
Enter passphrase (empty for no passphrase):
Enter same passphrase again:
Your identification has been saved in /root/.ssh/prod_rsa.
Your public key has been saved in /root/.ssh/prod_rsa.pub.
The key fingerprint is:
SHA256:jzN8wSstBr2kv5oxVds/1G4vbRcqE4zz4saNTClrRYk root@tecmint
The key's randomart image is:
+---[RSA 3072]----+
|                 |
|                 |
|       . o       |
|      E = o   .  |
|     . S B . . . |
|      B @ = o o  |
|      + ^ X . +.+|
|      0 % = ..o= |
|      +.=o. o  oo|
+----[SHA256]-----+
[root@tecmint ~]# █
```

*Figure 14-3.*  *Sample of how to generate a key pair*

## Key Facts

### Generating keys

- **ssh-keygen –t rsa**

  - id_ras – user's RSA private key

  - id_ras.pub – user's RSA public key

- **ssh-keygen –t dsa**

  - id_das – user's DSA private key

  - id_das.pub – user's DSA public key

- Public key is stored on remote host in the ~/.ssh/authorized_key file

You will now learn how to get the public key you just generated to the remote host. First you need to learn how to manually copy the public key files to a remote host using the remote file copy program or secure copy (**scp**). An example of the syntax of this command is **scp ~/.ss/id_dsa.pub sspade@linux.org:.ssh/authorized_keys**. Remember the user name, sspade in the example, is an account on the remote host and not on your local machine. You will then be asked for that user's password. It is a good idea to verify the ~/.ssh directory exists on the remote host before starting the copy.

You can also manually copy the public key from the .ssh_dsa.pub file using the **cat** command to view the file's contents. Open the ~/.ssh/authorized_keys file on the host with a text editor and paste the key there.

Those both seem easy enough but the automatic way of installing your public key is even easier. Using the **ssh-copy-id** command and a valid user name on the remote host copies the key and puts it in the proper file for you. You still have to supply the remote user's password though.

Now when you use ssh to connect to the remote host, you will be asked for the key pair's passphrase rather than the user's password.

---

## Key Facts

## Getting the Public Key to the Remote Host

## Manual

- scp ~/.ssh/id_dsa.pub  <username>@<domain>:.ssh/authorized_keys

- Enter password of user on remote host

## Manual

- cat ~/.ssh/id_dsa.pub

- Copy the key and Paste key in remote host's ~/.ssh/authorized_keys file using an editor

## Automatic

- ssh-copy-id username>@<domain>

- Enter password of user on remote host

---

# SSH-Agent Utility

Using the ssh-agent programs allows you to use the **ssh-add** command to add the user's passphrase to the ssh-agent so you will not be prompted for it each time it is required.

You can view the passwords and encryption keys from the GUI in Applications ➤ Accessories ➤ Passwords and Encryption Keys.

---

## Key Facts

### Using the ssh-agent utility

- Starts before X windows starts.
- All other X windows programs run through the ssh-agent.
- Use **ssh-add** to add your passphrase to the agent.
- After providing the passphrase, the user's identity is added to the ssh-agent.
- The ssh-agent will then automatically provide the passphrase when asked.

---

# SSH Configuration Options

The list below shares the various options that are often configured on the server and the client so they can communicate. The server side has to say what port is used and using what protocol. It can list users that are allowed access or denied access. The client side has to match the server side, or they can't establish a connection.

---

## Key Facts

### Configuring SSH

- Server configuration
    - /etc/ssh/sshd_config
        - Options – Protocol, AllowUsers, DenyUsers, Port, PasswordAuthentication

- Client configuration

  - ~/.ssh/config or /etc/ssh/ssh_config

    - Options – Protocol, Port, User, CheckHostIP

- Authentication and encryption between server and host has to match.

# SSH Port Tunneling

SSH port tunneling takes data that is usually not secure and encrypts it before sending it across the wire. Examples are X server and e-mail. In order to use SSH tunneling, each user has to generate their own key pair. The **ssh-keygen** command is used to create both the RSA and DSA key pair and the pair is stored in the ~/.ssh directory. You will need to make changes to the server's configuration file also.

### Key Facts

- Configure options in the server's configuration file – /etc/ssh/sshd_config

  - Options: X11Forwarding, ForwardX11, AllowTcpForwarding, ForwardX11Trusted

# SSH Authentication

SSH can use several different methods to authenticate. Challenge-response is the default method used by OpenSSH. This form of authentication asks a question (challenge) and expects a correct answer, such as a password (response). Kerberos can also be used. Another method is to use a file that lists the users and/or hosts that are trusted to make a connection.

Table 14-6 lists the types of encryption used by OpenSSH and a little information about each.

**Table 14-6.** *Encryption Standards Used with SSH*

| Standards | Key Length | Notes |
|---|---|---|
| Triple Data Encryption Standard (3DES) | 168-bit | Three stages – blocks |
| Advanced Encryption Standard (AES) | 128-, 192-, 256-bit | Improvement on 3DES |
| Blowfish | 448-bit | Faster than 3DES |
| Carlisle Adams Stafford Tavares (CAST) | 128-bit | General purpose |
| ARCfour | 2048-bit | Fast – streams |

# GNU Privacy Guard

Linux uses the open source version of PGP (Pretty Good Privacy) to digitally sign e-mail and to encrypt its content. When you digitally sign an e-mail, it shows that it has not been changed along the way to its recipient. It also uses RSA and DSA along with several others to encrypt and digitally sign e-mail.

You can view the keys on the key ring using the **gpg –list-keys** command or from the Passwords and Encryption Keys GUI interface.

---

### Key Facts

GNU Privacy Guard (GPG)

- Encrypts and digitally signs e-mail and encrypts content of e-mail

- Open source version of  Pretty Good Privacy (PGP)

- Uses RSA and others for encryption

- Uses DSA and ElGamal by default for digital signing

- Stored in ~/.gnupg directory

- Trust model – sender digitally signs content with recipient's public key – recipient decrypts with their private key

- Manage with gpg command or Passwords and Encryption Keys

---

# Key Exchange and Encryption Example

Figure 14-4 shows you how key exchange and encryption is done. Sam gives Susie his public key in any way he wants: e-mail, hand delivery, or adding it to a public key server. This key can be seen by anyone; it is not secret as is the private key. Susie uses Sam's public key to encrypt a file and then sends the encrypted file to Sam. Sam uses his private key to decrypt the encrypted file. Anyone that can get this encrypted file can't decipher its contents unless they have Sam's private key.

## Step 1 – Sam gives Susie his public key

## Step 2 –Susie uses Sam's public key to encrypt File_A

## Step 3 –Susie sends Sam the Encrypted File_A

## Step 4 –Sam uses his private key to decrypt Encrypted File_A

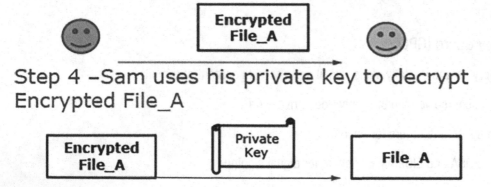

***Figure 14-4.*** *Example of key exchange and encryption*

# GPG Options

Table 14-7 describes the most commonly used **gpg** options. These options are the ones commonly used with this command and only represent a small portion of the available options.

Note the last option, **--gen-revoke <key-ID>**. If you need to stop using a key pair because of something such as the key pair has been compromised, you need to revoke that key-ID and notify anyone using that key pair. You can then start over by generating a new key pair.

***Table 14-7.*** *Most Commonly Used GPG Options*

| GPG/GPG2 Options | Description |
| --- | --- |
| --gen-key | Generates a key pair |
| --export <username>  >  <public.key> | Creates a public key file |
| --export-secret-key  <username>   > <priv.key> | Creates a private key file so it can be backed up for safekeeping |
| --import <public.key> | Imports public keys into key ring |
| --list-keys | Lists keys on key ring |
| --delete-secret-key <username> | Deletes the private key from key ring |
| --delete-key <uscrname> | Deletes the public key from key ring |
| --output <file.gpg> --recipient <username> --encrypt <file> | Encrypts a file to a new name |
| --output <file_ungpg> --decrypt <file.gpg> | Decrypts an encrypted file |
| --clearsign <file> | Digitally signs a file |
| --verify <filename> | Compares a file against all keys in key ring |
| --gen-revoke <key-ID> | Creates key revocation certificate |
| --sign | Creates a digital signature |
| -r | Encrypts for the given user |

# Summary

- Securing the password for the root user account is very important to the overall security of your host and network. Since root has "keys to the kingdom," it should be the most protected user account on any host. Rather than logging in as the root user, always use a regular account that has the appropriate access. If you have the root user's password, you can use the **su** command to switch users to root and perform any necessary task, then change back to your regular user account.

- Another way to execute a command that requires root access is to use **sudo** before the command. When the /etc/sudoers file is properly configured, a regular user can execute a command that requires root permissions without knowing the root password.

- Even though passwords are encrypted in the /etc/passwd and /etc/shadow files, permissions to access those files should be very limited. Special care in modifying those accounts and keeping them in sync is important.

- The **ulimit** command should be used to control the amount of resources that can be used by applications and processes. Without these limits, a hacker who gains access to your host could execute a process that would run it out of resources which would take down your host.

- Auditing files and folders periodically (according to corporate policy) will monitor who is accessing your resources. It is common for a user to be given too much access – more than they need to do their job. By performing audits, a sysadmin can catch improper access as well as suspicious activity.

- Removing unneeded applications, stopping services that don't need to run, and closing unused network connections further protect your system from intruders. Commands such as **netstat**, **chkconfig**, and **rpm** can help with this process.

- Properly configured firewalls can block unwanted traffic from coming into or leaving your host.

- Encryption is the method used to encode data that is traveling from one host to another. A key or a key pair is used to encrypt data so only the intended recipient can decode the data for review. Secure Shell (**SSH**) is the tool most commonly used to encrypt data.

# CHAPTER 15

# Working with Files, Directories, and Permissions

In this chapter, you'll acquire knowledge on effectively overseeing, finding, and organizing files and directories. Additionally, you'll grasp the customization of permissions and the utilization of text editors. By the conclusion of this chapter, you'll have the ability to

1. Efficiently handle files and directories

2. Locate both directories and files

3. Explain file structure and file linkage

4. Tailor permissions to your requirements

5. Employ Linux text editors to change files

## Managing Directories and Files

In order to maintain a well-structured system, it's essential to create directories and perform actions like moving, copying, and deleting files. Two instances of such actions are creating a directory using "mkdir" and removing a directory using "rmdir.

The key principle to bear in mind is that you move or copy FROM a location TO a location.

© Ahmed F. Sheikh 2024
A. F. Sheikh, *CompTIA Linux+ Certification Companion*, Certification Study Companion Series, https://doi.org/10.1007/979-8-8688-0128-0_15

Establishing an alias is a valuable function in Linux. When we define an alias, we essentially create an abbreviated form of a longer command. Think of it like programming a speed dial number on our phone. By pressing just one digit, we initiate a call to a lengthy string of numbers. Imagine we have a daily report that necessitates a command involving multiple options with precise variables – perhaps even up to 20 characters in length. Would we prefer to recall and type all 20 characters each time, or opt for a concise three- or four-letter name? This concise name becomes the alias for the lengthy 20-character command.

As a review, leveraging the period (.) and double period (..) significantly simplifies directory management. The period instructs the system to search for something within the present directory, sparing you from typing out the entire path name. On the other hand, the double period (..) enables us to navigate up one directory level. For instance, we can employ cd .. to ascend a level, avoiding the need to input the complete path.

Keep in mind the usefulness of wildcard characters, like * and ?, which prove invaluable when copying or moving multiple files that share similarities.

Commands for managing files and directories:

- mkdir <name> – creating a new directory

- mv <from> <to> – moving a directory or file

- cp <from> <to> – copying a directory or file

- rm <name> – removing a file

- rmdir <name> – removing a directory

- alias <name> <command> – generating a shortcut to another command

# Finding Directories and Files

Searching for directories or files can present its challenges. Fortunately, there are a few commands designed to assist with this task as shown in Table 15-1.

***Table 15-1.*** *Directories and Files Search*

| Command | Description |
|---|---|
| find  \<start dir> -\<criteria> \<name> | Scanning for a file from the root – slower<br>• Doesn't rely on a prebuilt database<br>• Conducts a thorough recursive search across the directory tree |
| which \<name> | Scans exclusively within directories listed in the $PATH environment variable |
| locate \<name> | Scans for a file from the root<br>• Relies on a prebuilt database that is updated regularly<br>• employ "updatedb" to manually update the database |

If you possess a starting point for your file or directory search, the find command proves useful. Unlike the locate command, it doesn't rely on the same database. Nevertheless, it systematically traverses through the directory tree starting from its current position.

The locate command initiates its search from the root, scanning through all available items. To optimize speed, a database meticulously logs the locations of all elements, constantly updated on a daily basis. If the need arises to reindex the database for any reason, simply execute the updatedb command.

The which command exclusively scans directories specified in the $PATH environment variable.

# Structure of Files

Every file system possesses a superblock, which contains crucial information like the count of data blocks and inodes.

A data block holds both the filename and the file's contents.

An inode, essentially an index node, uniquely identifies specific metadata within a given filesystem. The inode table comprehensively stores details about all inodes within the file system. Each file or directory corresponds to an inode, which holds metadata about them. Metadata includes ownership, the last update timestamp, and permissions – essentially, information about the data.

When a file is deleted, the file's content remains intact, but the inode associated with it is removed. This behavior is consistent in Windows as well, where the data persists, but the system loses knowledge of its location.

## Linking Files

In Linux, links are used when dealing with specific files and processes.

A symbolic link, analogous to a Windows shortcut, directs to another file. If a symbolic link is deleted, the original file or data remains unaffected. The two files are not obligated to reside on the same file system.

A hard link generates two distinct files that share identical data and the same inode, albeit potentially having different names. However, both files must coexist within the same file system.

Symbolic links have the capability to link directories to files or directories located on remote systems. Furthermore, they aid in conserving hard drive space by not storing actual data.

The "ln" command-line utility creates links between files, typically creating hard links by default. To create a symbolic link, utilize the -s option (Table 15-2).

***Table 15-2.***  *Commands for Linking Files*

| Command | Link Type |
| --- | --- |
| ln <file> <target file> | Hard link |
| ln –s <file> <target file> | Symbolic link |

# Ownership and Permissions

## Directory and File Permissions

Specific permissions are needed to access and modify a resource such as a file or directory. In Linux, there are three types of permissions, read, write, and execute, that can be granted to three different entities: users, groups, and everyone else. These three permissions are stored in the mode section of the inode. By default, users, groups, and everyone else get read and write permissions for newly created files, and the read, write, and execute permissions for directories.

The three permissions read, write, and execute have specific functions that are described below:

- The read permission (r) enables entities to open and read the contents of a file. They also allow the entities to list the contents of a directory, provided they have the execute permission as well.

- Write permission (w) allows entities to add and remove files from a directory, provided they also possess the execute permission. This permission also permits the entity to open and edit a file.

- Execute permission (x), in combination with read and/or write, allows entities to interact with the contents of a directory and execute a file.

# Ownership

"Ownership" and "Groups" are two terms that are commonly used when working with permissions. These are described below.

- **Ownership** pertains to the specific individual accountable for a file or directory, typically the user who initiated its creation. However, this ownership can be transferred to other users if the need arises.

- **Groups** operate in a manner akin to their counterparts in Windows. They serve as collections of user accounts, often organized based on roles or geographic locations.

Managers often require access to particular information that ordinary users cannot access. To simplify this process, a group named "Managers" can be established, with all the managers' user IDs added to the group. Permissions can then be applied to the entire group, streamlining the process rather than assigning permissions to each individual user.

This principle applies similarly to different geographic locations. For instance, users in Germany might require access to a set of documents written in German. To limit access to only those who need it, permissions can be allocated to a specific group for the users in Germany, ensuring that users in other locations do not have unnecessary access to that material.

# Setting Up Permissions and Ownership

The commands chown and chgrp are instrumental in handling ownership settings. Through these commands, a user can assume ownership of a file or a specific group.

In the two subsequent sections, you'll learn about methods to allocate or modify permissions, either through letter or value commands.

## Modifying Permissions Using Operators

Use the chmod command to configure permissions using letters. With this command, you can add permissions by using the plus sign followed by the necessary letter. Conversely, permissions can be removed by employing a minus sign with the corresponding letter. Lastly, the equal sign can be used to set permissions equal to a specific entity.

## Change Permissions Using Numbers

Permissions are typically set using numerical values corresponding to the rwx (read, write, execute) attributes. This system mirrors the principles of IPv4 subnetting. In this context, each permission bit holds a specific value: x in the 1st bit equals 1, w in the 2nd bit equals 2, and r in the 3rd bit equals 4. These permissions are stored in the inode as binary powers of two ($2^2$=4, $2^1$=2, $2^0$=1). To determine the permission number for an entity, you add up the values of the relevant bits.

**Example**

- For instance, the command "chmod 544 <file>" can assign read and execute permissions to the user, read permission to the group, and read permission to other on the specified file.

# Default Permission

It is crucial to understand the default permissions set for both files and directories.

For individuals accustomed to Windows systems, the concept of the umask command might be new. It operates similarly to the option in Novell that allows administrators to block the inheritance of permissions for files and directories. The unmask command enables you to establish default permissions for newly created files and folders.

With the umask command, you have the ability to adjust these default permissions. Typically, the default settings offer excessive access, which can pose security risks. The fundamental principle here is to provide only the necessary permissions and nothing more. It's important to note that in older versions of Windows, new files or directories were automatically given full control, allowing anyone to perform any action on them.

The umask command becomes valuable in this context, as it automatically reduces the default permissions. You can think of the umask number as a value you subtract from the maximum permissions to determine the actual permissions that are granted. By utilizing umask, you can ensure that files and directories start with the appropriate level of access, aligning with the principle of least privilege.

*Table 15-3.* *Set of Unmask Command*

| Command | Description |
| --- | --- |
| Umask | Dsiplays umask setting |
| umask 007 | Removes all permissions from other |

To check how the umask command is defined in your system, simply use the umask command (Table 15-3) on its own. If you decide to alter this default setting, ensure you add it to the /etc/bashrc or /etc/profile files. This guarantees that the modified permissions are applied universally for all users.

# Special Permissions

There are three specific permissions – SUID, SGID, and sticky bit – that can be applied to simplify the process of setting permissions. These specific permissions are relevant only when the execute permission is granted.

When the SUID is assigned to a file using a value of 4, the user executing the file temporarily assumes ownership of it. A practical example is the ping command: rather than granting separate permission to the user for the ping file, a value 4 can be added alongside the regular permissions.

Similarly, the SGID operates on the principle of temporarily granting group membership. If a user needs to execute a file requiring membership in a specific group, setting a value of 2 for SGID temporarily assigns group membership, allowing the user to execute the file without being a permanent member of that group.

The sticky bit can be used to modify the write permission on a directory. It allows a user to add files and delete files they added to that directory; however, it does not allow the user to delete any other files.

It is important to remember that these special permissions only come into effect if the execute permission has been granted.

Special permissions are incorporated alongside regular permissions by adding their respective values at the front. You have the flexibility to use SGID alone with a value of 2, SUID on its own with 4, the sticky bit alone with 1, or any combination of these. For instance, using all three special permissions together would result in a value of 7 (4+2+1).

Upon inspecting the permissions of a directory or file following the setup of a special permission, the representation might resemble the examples in Figure 15-1. In cases where the execute permission bit is not set, lowercase letters replace the "x." Alternatively, if the execute permission is absent, you would observe a capital "S" or "T" in its place.

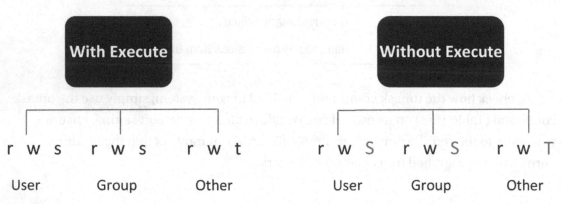

*Figure 15-1.* *Special permissions*

# Text Editors

There are two popular text editors frequently utilized in Linux:

- Vi (pronounced vee eye) is likely the oldest text editor and is utilized in both Linux and in UNIX.

- Gedit is a graphical user interface (GUI) text editor resembling Notepad in Windows. Gedit possesses fewer features compared to vi but is more user-friendly.

To establish yourself as a proficient Linux user, mastering the use of vi is essential.

# The vi Editor

In Linux systems, the equivalent of the vi text editor is Vim, an enhanced and refined version of the original vi. During installation, an alias is established, allowing users to employ either the "vi" or "vim" command interchangeably. An alias essentially acts as a shortcut that invokes and executes another command. The popularity of vi in UNIX led to its inclusion in Linux, as many original users favored it over graphical user interface (GUI) applications.

The transition to using vi might initially prove challenging for those accustomed to a mouse-driven interface, as vi relies solely on keyboard input. It's worth noting that many Linux experts predominantly work in terminal sessions, sometimes even text-only environments devoid of a GUI. In many scenarios, working with the keyboard alone can actually be more efficient when utilizing the right tools.

---

### The vi Editor

- Vim, often referred to as "vi," is the enhanced version of the original vi editor.

- Vim is a standard and indispensable tool found in nearly all Linux and UNIX distributions, making it a valuable skill to acquire.

- Vi can be a bit challenging to master, particularly because it doesn't support mouse input. You'll rely solely on keyboard commands, so learning the shortcuts is essential.

---

One aspect that can pose challenges when first using vi is understanding and transitioning between its two primary modes: Command mode and Insert mode.

- Command mode – In this mode, you can perform tasks such as saving edited text, searching within a document, and exiting vi.

- Insert mode – This is where you actually edit the text. You need to switch out of Insert mode to save a file.

## Gedit Editor

The gedit text editor is known for its versatility in editing text files. Users can open multiple files simultaneously and utilize various encodings. Additionally, its integration with both the terminal and GUI enhances its flexibility and user-friendliness. While suitable for quick edits, gedit lacks the extensive capabilities of vi.

In Fedora, you can locate gedit under the Accessories category.

# Summary

After reading this chapter, you've gained knowledge about managing directories, files, and permissions. Here are the key takeaways:

- The move (mv), make directory (mkdir), remove (rm), copy (cp), and remove directory (rmdir) commands facilitate file system operations.

- The commands locate and find aid in searching for directories and files.

- Wildcards prove helpful when working with files, allowing for versatile and efficient file operations.

- Creating symbolic and hard links between files is useful to save storage space and reduce the necessity for multiple inodes, optimizing file management.

- Access permissions for files and directories are granted to the user owner, group owner, and others, controlling their access levels.

- Vi stands out as a potent text editor widely used for its extensive functionality.

- If you prefer a graphical interface, gedit is a user-friendly text editor based on GUI.

# Index

## A

Accessibility, 97–102

/acct/acct.cpio, 213

acct.tar, 212

acct.tar.gz, 212

Addresses
  binary values, 222, 223
  IPv4 address, 220–222
  IPv4 address classes, 223, 224
  physical and logical, 219, 220
  subnet mask, 224

Advanced Research Project Agency
      Network (ARPANET), 216

Aliases, 258, 259

&& chaining operator, 43, 44

ANDing process, 224
  broadcast address, 225
  converting hex to binary/decimal,
      229, 230
  default gateway, 225
  examples, 225
  IPv4 addresses, 226
  IPv4 vs. IPv6, 226–228
  IPv6 address, 228, 230

Application Programming Interface
      (API), 78

Archiving
  backup, 210, 211
  cpio, 211–213
  tar, 211–212
  Tarballs, 211

utilities, 211

Assistive Technologies (AT), 98, 109

Asymmetric key encryption, 270

AT Preferred Applications, 104

Auditing files, 263, 264

Automatic Private Internet Protocol
      Addressing (APIPA), 234

## B

Bash (Bourne Again SHell), 165

BASH functions, 26

Basic input/output system (BIOS), 58, 59

Binary values, 222, 223

32-bit address, 220

Bit values, 221, 222

Boot loader
  common, 60
  GRUB, 60, 61
  GRUB2, 62–64
  GRUB parameters, 61, 62
  GRUB_TIMEOUT option, 64
  kernel, 59
  LILO, 60
  Linux installations, 59
  operating systems, 59
  options, /etc/default/grub file, 65

Boot process
  BIOS, 58, 59
  Fedora, 57, 58

Bourne shell (sh), 165

Broadcast address, 223, 225, 226

© Ahmed F. Sheikh 2024
A. F. Sheikh, *CompTIA Linux+ Certification Companion*, Certification Study Companion Series,
https://doi.org/10.1007/979-8-8688-0128-0

BSD distributions, 69
Bzip2 utility, 209, 210

## C

Case construct, 39–41
Case statement, 40, 41
Central Standard Time (CST), 159
|| chaining operators, 43, 44
Changing limits, 262, 263
chkconfig command, 70
chmod command, 33
CIDR notation, 224
Classless InterDomain Routing
        (CIDR), 223
Client/server model, 53, 54
Cmnd_Alias, 259
Coldplug devices, 117
Command line interface (CLI), 164
Common regular expressions, 205
Common shells, 164, 165
Common Unix Printing System
        (CUPS), 190–192
    configuration, 193
    print job management, 194, 195
Complementary metal-oxide
        semiconductor chip (CMOS), 58
Compression
    bzip2 utility, 209, 210
    commands used, 208
    GNU Utility, 208, 209
    utilities, 207, 208
CompTIA's Linux+, 6
Connection-oriented protocol, 218
Constructs, 33
Cpio, 212, 213
cron command, 147, 151

## D

Databases, 125
    client/server model, 53, 54
    design, 53
    relational, 52
    SQL, 52
D-Bus daemon, 117
Debian Package Manager (DPM), 247, 251
Debian's Advanced Packaging Tool
        (APT), 251
Decision construct, 34
Default gateway, 225
Default permissions, 288, 289
Default router, 236
Dependency, 246
Desktop environment, 79–81, 88, 109
Desktop Themes, 107, 108
Device drivers, 111
    implementation, 111, 112
    /proc directory, 112
    /sys directory, 113
    tools, 113, 114
Device management, 117
dig, 241
Direct memory access (DMA), 112
Directories
    commands, 284
    creation, 283
    double period, 284
    and file permissions, 286, 287
    and files search, 284, 285
    mkdir, 283
    period instructs, 284
    rmdir, 283
Directory structure
    filename extensions, 203
    filesystem hierarchy, 201, 202

file types, 202, 203

hierarchical tree structure, 199

Linux, 199, 200

Windows, 199, 200

Display Managers

accessibility, 97–102

accessibility key controls, 101

configuration, 90

configuration steps, X Server, 92

Desktop Themes, 107, 108

enable AT Support, 103

GDM, 96, 97

gdm.conf file sections, 97

GOK main menu, 104

KDM, 96

Mouse Accessibility, 102, 103

Onscreen keyboards, 106

options, Orca Application, 104

Preferred Applications menu, 105

Remote X Window, 95

Screen readers, 107

visual and mobility accessibility
    options, 105, 106

Windows, 90

XDM, 93

Xresources file options, 94

X terminal/X station, 91, 92

DNS configuration

/etc/hosts, 238

/etc/nsswitch.conf file, 239

/etc/resolv.conf, 238, 239

name resolution, 237, 238

DOS shell, 164

Dumb terminal, 91

Dynamic configuration, 234

Dynamic Host Configuration Protocol
    (DHCP), 220, 234, 235, 239,
    242, 243

Dynamic ports, 231

Dynamic shared libraries, 252

## E

echo command, 30

elif commands, 38

Encryption

asymmetric key encryption, 270

GPG, 277, 279, 280

and key exchange, 278

RSA, 271

SSH (*see* Secure Shell (SSH))

standards, 270, 271

symmetric key encryption, 270

telnet, 269

End-user applications, 219

Enhanced Simple Mail Transfer Protocol
    (ESMTP), 187

Entity, 262, 264

Environment variables, 23, 24, 167

PATH, 168, 169

types, 167, 168

used in Linux, 168

Epson's ESC/P (Epson Standard Code for
    Printers), 192

Essential system services

print management, 190–195

system logging, 180–190

system time management, 177–180

/etc/hosts, 238

/etc/nsswitch.conf file, 239

/etc/resolv.conf, 238, 239

/etc/udev/rules.d/ file, 117

/etc/udev/udev.conf file, 117

Execute permission, 287

Ext2, 16

Ext3, 16

Ext4, 16
Extended regular expressions, 205, 206

**F**

Fedora, 11, 12, 66, 85–87
Fedora Boot process, 57, 58
Files
    and directories search, 284, 285
    linking, 286
    permissions, 286, 287
    structure, 285, 286
Filesystem hierarchy, 201, 202
Filesystem Hierarchy Standard (FHS), 201
File types, 202, 203
Firewalls, 267
Forking process, 119

**G**

Gateway router, 236
Gedit text editor, 292
Gnome Display Manager (GDM), 96, 97
GNU privacy guard (GPG), 277
GNU project, 3
GNU Public License (GPL), 3
GNU Utility, 208, 209
GPG options, 279, 280
Graphical user interface (GUI), 291, 292
    configuration
        network configuration tool, 239
        troubleshooting, 239–241
        interface, 164
    problem-solving utilities, 89
Group accounts, 130
    add group, 141
    best practices, 143, 144
    commands, 143, 145

default configurations, 134
deletion, 142
/etc/group file, 132
/etc/gshadow file, 132, 133
files, 145
location, 145
management, 142, 143, 145
managers, 130
modification, 141
primary, 131, 145
secondary, 131, 145
setting up, 131
Groups, 287
GRUB, 60, 61
GRUB2, 62–64
GRUB parameters, 61, 62
GUID Partition Table (GPT), 59

**H**

Hardware abstraction layer (HAL), 78
Hardware clock, 177, 178
Hardware platforms, 5
Hewlett Packard's (HP) Printer Control
        Language (PCL), 192
host, 241
Host_Alias, 259
hostname, 241
Host security
    chkconfig, init, and insserv
        commands, 265
    firewalls, 267
    man command, 265
    open network connections (sockets),
        265, 266
    open ports, 266, 267
    password protection, 264
    rpm command, 265

TCP wrappers, 268, 269

user running a service, 268

Hotplug devices, 116

hwclock command, 177

# I, J

ifconfig command, 236

if/ else/elseif statement, 36

if statement, 34, 35, 37, 38, 41

if/then/else statement, 35

Industry Standard Architecture (ISA), 112

initrd, 59

Init scripts

BSD distributions, 69

configuration, 70, 71

init.d directory, 72

Linux, 68

service parameters, 69

status parameter, 69

Systemd, 74

System V distros, 68

upstart, 73

insmod command, 115, 116, 233

Installation packages, 245

Integrated Drive Electronics (IDE), 12

Interface configuration

DHCP settings, 235

ifconfig command, 236

NIC, 233, 234

static settings, 234, 235

Interface ID, 230

Internet Assigned Number Authority
    (IANA), 220

Internet Control Message Protocol
    (ICMP), 217–219

Internet Corporation for Assigned Names
    and Numbers (ICANN), 231

Internet Message Access Protocol
    (IMAP4), 187

Internet protocol (IP)

configuration, 216

ICMP, 218, 219

networking models, 216

OSI model, 217

procedures/conventions, 215

TCP, 218

TCP/IP model, 217

UDP, 218

iptables, 267

IPv4 address, 220–222, 226

IPv4 address classes, 223, 224

IPv4 vs. IPv6, 226–228

IPv6 addresses

in hexadecimal, 229

NAT, 226

Prefix and Interface ID, 230

vs. IPv4, 226–228

# K

KDM, 96

Kerberos, 276

Kernel, 59, 163

architecture, 166

modules

command lists, 115

configuration files, 114, 115

dynamic, 111

tools, 115, 116

Kernel Log Daemon, 186

Keyboard Accessibility, 101

Key exchange, 278

Key pair, 272–274

killall command, 123

kill command, 123

Kool Desktop Environment (KDE), 80
KPackageKit package managers, 252
ksh (Korn shell), 165

# L

Libraries, 252, 253
Lightweight Directory Access Protocol
    (LDAP), 125
Limits, 262
Line Printer Daemon, 190
Linux, 1
    clocks, 158, 161
    creation, 3
    distributions, 4
    GNU project, 3
    increases security and stability, 5
    license, 3
    MULTICS Project, 2
    multiple hardware platforms, 5, 6
    reduces total cost, 4
    software availability, 5
    system, man and info pages, 175
    UNIX, 2
Linux certification
    CompTIA's Linux+, 6
    LPI
        Introductory Certification, 7
        Linux Essentials, 7
        Professional Certifications, 7
Linux Commands
    display file contents, 204
    symbols, 204
    terminal session, 203
    Wildcard Characters, 204, 205
Linux installation
    additional information needs, 17
    default bootloader, 15

distribution, 10
file system
    Ext2, 16
    Ext3, 16
    Ext4, 16
    key players, 10
    Linux File System, 17
    methods, 18
    naming conventions
        PATA/IDE, 12
        SATA/SCSI, 13
    partition, 13–15
    questions, 9
    resource requirements
        Fedora, 11, 12
        Ubuntu, 11
    Windows File System, 17
LInux LOader (LILO), 60
Linux printing systems, 190
Linux Professional Institute, (LPI), 7
linuxrc, 59
Local address, 220
Locale
    code, 155, 156
    commands, 156
    definition, 155
    environment variables, 157
    parameters, 155
Local routing table, 237
Login shells, 172
Logrorate
    binary files, 185
    configure, 182
    Kernel Log Daemon, 186
    Rotations/backups, 183
    text-based log files, 184, 185
    utility, 182
Loop Back, 220

LPD printing, 190, 191, 194
lsmod command, 115, 116, 233

## M

Mail Distribution Agent (MDA), 186, 189
Mail protocols, 187, 188
Mail Transfer Agents (MTAs)
 Cron, 186
 Exim, 188
 Postfix, 188
 Qmail, 188
 Sendmail, 188
Mail User Agent (MUA), 186, 187, 189
Managers, 287
Master Boot Record (MBR), 59
Media Access Control (MAC), 219
Metacharacters, 174
Modifier key, 101
modprobe, 233
Mouse Accessibility, 102, 103
Mouse keys, 101
Multiplexed Information and Computing
 Service (MULTICS) project, 1, 2
MySQL, 53, 55

## N

Name resolution, 237, 238
Naming Convention for ntp Installer, 247
netstat command, 240, 265, 266
Network Address Translation (NAT), 226
Network Information Services (NIS), 125
Networking
 addresses, 219–224
 ANDing process, 224–231
 DNS configuration, 237–239
 GUI configuring, 239–241

interface configuring, 233–236
 Internet Protocol (IP), 216–220
 ports, 231–233
 routers configuration, 236, 237
Network interface card (NIC), 233, 234
Network Mapper (nmap), 266
Network time protocol (NTP), 179, 180
New Technology File System (NTFS), 17
nohup command, 121
Non-login shells, 172
Novell Directory Services (NDS), 125
nslookup, 241
Numbers, 288

## O

Open network connections (sockets),
 265, 266
Open ports, 265–267
Open socket, 265
OpenSSH, 271, 276
Operators, 288
OSI model, 216, 217
Ownership, 287

## P, Q

Package managers
 32-bit and 64-bit systems, 245
 Debian's APT, 251
 DPM, 251
 installation CD/DVD, 246
 installation packages, 245
 KPackageKit, 252
 RPM, 247–249
 source/binary, 246, 247
 YUM, 249–251
Page Description Language (PDL), 191

Parallel AT Attachment (PATA), 12
Parent Process ID (PPID), 118, 119
PATH environment variable, 168, 169
PATH variable, 24
Permissions
    default, 288, 289
    execute permission, 287
    file, 286, 287
    numbers, 288
    read permission, 287
    security risk, 264
    special, 289, 290
    using operators, 288
    write permission, 287
Physical and logical addresses, 219, 220
ping command, 219, 240, 264
Ports, 231–233
Ports numbers, 231–233
Post Office Protocol (POP3), 187
Power-on self-test (POST), 58
Prefix ID, 230
Pre-shared key, 270
Pretty Good Privacy (PGP), 277
Printer set-up, 194, 195
Print job flow, 192, 193
Print management
    CUPS, 191, 192
        configuration, 193
        print job management, 194, 195
    Linux printing systems, 190
    LPD printing system, 191
    print job flow, 192, 193
Private key, 270
Process
    CPU, 118
    definition, 118
    forking, 119
    management

background process, 121
foreground processing, 121
nohup command, 121
prioritization, 122
termination, 122, 123
PID, 118, 119
ps command, 120
pstree command, 120
top command, 120
user process, 118
zombie, 119
ps command, 120

R

RAM disk, 59
Read-only memory (ROM), 58
Read permission, 287
Redhat Package Manager (RPM), 247–249
    commands, 248, 249
Registered ports, 231
Regular expressions
    common, 205
    extended, 205, 206
Relational database, 52
Remote host, 274
Remote logging, 181
Remote X Window, 95
rmmod, 233
Root user security
    best practices, 260, 261
    su command, 257, 258
    sudo command, 258
    sudoers file, 258, 259
    user security administration, 259, 260
Routers configuration, 236, 237
Runas_Alias, 259
Runlevels, 89

commands, 67

Fedora, 66

Kernel options, 67

Linux, 65

Ubuntu, 66

# S

sar, 241

Scripts

&& chaining operator, 43, 44

case construct, 39–41

|| chaining operators, 43, 44

command substitution, 32

complexity, 29

constructs, 33

create text file, 29

decision construct, 34

echo command, 30

execute permission, 33

function, 26–28

if statement, 34, 35, 37, 38

if *vs.* case statements, 41

input, 32

multithreading, 28

NOT operator, while statement, 48

repetition construct, 45, 46

run, 29

sequence construct, 34

for statement

seq(), 46, 47

values list, 45

status, 49, 50

test, if and case statements, 41, 42

types, 29, 30

while statement, 47, 48

Secret key, 270

Secure Shell (SSH)

agent utility, 275

authentication, 276, 277

configuration options, 275, 276

connection with, 272

key pair, 272–274

OpenSSH, 271

port tunneling, 276

remote connection, 272

sshd, 271

Security

auditing files, 263, 264

encryption (*see* Encryption)

host security, 264–269

root user, 257–261

user limits, 261–263

seq (sequence) command, 46

Sequence construct, 34

Serial AT Attachment (SATA), 13

SGID, 289, 290

Shell, 21, 22, 164

commands, 25

configuration, 22

environment variables, 23

in Linux, 164, 165

PATH variable, 24

special characters, 25

types, configuration, 23

Shell commands

basic commands, 173, 174

case sensitive, 170

characters with special
meaning, 169

configuration files, 172, 173

history file, 171, 172

Metacharacters, 174

PATH, 170, 171

period, 171

terminal session, 173

Shutting Down Linux
-a, 75
-c option, 75
-h, 75
-r, 75
SIGTERM, 74
Simple Mail Transfer Protocol
(SMTP), 187
Slow keys, 101
Small Computer System Interface
(SCSI), 13
Software-installation
libraries, 252, 253
package managers (*see* Package
managers)
troubleshooting, 253, 254
Special permissions, 289, 290
SQL commands, 54
ssh-copy-id command, 274
Standard Directories, 201, 202
Static shared libraries, 252, 253
Sticky keys, 101
Structured Query Language (SQL), 51, 52
Subnet mask, 224
su command, 257, 258
sudo command, 258
Sudoers file, 258, 259
SUID, 263, 289, 290
Symmetric key encryption, 270
Sysfs, 117
System clock, 178
System cron jobs, 153
Systemd, 74
System logging
binary file, 181
facility, 180, 181
logrotate, 182–186
mail protocols, 187, 188

MTAs (*see* Mail Transfer
Agents (MTAs))
priority, 180, 181
redirecting mail, 189, 190
remote logging, 181
utility, 180
System time management
hardware clock, 177, 178
NTP, 179, 180
system clock, 178
System V distros, 68

T

Tar, 211, 212
Task management, 160
at command, 148
control, 151
optional additions, 149, 150
results, 151
atd daemon, 147, 148
configuration files, 152, 153
cron command, 147, 151
cron files, 154
cron jobs, 152, 154
shell script, 148
TCP/IP model, 216, 217
TCP/IP Suite, 219
Telnet, 241, 269
Terminal session, 164, 166, 167
Text editors, 290–292
The Borne Again Shell (bash), 21
Time management
Linux clocks, 158, 161
local time, 158, 159
time zone, 159–161
tzselect command, 160, 161
UTC, 158, 159

Toggle keys, 101
top command, 120
Total cost of ownership (TCO), 4
Traceroute, 219, 240
Transmission Control
        Protocol (TCP), 92, 217, 218
  *vs.* UDP, 218
  wrappers, 268, 269
Troubleshooting
  dig, 241
  host, 241
  hostname, 241
  netstat, 240
  nslookup, 241
  ping, 240
  sar, 241
  software-installation, 253, 254
  telnet, 241
  traceroute, 240
Type, 262

**U**

Ubuntu, 11, 66
UDP *vs.* TCP, 218
ulimit command, 261
umask command, 288, 289
Universal Time Coordinated (UTC), 158,
      159, 161
UNIX, 2, 3
Unmask command, 289
Upstart, 73
User accounts
  best practices, 143, 144
  chage command, 138
  commands, 129
  default configurations, 134
  deletion, 140, 141

/etc/default/useradd file, 135
/etc/login.defs file, 134
/etc/passwd file, 127
/etc/shadow file, 127, 128
files, 126
filesuser, 145
locations, 125, 144
lock/unlock, 139
modification, 137
password, 136
shadow files, 130
skeleton directory, 135
standard, 126, 144
synchronization, 130
system user, 126, 144
useradd command, 136
User_Alias, 259
User Datagram Protocol (UDP), 217
User-defined variables, 167
User ID (UID), 126
User limits, 261–263
User security administration
  chage command, 260
  passwd command, 260
  password and shadow file, 259
  usermod command, 260

**V**

Value, 262
Video hardware, 78, 79
Virtual memory, 14
vi text editor, 291

**W**

Well-known ports, 231, 232
while statement, 47, 48

Wildcard characters, 204, 205
Window Manager, 79, 88
Windows directory structure, 199
Write permission, 287

# X

Xaccess, 94
X client, 83
X Display Manager (XDM), 93
Xdm-config, 94
X Font Servers, 83
xkill command, 123
Xresources, 93
X Server, 79, 109
X Server configuration
   Fedora
      XF86Conf file, 86, 87
      xorg.conf files, 85, 86
   restart X server, 87
   sections, configuration files, 84, 85
Xservers, 94
X terminal/X station, 91, 92

X Window System
   components, 77, 78
   desktop environment, 80, 81
   GNOME desktop example, 81
   KDE Desktop, 82
   modular design, 108
   Video Hardware, 78, 79
   Window Manager, 79
   X client, 83
   X Font Servers, 83
   X Server, 79

# Y

Yellowdog Updater Modified (YUM)
   commands, 250
   configuration files, 250, 251
   dependencies, 249
   installation, 249

# Z

Zombie process, 119

Printed in the United States
by Baker & Taylor Publisher Services